In the HANDS of TIME

BJ Speer

WestBow Press books may be ordered through booksellers or by contacting:

WestBow Press
A Division of Thomas Nelson & Zondervan
1663 Liberty Drive
Bloomington, IN 47403
www.westbowpress.com
844-714-3454

ISBN: 978-1-6642-4795-6 (sc)
ISBN: 978-1-6642-4796-3 (e)

Print information available on the last page.

WestBow Press rev. date: 11/01/2021

DEDICATION

I can't imagine what my life would have been like without meeting Stone "Stoney" Mountain Dartt. I would have missed out on a lot of adventures, never tried outrageous foods, nor seen such pain through someone else's eyes.

So… to the best friend I have ever had in my entire life. To the one who made me smile and laugh like no one else ever could or will. To the one who showed me the TRUE meaning of Joy, Love, Compassion and Strength. I dedicate this to you… I was honored to walk life with you, to care for you and to love you through it all! I was honored to be your friend, and so much more. Thank you… My life is forever changed, because of you.

Heaven is just around the corner, so, "I'll see you up the road…."

ACKNOWLEDGEMENTS

I guess this is the place that I am suppose to Thank those that were apart of this journey, or who made an impact. I think I would have another books worth of information on this section alone.

However, I would not have been able to complete many legs of this journey without my mom, and my friends Liz and Debra. My mom was a rock in my life through this whole process. Being there from the day of diagnosis to the day he took his final breath. I could not have walked the road without her prayers, her love, and encouragement.

To Elizabeth, who cooked meals, who cleaned up, who took care of all the needs at home when we were gone. Words cannot express my gratitude for all you do. The list is too long to mention. You are a joy, and a gift from God. Stoney loved you, and he always thought you were someone special, an angel in our lives.

Debra, I would have been lost without you at the end. Your dedication in putting gloves on, getting dirty, sleepless nights, your compassion to your dearest friend was evident and abundantly clear. You were my shoulder to cry on, and confidant in moments of unclarity and despair. I am forever grateful for your friendship not only to me, but to Stoney.

To CTCA, Kristen Nigro, the Oncology team, the doctors, the nurses, the culinary team, the cleaning crew, the pastoral care, nutrition team, and reception greeters…YOU should be proud of yourselves. The love, grace and kindness you showed was something care facilities dream to have. You carried me, you encouraged me, you loved me, you lifted me. I am blessed to know you all, and honored to call you my friends, and family. My heart was changed because of each one of you.

To the Dartt Family, it was an honor, and a privilege to be the caregiver to your son, brother, uncle. I am deeply humbled for the way God brought our families together for such a time as this. The bond He weaved together between us all, and the love we have. You are my family, my brothers and sister, and its an honor to be called another Uncle to all of the nephews and nieces. Stoney loved each one of you more than he had words to tell. He and I talked about each one of you so many times, and he was so proud of all of the work you had done. He is now looking down from Heaven with joy in his heart for the incredible people you have become.

To the churches, prayer warriors, and financial givers that kept us going for nearly 3 years....my heart is so full and overflowing. You will never know how much the cards, gifts, texts, emails and love you showed us meant to us. How much it continues to mean to me. I am overwhelmed looking back and seeing Gods faithfulness THROUGH each of you! Thank you for be a part of US, our LIVES, our MINISTRY!

To the patients and caregivers around the world, reading this book...may you know that every chapter of our lives is different. Our stories are unique and are emotions are a choice. May you choose to LOVE, to show KINDNESS, and receive STRENGTH from above. May you feel wrapped in peace as you each experience the uncertainties ahead. May you find comfort in knowing our lives belong to God above, and He alone will show you the light to lead you forward on your journey. Do not let the darkness of sickness and death, shadow the light that comes from above. May you each find JOY on the journey and REST in the Redeemer.

To God my Father, the Almighty, the Creator of the Universe, YOU ALONE ARE WORTHY! Thank you Lord for guiding me, for moving me, for loving me, for strengthening me, for comforting me in my time of need and beyond. You Oh Lord, are MORE than I deserve, and I am unworthy of the kindness and love you have showed on this journey. My life is in your hands, and they will remain "In your Hands of Time" THROUGH eternity!

INTRODUCTION

Cancer Stinks!

I tried to figure out how to title this journey we've been on, but all I could come up with is Cancer Stinks! When someone hears that little word, life changes, and never for the better. I will never forget the day on January 9, 2019 when I was with Stoney at our local hospital in Springfield, TN where a nurse practitioner read a radiology report that said Stoney had tumors in his pancreas with metastasis to the liver. She even mentioned the word, cancer, which goes against most policies in any hospitals without biopsies and more information, not to mention she wasn't even a doctor. She offered to pray with us, which was very kind, but that didn't make a difference after what she had just told us. I remember shaking uncontrollably, but trying to be positive for Stoney in that moment of complete fear. I stepped out in the hallway where she even went on to say he would most likely only have 5 months to live. It was shocking, devastating, depressing, and life changing news that would disrupt the lives of Stoney, myself, and our families for the next two plus years. We were about to venture into the great unknown. The journey I am about to share includes the vivid memories, daily social media updates, and deep heart felt emotions that took us on an unforgettable adventure into the world of cancer. We saw God guide and provide through the darkest days, and found friends in the strangest places. We found peace in the presence of Jehovah. We experienced supernatural strength in our weakest moments. We found ourselves being tested and tried, while our faith was shaken at times. Cancer is a word that changes every part of our lives. From eating, social activities, sleep, daily schedules, etc… It ruins families, it splits marriages, it rips people a part and can even push them away from the truth they know.

Cancer Stinks!

Once you have it, you always have it. It can stay silent for a time, but never goes away. Most of the time it will come back with a vengeance. Cancer changes your looks, your attitude, your abilities to engage in daily activities with friends and family….

Cancer Stinks!

Let me tell you how Cancer changed our lives, how it grew our faith in Christ, and our ability to trust Him more. Let me tell you about the people we met, the plans and promises God provided, and stability in the unknown. How I found comfort in the loss of a dear friend, and new purpose in the legacy that lives on.

Cancer Stinks, BUT GOD!…..

CONTENTS

Chapter 1 "Living Through Time" 1
Chapter 2 Learning About Time 9
Chapter 3 Listening To Time 21
Chapter 4 Loving Our Time 31
Chapter 5 Leaning on Time… 39
Chapter 6 Losing Time 53
Chapter 7 Laughing at Time 71
Chapter 8 Lasting Through Time 81
Chapter 9 Longing For Time 105
Chapter 10 Loneliness of Time 135
Chapter 11 Leaving Time 191
Chapter 12 Lifting Up Time 241

1

"Living Through Time"

Psalm 31:15 - "My time is in your hands. Deliver me from the hands of my enemies..." -NIV

It was a beautiful morning in Northern California as Stoney, Elizabeth (one of our best friends) and I headed to the airport to celebrate Stoney's 40th birthday. We were traveling to Narita, Japan headed to Tokyo Disney, where we would meet up with our friends from Washington State. We would spend several days in Tokyo, then move onto Hong Kong, and finish up in Shanghai, hitting all the Disney parks in Asia. Stoney was a Disney Fanatic! In fact, that was even part of his personal email address. He loved the Disney parks since a young boy, and his birthday wish was to visit all 6 theme parks during his 40th celebratory year.

We arrived in Tokyo and had the time of our lives. Experiencing the theme parks in a completely different country, with all of their cultural differences, designs, but the same love for a man with a vision, and a very wealthy mouse! Stoney always admired Walt Disney and his ability to fail, yet rise again with an even greater vision than before. To have the ability to create something that would make people happy and last for years to come. We had many conversations about Walt and his love for family, friends and all things Disney, and even wondered if we would see him in heaven some day.

On this trip, we spent all of our time in the parks and never even ventured out into other parts of the country to see what they had to offer, but boy did we have fun! As we traveled through Asia, I began to notice a change in Stoneys health. He was someone who drank barley greens, took vitamins, and stayed very healthy most of the year, that when there was a problem, it was more obvious to me. I noticed that Stoney was spending more time in the bathroom than usual and he complained more about his stomach bothering him. Stoney loved food...ALL things food. He loved trying new things, and was never afraid of it. He liked things spicy, he even enjoyed crying when he ate hot foods. Another thing about Stoney, is he always joked about "poop". He loved to tell poop jokes, and torment his nephews and nieces. He invented games like "Poop on a stick", which I will let you make up your own visual and idea of what that game was like, but it always ended with someone getting dog poop on them. We had many laughs, and the word "poop" almost always came up at every meal. So, when he started talking about it, we just made more jokes and didn't give it too much thought.

We finished our grand vacation of Asia, and flew back to California to load up our tour bus to finish the remainder of our music schedule. For those of you reading this who may not know Stoney or myself personally, we were a part of a Gospel music quartet, traveling to churches all around the world singing over 200 nights a year. We would leave our Nashville home and go out for 3-4 months at a time, sharing our own personal written gospel songs to many people. We recorded over 20 different recordings between Stoneys family and myself. (All available on iTunes!) For the last few years of the ministry, Stoney and myself performed as a duet as his dad was home with health issues. We have many wonderful memories of our time on the road, and many we would like to forget. Mainly the bus breakdowns, and a few events and people we might have erased from our minds! haha!

As our touring continued through the summer, we were planning on a major change to our lives in July 2018. We would retire the music ministry, and return home to Nashville to do something entirely different. With church music programs changing, financial obligations rising, and the overwhelming health crisis from home, it was evident that we needed to make these changes for the well-being of our future. Seeing how God orchestrated this movement was another factor in how Stoneys future would become clear that God had a plan that we couldn't see.

As we finished up on the road, Stoney was noticing more issues internally with his stomach, but since we were so busy at the time, it was easier to ignore. He blamed it on nerves, something he ate, or just life in general making his stomach upset. We finished our tour July 15th, 2018 just outside of Springfield, Missouri at a small church in the country. When the concert was over, we packed up and headed home to start a new life. Stoney would begin driving as an Uber/Lyft driver, something he did when we had breaks in our already busy schedule. I would start full time as owner and director of my travel agency, "Where U Wanna Go Travel". I had tours already scheduled and people lined up for travel a year in advance. I had worked some tours for our music group through my travel agency, so I had my feet on the ground and was looking forward to dive into this travel world full time.

August was exciting as we set sail on a cruise to Alaska with many friends and family members who booked this trip as part of my agency group tours. We had so much fun exploring the unique cities of Juneau, Skagway, Ketchikan and Victoria, BC. We made many memories with new and old friends, and at that time it was evident to me that I was doing exactly what I loved. Stoney enjoyed the opportunities of being able to travel with me when I had tours, and that he could create his own flexible hours driving in and around town. Neither of us had a life of such flexibility until now. In the past, we would leave for long concert tours and have a schedule that could not be changed or moved, and they were booked months, if not years in advance, so having this freedom was liberating! Life seemed to be going well, and we were enjoying its prosperity.

Each night at home, Stoney and I would discuss the events of the day, our goals, our fears, and our joys. We would make plans to spend with our families, set goals for the future and always found time to make a plan to visit Disneyland or Walt Disney World throughout the year. We had days where we fretted about paying bills, and how many hours he would need to pick up, or how many clients I needed to add. We prayed for one another, and our business endeavors, but also found time to enjoy a movie or two at home while eating dinner. My mom and our good friend Liz, live next door so we were able to have many enjoyable evenings of cooking dinner together, and watching TV. Life seemed too good to be true….little did we know, it was.

As the Fall rolled in, I had a "Where U Wanna Go Travel" group tour booked for Ireland/Scotland and Stoney was very excited! We talked so many times about the places we wanted to explore when we came off the road and we had a long list. For this tour, we would fly from Nashville to Dublin, spend 4 days sightseeing with an Irish guide, then fly to Edinburgh Scotland for 3 days before heading home. We knew everyone on the tour that was traveling with us, so we became quite excited to see everyone and experience these beautiful countries.

Leading up to that trip, Stoney began having more issues with his digestive track and took several days off from work, before making a virtual appointment online with a specialist. Approximately a week before we left, he made an appointment at the doctors office to get checked out because he knew something didn't feel right and with making such a long trip overseas, we didn't want to get stuck or have any problems in a foreign country. They tested him for a parasite, which came back positive to which they believed he picked up in Asia. We thought to ourselves, "how could he have picked this up in Asia in May, and only now really start to have this many issues?" Not to mention that I was noticing changes while we were in Asia earlier in the year, but at the time we didn't really think too much about it, figuring that anything could be possible. It seemed highly unlikely that he could have anything different, so they prescribed him an antibiotic to help with his symptoms of ongoing diarrhea and stomach cramping.

While in Ireland and Scotland, he made several bathroom visits during the days we toured, but we both felt like he was on the right track by taking this new antibiotic and we kept trying to think positive. We kept praying that this would all go away, and we go home where things would return to normal as quickly as possible. We figured over time he would start feeling better, and the amount, along with volume would continue to decrease. He became more cautious in what he was eating, and tried to be careful with what kind of water he was drinking overseas as when as at home; however, upon returning home, he seemed to notice more issues, not less.

As we were into November and December was quickly approaching, we fell into that rut of the holiday festivities. We both worked longer hours, and tried to do as much as we could with family and friends. We were going to more parties, out to dinner with friends, concerts, and taking in the sights and sounds of the holidays that we never really enjoyed from being on the road. We were always out on tour singing right up until a few days before Christmas. The only concerts we were able to attend during the holidays, were our own!

Stoney found himself making more stops during the day to use the restroom while he was out driving and he would call me to say that he felt like the urgency was increasing and he began to do what we all do…. use Dr Google! We had a trip planned in December to go to Las Vegas with my cousin and her husband, who both work in the medical field so I knew I would have a list of questions for them on our trip. We had an enjoyable time even though Stoneys urgency was shifting. Even they noticed the changes that were developing in Stoneys health. Kristen, my cousin, encouraged me to get him into the hospital at home for scans and more information even as scary as it may be to get answers. She said the longer we wait, the worse it could be and if it was indeed cancer, it could be spreading, and we needed answers. We tried not to dwell too much on it and enjoy the time in Las Vegas seeing shows and eating the best food we could. We tried to laugh, relax and not dwell on what information we may get at home.

We came home to celebrate Christmas with family and friends, not realizing that this would be the very last Christmas that things would be remotely normal. It would be our last Christmas at home, as things would soon turn terribly wrong. During the holidays, Stoney took more time off. He would try going into Nashville earlier in the day to get some work so he could get home and rest as he noticed his energy levels were decreasing. I blamed it on his new "old age". They always say "things go downhill at 40", and I was beginning to think whoever "they" were, were right! New Years Eve was busy for Stoney, but he came home early after one of his passengers had an accident in the van. He decided not to work for a couple days and to just stay home and rest. He began taking Imodium, pepto, and whatever else he could to limit the time spent in the bathroom. Still, it wasn't making much difference.

During the week following Christmas, I began to have some health issues myself. I was experiencing pain in the joints of my feet, and ankles. I made an appointment for bloodwork after my mom, Stoney and Liz begged. I didn't have health insurance at the time, neither Stoney or myself did. Being on the road and in ministry, we weren't rolling in any extra finances so I couldn't afford the $220 policy they were asking. Stoney had called the insurance company, and they came out to assess him the last week of December because he knew he might be headed for some major medical expenses. Nothing was approved, and he never heard anything for several weeks. (More on that later…) For me, I just went to the doctor and hoped it wasn't going to cost me a fortune, but as we all know for those without insurance, its never cheap. They must have drawn enough blood from me in one afternoon to create a country of clones. I thought I was going to pass out since I am not a big fan of needles, and blood. I guess looking back, God was preparing me then for what job He was going to have for me in the future.

I would have to wait a couple weeks for results, so in the meantime I went home and shared with Stoney the events of my day. He told me he wasn't feeling great, but that he needed to work some longer hours, because taking so much time off during the holidays hit him financially. He was planning on going in early the next morning at 5:00am to get some earlier riders.

January 9, 2019…a colder rainy morning if my memory serves me right. Here in Nashville we don't have real bad winters. We get snow, and it gets cold, but its fairly mild. Stoney left early, but not at 5:00. He never really was on time, although he tried doing better at it when he was working for Lyft/Uber. He called me around 9:00 that morning to tell me he had already stopped about 5 times to use the bathroom and was feeling dehydrated and tired. Going to the bathroom that many times, and losing that much fluid would make anyone exhausted! Around lunch time he called again, and I said, "that's it! come on home, we are going to the ER here in town". He didn't love the idea, and he argued with me awhile because he was scared to go to the ER with no insurance, knowing he didn't have the money to pay for what they were going to charge. I told him that we had lived by faith our entire lives, and that God didn't have a plan to leave us now, so we would figure it out when the time came to pay. Once he got home, he wanted to nap, and I told him he could nap later. We needed to get to the bottom of this and find out what was going on. So, I got him in the car and took him to our local hospital which is about 7-10 minutes away. This little hospital doesn't have the best reputation in town by some locals, but trying to get into an ER in downtown Nashville would have taken us many more hours.

We were met at the door by a nice gal who took his information and told us to have a seat. There was not that many people in the waiting room, so we thought that maybe that was a good thing. It was too long and a door opened up and as Stoney likes to describe it, "Ernest Goes to Camp" like character called him into the next room. We grabbed our coats and went to the next room where they asked him questions about why he was there. Stoney always handled things with grace in my opinion, as for me, I listened to this guy ask questions and thought to myself, "how are you working in a hospital?" Once we got roomed, Stoney said to me, "Why did you bring me here?" We both laughed, and told some jokes and perhaps insulted the poor guy amongst ourselves, but we are passed that stage now, and I know God forgave us when we asked! haha! If he is still working at the hospital today, I hope he has a translator, especially if he's wearing a mask!

As we continue on this journey, I would like to say this is where my records of journaling, as well as Facebook posts and texts, will come in handy as we move forward. You will read several posts of what happened earlier on in the diagnosis, with me providing updates with more informational materials, and then almost daily towards the end of our journey.

As we officially begin this adventure, may you open your ears and eyes to the Goodness of God we experienced through it all…

"January 9, 2019…

Hey friends! I have a HUGE prayer request!! Yesterday I found myself in the hospital having lots of bloodwork and tests done for severe pain making it nearly impossible to walk. I am still waiting on results... Today, Stoney and I are headed to the ER to take care of gastro issues he has had for 9 months now. A parasite he picked up on a trip to Asia in May has been treated for, but the issues remain prevalent and finally today is the need for a hospital visit. Neither of us have any health insurance, and so it is a scary time as we both have entered new journeys in our life. If any of you would like to help in these unexpected medical expenses, we have a go fund me page, as well as PayPal... However, we know the power of prayer is supernatural and Gods healing is possible! Stoney needs a miracle and I believe God can do it, but he needs prayer! PM me for ways you can help... Thanks for all your love and support!! "In His hands!"

Prayers for stoney!!

January 9, 2019…EVENING…..LATER UPDATE….

The prognosis is not good....doctors are talking cancer in liver, pancreas and colon. He is being transported to Centennial hospital in Nashville for lots more testing. He is scared about not having insurance and the news is shocking, discouraging and frightening.

He needs your prayers and support as we work out these next several days for more answers and treatment options."

2

Learning About Time

Psalm 90:12 - "Teach us to number our days, that we may gain a heart of wisdom". -NIV

While we waited at our local hospital for the ambulance to come, and begin the transport to a downtown hospital, the room was silent. A CT scan had been done, while fluids were being given to help with dehydration. The Nurse Practitioner was very kind, and seemed obvious a Christian woman. She asked Stoney about his name, and how it came to be, as so many people do. She went out to get the results of the scan, and when she came back in the tension in the room could be cut with a knife. You could tell she was carrying the weight of the world on her shoulders, and was not wanting to deliver any news. I remember the conversation so well, and so clear. "Mr Dartt, your scan has showed a mass on your pancreas, as well as in the liver and colon. We are going to send you to Centennial Hospital in Nashville tonight for a biopsy and MRI. Would that be ok with you? Honestly, at that point, what is he supposed to say? No? Try again? Instead, Stoney looked up with fear in his eyes, and said that would be fine, and asked me to call our moms and let them know whats going on. Stoney asked the nurse, is this cancer? She paused, almost for dramatic effect, and then looked at him and said "yes". She said "we aren't supposed to say that without further scans, and biopsies, but the radiologist sees these everyday and is quite certain it is". My heart sunk as I knew our lives were going to change. No-one likes hearing they are sick, and cancer is almost always a death sentence, especially pancreatic.

As the nurse went out into the hallway, I followed her and when the door shut, I asked, "how long?" She said, "I honestly don't know, but its not good, and there are several in the liver, so maybe 5-6 months". I began to shake… I started crying and she put her arm around me, and asked how long we had known each other. I told her I had worked with his family for 15 years. I told her what we did for a living in our previous career and told her God took us off the road for a new adventure, not knowing this would be the direction. She went on ahead, and I leaned up against the wall, and my body slid down. I put my hands over my eyes and began to weep. I knew Stoney was alone, and I did not want to be gone long, so I dried my eyes, stood up, and decided to be strong for Stoney during this time. I called our moms, they were having lunch, so they packed their food up and hurried over. Stoney had asked me if I knew anymore, and in that moment I thought about lying to my best friend. If I had said yes, it would make him sick, and if I had said no, I would have carried guilt. I told him that she told me 5-6 months, but she was unsure. I could tell in that very moment, his mind went to a place no human should go. "Time". How long do I have? How long will my body fight or can it fight? I could tell he was processing what he could, but was adjusting to this news. Within a few moments, the kind nurse made her way back into the room and asked if she could pray with us. We said "yes, we would love that." She began to pray a prayer that was powerful, even for a nurse. A prayer that could make a pastor question himself. It was real, it was true and genuine. She told us she would be back in a little while to give us updates, but planned to keep Stoney hydrated until transport. Stoney's mom Sharon and my mom, Paula, both arrived and we broke the news to them. CANCER… It truly is amazing how harsh, how scary, how real that word is. My mom started crying, and Sharon pet Stoneys head and told him he was going to be ok. She said God knows all about it, and he is going to watch over him. The nurse stepped back into the room and asked if we wanted to drive down to the hospital and save money, because the ambulance would be expensive and she knew Stoney didn't have insurance. She told us she would have everything lined up with the ER downtown, she would discharge us to leave and go directly there, to be greeted and admitted immediately upon arrival. So, we did. I drove my mom in her car, and Stoney drove his mom in her car.

We arrived at Centennial, and everything worked quickly. He was sent to a room and I stayed by his side. Family came to visit after hearing the news and we gathered around Stoney and prayed for him before they all went home. A tall doctor from somewhere in the islands came into the room and addressed the scans. We said, "cancer?" He said, "We can't know for sure until we have a biopsy, which is scheduled first thing in the morning". So, we wait some more. During this time of waiting, my feet and ankles were sore. I was struggling with the pain, and it seemed to be hurting more. I spent the night in a chair next to Stoneys bed, and while we talked some that night, he was more quiet than I had ever seen him. I wanted to get in his mind, and know what he was thinking. I wanted to tell him what his mother told him…that it would be ok…but I didn't believe it myself. I was scared that time was over, and my best friend would soon slip away from me faster than I wanted.

"January 10, 2019…

As I stayed in the hospital with Stoney all night, my mind could not shut off. It's amazing how we let ourselves think the absolute worst when we KNOW The Great Physician, The Healer, The Shepherd, our Father. The road I walked with my dad was awful, but taught me so many lessons. This is different...

So thankful for all the prayers, kind words and love you've sent to me, Stoney, and our families. As more testing begins this morning, I call upon the name of Jesus to anoint the doctors, to somehow show healing through a miracle, but if another path is certain, that we might all show Christ in our actions. That we would all be given grace and mercy, peace and strength, that others would see our faith. There is nothing here that is surprising to our Lord and Savior...the outcome is already decided, how we choose to follow and respond is up to us. As I think of so many songs, and scriptures, I can't stop thinking about "Does Jesus Care". When I recorded that song, I never knew how much it was going to impact my life and others around me. We are abiding in Him, under His wings! More to come....please keep praying!! We all need it!"

"January 11, 2019…

After a very busy long day yesterday waiting and waiting...which FYI- I am NOT good at... Stoney was released to go home until we get the results. As we were packing things up, the oncologist came in and gave us a little brighter hope for the time being. Since he had not seen the biopsy report, he could not give defined answers, but could say that if Stoney has what they originally thought, he would be Superman! We went in Thursday from one hospital to another with a basic death sentence from one place, to glimpses of hope and light by the end of day last night. We still have to WAIT and see the oncologist for the next bit of news and treatment options. Until then, we continue to pray for healing, for miracles, for direction and for comfort for the entire family. You can still help with financial support as well if you' d like.. God knows and He Cares!! Resting Under His Wings"

January 12th, was a very different day for us, as we had received the news from the Oncologist before leaving the hospital the night before as you read in that post. We felt, maybe this is going to be ok. Maybe we don't need to worry as much right now, trust the Lord like we are suppose too, and lean not on our own understanding. We had plans to leave on January 14th for a much needed vacation with family. Stoneys brother, Don, and his wife and their daughter, my mom, Liz and my cousin in Florida and her family were all supposed to meet in Hawaii. The stress of Stoneys health issues had made me forget all about going anywhere. The morning of the 12th, I got in the shower and noticed my feet were purple. They looked bruised all over the tops and side, and up the ankle. I began to get scared, but didn't want to say anything because I knew this close to a trip, people would overreact and want to cancel. We were going to HAWAII!!! I can't cancel this trip and not go…Stoney needed the distraction with his family and a break from the depressing cloud hanging over us waiting on the tests results. By the end of the day, I couldn't walk, or put any pressure on my feet without extreme pain. I often made fun of Stoney, because he did not have much of a threshold for pain. I refuse to take anything for a headache unless I know I can't function, so for me this was bad! We tried everything from epson salt baths, to cherry juice, to turmeric and ginger pills. I would have crawled through the airport to get on that plane. With just 36 hours before boarding the flight, I told them we were all going. My mom was so upset. I remember her crying and telling me I didn't have to do this. I told her I was fine...clearly that was a lie. Well, January 14th came, and I managed to bite my tongue, grit my teeth and get myself to the airport. Stoney got me a wheelchair and pushed me through the Nashville airport and again in Houston. The trip was long, and my feet and ankles began to hurt. Mom was worried about blood clots, among other things. Stoney was more focused on me than his own problems, which probably helped his mental status for the time being. We arrived in Hawaii and my legs were so swollen, I looked like the marshmallow man. The purple color was creeping up my ankle and looked more bruised. Mom, Liz and probably Stoney were all on Dr Google trying to figure out what I had and how long I had. Looking back, it was not fun but truly interesting how God used this time to make us all depend on Him even more. We had all the puzzle pieces of life thrown up in the air, they had fallen upside down, and some were even missing, but God saw the whole broken puzzle as a finished product. This trip was allowing us to stop thinking about Stoneys cancer diagnosis and focus on something different. Yes, it was my swollen purple feet, but at least it wasn't cancer! The week was much needed, and oh so fun! We laughed, and made many memories that I still think about today. I started juicing on the trip, and by the end of the week, the color was better and the swelling was down.

Stoney was not much for Facebook, or any social media for that matter. He stayed away from it, unless he was sharing my posts, prayer requests or our concert schedule. However when he returned home from our trip, he decided to make a post on his page about how he was feeling. I do not have many of them to record in this book, but I have a few, and this was his first post pertaining to his diagnosis...

FROM STONEY...

January 24, 2019

14 days plus a few hours or so ago from right now - I had received my discharge papers at the hospital & changed back into my "civilian" clothes. I put on my fedora too. It had been beautiful & sunny that day - I had very nice windows in my private room which let in the energizing sunbeams to recharge the solar batteries in this California boy… but rest assured, it was freezing cold outside despite the sunshine… I put on my coat. One more check around the room to make sure I wasn't leaving anything & then we started for the door. At that moment entered a kind looking man - wearing rubber gloves on his hands & a protective paper gown over the top of his suit & tie. Over the next several minutes we had an important conversation about the realities of where we were at in my journey & he gave some very welcome words of some hopeful possibilities. "We can't rule anything out until we have the results of the biopsy, but…." He went on to share his personal observation that due to how healthy I appear to be… without pain… great lab numbers… he would be very surprised if I was facing some aggressive type or advanced stage of cancer. This was quite a contrast to the initial message of hopelessness I had been given by the hospital I had been transferred from the day before… a leading staff member there had literally pulled BJ aside privately out in the hallway & told him that what I had was untreatable.

…Shortly after I arrived home from the hospital, I was composing a text message to send out to my immediate family members. As I searched my brain for the correct word to use for "cancer doctor", I thought I remembered hearing the word "oncologist"… I typed it into Google to make sure of the definition. "Yep, that's the right word…" It's interesting the terminologies we add to our vocabulary as we see the illnesses and ailments of this earth enter into the lives of those close to us… [January 1st, 2009 - the word "dialysis" was added to my vocabulary as we learned that Dad's kidneys had failed…] and sometimes we learn those new words as those ailments touch us directly… [January 10th, 2019 - I learned the word "oncologist".]

…Cut to today - Thursday, January 24th, 2019 - The day I was officially diagnosed with "low-grade neuroendocrine carcinoma" - a cancer that is affecting my pancreas and liver. My oncologist feels that I've had this for a couple years or more. We are fortunate & blessed that it was stumbled upon in the CT scan from 2 weeks ago. It is in my favor that I really don't seem to be showing any symptoms from the tumors. The good news is that he feels he has 100% certainty that I do NOT have the biggest baddest pancreatic cancer - pancreatic adenocarcinoma. At present, there is much still to be learned about what my particular cancer diagnosis means… and the days ahead will show us, one step at a time, what direction we need to take as far as treatment. I

am currently scheduled for a new type of PET scan on Monday, February 4th, using a technology that has only been available in the Nashville area for about a year. It should be an excellent tool to help us find out how active my tumors are & with the resulting images, we will be able to create a baseline as we keep them under observation in the days, weeks, months, & hopefully years ahead & adjust my treatment accordingly. In the meantime, Lord willing, I've got some time to get healed up from this awful bout of C-Diff that I continue to deal with… and, Lord willing, time to find the best ways to live the healthiest lifestyle I can in order to keep strong & to help equip my body to heal itself as we also pray for God's healing & enabling touch & for strength for the journey.

God bless you all & a happy belated 75th birthday to the wonderful & amazing Tracy Dartt! I love you, Dad! Thank you for writing so many wonderful, practical, & applicable songs that can speak to us in so many of life's experiences & hardships… songs like the one that popped into my head early today as I was getting ready to go to the Dr. I wasn't even trying to think of any music or songs at the time and BOOM! a Tracy Dartt song started playing in the 8-track player of my brain… a song I've been listening to for as long as I can remember anything… I used to listen to it on 8-track & LP record album… then cassette tape and compact disc… now, to make sure I get the lyrics right, I'll just stream it from Apple Music on my iPhone…

"BE STILL AND KNOW" words & music by Tracy Dartt

"Be still & know that He is God… Now's the time to start… to worship Him and praise Him in the quiet of your heart… Let His Holy Spirit, deep within, whisper peace unto your soul. He'll calm each doubt and fear… If you'll just Be Still & Know"

"He knows the end from the beginning… He knows the hidden things ahead… There's no need of doubt or worry… There's no need of fear or dread… He holds the key to your tomorrow… The whole world is in His hands… Won't you just be still & know He understands"

"Be still & know that He is God… Now's the time to start… to worship Him and praise Him in the quiet of your heart… Let His Holy Spirit, deep within, whisper peace unto your soul. He'll calm each doubt and fear… If you'll just Be Still & Know"

-Stoney

ps. Until I know that I'm not contagious, I cannot return to work… and I'm doing what I can to get the bacteria in my gut back to a strong and safe enough level so that I am not so susceptible to further GI illness. I am most likely going to be off work for another 4 or 5 weeks. I am OVERWHELMED & so appreciative to the individuals, & the families, & the church congregations who have so lovingly & generously helped me with a financial gift during this challenging time.

When we arrived home from our trip, it was as if the burden had been thrown right back onto us. We listened for calls while we were gone, and waited for emails to give us some idea of when we would find out what was next. Finally, the Oncologist called! A date was set for February 4th to have a detailed Pet Scan with a reading to follow. We wanted more information, so even though this wasn't what we were hoping for, it was the next step to get us there. Leading up to the dreaded day of February 4th, I began to change my eating habits and went all plant based. Within days, my strength came back in my feet, the color moved away, and swelling was gone. My results came back as a rare form of Vasculitis found in those who experience shock, or devastating news. Well, I couldn't imagine what kind of shock I had experienced, haha. Even for me, cancer had a way of eating at my gut and causing a rare inflammatory auto-immune disease. The Dr said it could come back in months, or years, or never again. So, basically he was telling me to stay away from devastation, and shocking news. It's amazing I didn't have more trouble when covid hit!

February 4, 2019 had arrived…and boy was it going to be an early morning!

"February 4, 2019…

5:30am and on the road with stoney to Centennial hospital in Nashville for the much anticipated Pet Scan (7:00am) We are hoping for answers at 3:00 today as to the treatment in Stoneys cancer care. Please pray for miracles, but also that God's Will be done and for peace, strength, grace and loads of faith to cope and process the next steps.... Lord, you are the GREAT PHYSICIAN AND HEALER! We need YOU today!!

….EVENING UPDATE…

So many people have been texting and messaging about today's appointment. Stoney's Pet scan revealed that he does indeed have cancerous tumors on the pancreas, liver and lymph nodes around the abdomen. The oncologist recommended a clinical treatment that was available, but would need insurance to help cover the extra costs involved because it's a new study that is very expensive. So, being uninsured means lots of questions. There are a couple other options to think about, which we are taking some time for and praying for God's leading. This type of cancer is chronic, meaning there is no technical cure, but something he can live with for several years with the right treatment. Just needing to find the right one!! Stoney will be updating Facebook tomorrow. We've been up since 4:30 and it's been a long emotional day, so he will post his thoughts tomorrow and I will share them here on my page!! Thanks so much for all the prayers and support!! There are several ways you can help financially as well. If you are interested, please let me know!! Thanks so much!!"

A MESSAGE FROM STONEY….

February 6, 2019

Greetings, praying friends! Sorry it took so long to get this posted. There's a lot going on & a lot to process right now. Over the weekend & leading up to my PET/CT scan Monday morning & the subsequent visit to the oncologist in the afternoon there was a lot of wondering about what more they might find. When I found out the scan would be from the top of my head down nearly to my knees you can imagine my mind went wild with all the possible areas to find cancer. I tried to remain calm & trust & be patient… "be still and know".

Several hours later the verdict came in from the oncologist after he took time to look over the findings. The only surprises were that I apparently do NOT have cancer in the duodenum colon as I was originally told at the first hospital I went to back on January 9th. I do have the 10 masses in my liver & at least 1 mass in my pancreas, & I'm told that the lymph nodes behind the pancreas "lit up" a bit in the image as well, meaning there are cancer cells present. It was a relief that nothing else was found, & a relief to know my intestine/colon are cancer free… though the lymph nodes sound a bit on the scary side. I'll be getting more clarification on that soon hopefully. What I have is not considered curable by the medical community. For those who aren't aware, my diagnosis is a chronic low-grade neuroendocrine carcinoma (cancer) affecting the pancreas & liver. The oncologist feels that this is not something that will cause my "immediate demise"... he says some people live for years with it... & it tends to become more problematic & exhibit more troublesome symptoms over time. I'm told the liver is inoperable due to the fact of the multitude & sizes of the liver tumors. In my present condition, there's only one type of medication available - one that only treats symptoms - & the jury is still out on whether I need it right now. I've been offered participation in a research study, but for now I've decided not to take part as it would completely up-end my life for only a 7-10% chance of tumor shrinkage. I' d much rather spend my time & efforts in dedicating myself to healthy living & diet with the hope of trying to reverse tumor growth.

All that being said, today is a good day. I feel well & good. Day by day I'm seeing some varied progress against the retched C-Diff bug I've been fighting. Making dietary changes, watching the symptoms, and treating with a probiotic & a high-potency manuka honey which has shown some promise. I' ll be finished with my 2nd round of antibiotics tomorrow (Thursday) & then hopefully I can begin the process of building back my gut bacteria. I expect to be off work through the end of the month in order to get plenty of rest, to regain my physical strength & get my immune system strong again, and to get some new lifestyle routines in place.

I am so very thankful that I don't have to go through what I'm going through without the wonderful blessings of so many of you who have shared words of encouragement, prayer coverage, & financial assistance to help with the mountain of medical & living expenses in the face of being presently unable to work. I cannot thank you enough! Blessings to you all!

As we processed all this news together, it was no surprise that things became clear that time was of the essence. We began talking through life in a different way. Making plans, not knowing if next month or next year would be his last. Looking to the future with different eyes. We wanted more time, but who doesn't? We wanted to go to more places, and experience more adventures with family and friends. I wanted my best friend to be healed, and he wanted his life back. As we went on each day, we learned more about this rare cancer the oncologist had talked about with us. Only 1 in I don't know how many get this cancer, so rare is an understatement. We heard people say that if you get cancer, this is the one to get. The best kind and the one that wont kill you as fast as stage 4 pancreatic cancer. Here is my personal opinion…not asked, but its my book… "Diagnosis does not define you or your lifeline". Meaning, if you get stage 4 pancreatic cancer and are told that means 6-12 months, you may live 10 years! Don't live like life is over because of a diagnosis. I think that is why Stoney did as well as he did. He did not let this cancer define him and how he chose to live. You could get a cold and die. Now we know, you can get coronavirus and die within days, or weeks and yet some can live and heal. Do I believe cancer is a death sentence like I said before? YES. I believe that when people get a cancer diagnosis, your clock is ticking; however, the truth is…our clock was ticking the day we were born. A diagnosis of any stage of cancer, or any other disease, does not give you an estimate of time, but of LIFE! When you hear those words… thats when its time to LIVE. I saw that in Stoney… I saw his desire to do as much as possible increase, along with his ability to encourage others through his diagnosis. Ask any one of his nurses during the final months of his life, and not one will tell you he didn't love life, smile and make the best of his disease.

It still hurts. It's still hard. It still doesn't make sense, but then again nothing does.

The next few weeks were so difficult. The oncologist said he would have someone on his team call us and schedule us for an appointment to start some trials. Basically, to be a guinea pig in the medical world. For some it works, and others it doesn't. We were in and out of ER's due to hydration issues due to fluids loss from diarrhea. The stress of not paying bills were mounting, but yet the power of prayer, and Gods people providing in ways for us, I cant even put into words…Some doctors said he had C-diff, so they treated him with antibiotics, others said his colon was just inflamed so treated him with more drugs. We were running out of answers and feeling like we weren't going anywhere. I was running my travel agency on fumes, and trying to juggle taking calls, booking trips and taking Stoney to appointments as well as treating his symptoms at home. I was running out of energy, and beginning to think we had no more options.

"February 15, 2019…

Prayers appreciated!! Was back in the ER with stoney last night until 2:00 this morning. 6 more weeks of antibiotics for him!! Praying the C-diff infection will clear up this go around. Be in prayer, as this means no work for another month for him, and a set back in his "all natural" cancer treatments. Pray for miraculous healing!!

3

Listening To Time

Psalm 16:9 - "In their hearts humans plan their course, but the LORD establishes their steps." -NIV

March had arrived, and I was planning on taking my mom to Florida to visit some friends, but she went on ahead of me. I still had to fly down for some business to take care of at another travel agency office to get my validation renewed to continue selling group tours. I asked Stoney if he was ok with me still going, or if he wanted me to stay. He assured me he would be fine, and wanted me to get away and rest. That's one thing that I would say about Stoney, he always encouraged me to get away when I could and catch my breath. If I ever stayed behind, it was my own choosing.

My mom was already situated in Florida, and I was headed down to meet her. Stoney and I went and had lunch and coffee at a new hipster place in Nashville before he dropped me off. He seemed fine, and was not in any pain nor did he seem to make me worried. He dropped me off at the airport, and I waved goodbye as I went in and headed to the Sunshine State. Once I arrived in Florida, I called him and he sounded fine, but said he went home after dropping me off because his stomach didn't feel right. At this time, we still had not heard from anyone at the Nashville Cancer center, so he was just managing as he had been, taking it one day at a time. His days driving for Lyft/Uber were taking a toll, and he began to struggle mentally about the time off and financial hardships.

I spent the first day with my mom, and although I was still taking calls, for some reason my phone was not sending everything through. Stoney had tried calling me, and things were already changing back home....

March 2, 2019...

Please pray for my best friend, Stoney!! He dropped me off at the airport Thursday so I could fly to Florida for work. He was in the ER yesterday for more health related issues. He needs so much prayer and healing coverage!!! He has not been able to work for nearly 3 months and it's been quite stressful. Also we are figuring out options on the best cancer treatments and the cost is a HUGE issue. Even with some insurance, the companies are not covering everything. We need miracles and especially a miracle HEALING!!

Come to find out, Stoney's blood pressure that morning was 60/45 and he nearly passed out, so he called 911. The ambulance arrived to take him to the ER for bloodwork and fluids. By this time, my mind was beginning to wonder how things could turn around or even get better. I remember staying with our friends from Canada in their condo, and in my room crying. I was asking God to send some good news, to give Stoney some good days. I would text and call him from Florida, and hearing his voice shaky and fearful made me wonder if I should go home early. He pleaded with me not to. He told me to stay and enjoy time with my mom and friends and that he would be fine. He had 2 brothers and a sister that lived within 35-40 minutes so I felt comfortable knowing he would have someone if I stayed. I was messaging with a distant relative of mine, who I sent the scans to for review. I was not settling for the pathetic hospital in Nashville, who vowed to reach out to us with information, and after 4 weeks of no news...I took matters in my own hands! Laurie called me and said she had the scans reviewed and both she and the surgeon confirmed what the Nashville oncology team had found, but her surgeon gave her a number for me to call. He told her that he had heard amazing things from the Cancer Treatment Centers of American and that I should call them and find out what region (or State) the pancreatic oncology team was located. I wasted NO time! I took the number down, and I believe this was a Saturday if I'm not mistaken, and I called! A young lady listened to my story, and offered her condolences and support, but then told me she would forward my information on to a team member, but it could be a few days for it to be reviewed. Within 15 minutes a gentleman called me from CTCA, and went over my case. I had all the scans and documents on my phone, so I sent them over to him and had my friend Laurie email the scans directly to them. The gentleman asked about insurance and I told him we were not covered, and he seemed quite concerned but told me he would do what he could. He made an appointment for April, but asked me if it was alright if they had an opening if we could come sooner. I said, "the sooner the better!" He told me that normally he would send us to Philadelphia but the Pancreatic specialist he recommended was in Atlanta, which worked better for us anyway. Only a 5 hour drive each way! Things were starting to look up, and I began to think we had a chance.

I hung up and called Stoney and told him what I had done, and he seemed upset. He said, "Beej, I don't have insurance…this is going to cost too much and I cant afford it." I told him I refused to give up, and I refuse to think God didn't have a plan, with or without insurance. After seeing what God did for my family after my dad was diagnosed with Lewy Body Dementia, I knew there was nothing too big for my God! (…read Dusty Road, A Journey into Faith for that story!)

I arrived home just a couple of days before my birthday (March 9th), and two things happened…One, A letter from the insurance company Stoney had looked into back in December (he even had completed the health check at home), had approved his insurance, as well as mine and wrote the start date back to January 1, 2019!!! HALLELUJAH!! Tell me that wasn't a God thing?! The poor insurance company didn't know what was about to hit them! haha! This means, that all the ER visits and all the scans he had already completed were covered. This also meant our chances of being approved at the Cancer Center would be greater. Blessing TWO… I called CTCA back and they bumped up our appointment by 2 plus weeks! Best Birthday gift for me, and answered prayers for Stoney.

March 10, 2019…

Thank you to everyone who wished me a Happy Birthday! It was amazing how many thoughtful notes and wishes were left on my page. It was a very interesting day... We canceled the plans that were made, because Stoney was having some health issues. The cancerous tumors he has are causing some issues and it keeps him close to home and feeling quite nauseated. We have an appointment at the Cancer Center of America on April 1-3 to get a second opinion as well as find out what they can do for the symptoms that have gotten worse. We are praying they can find an answer and that he can go on with life normal as possible. Right now, he still cannot work and needs full time care for the most part due to feelings of passing out, nausea, diarrhea, low blood pressure and more. We continue to trust the Lord for financial provisions. I must say this is expanding my faith, and stressing me out all at the same time. Yes, Jesus Cares!!!

March 11, 2019…

Friends and Family...

Many of you have been praying for Stoney Dartt on this cancer journey and I am so appreciative! I have been taking him to Dr's appointments and the next big one has now been moved up to March 18-21 at the Cancer Center of America in Atlanta. I'm still working my travel agency (Where U Wanna Go Travel) but taking a back seat to that right now due to taking care of the necessities for Stoney. Financially, things have been a bit of a nightmare, but I know this is what I'm suppose to be doing. Sharon is taking care of her husband, and Stoneys siblings and family work full time and don't have as much flexibility as I have. I'm thankful for Elizabeth Kieser, and my mom Paula Speer for their support and help at this challenging time. I am asking (once again) if any of you or your church family would like to help in partaking in the special needs we have right now, we would greatly appreciate it. So many people have sent letters and cards, love gifts and so many prayers!! THANK YOU!!! Stoney will not be able to work for awhile since he will be going back and forth for treatments in Atlanta (we will have a more defined schedule in 10 days) and so we need a tremendous amount of help on the financial side of things. Thankfully, we have worked out a new insurance plan that will help him, but have to pay $5,000 in deductibles up front to help with the previous medical expenses. PRAY!!! The cancer center would like this paid before we arrive next Tuesday...miracles needed!!!

As we continued to live in this upside down universe, I just had this gut feeling that God was going to provide. I kept hearing that still small voice inside and kept sharing the needs on facebook. I don't think a day went by that I didn't share a link where people could give. It actually makes me sick thinking back how much I pressured people to give, but I listened to my heart, and God provided. I did a fundraiser on facebook, followed by PayPal links. You would think I was earning stock in posting it, but I was positive God was going to supply ours needs. I had put my work on hold, Stoney couldn't work if he had wanted too, and believe me…he wanted to work! I would say in a matter of minutes from posting the first campaign, we had what we needed for the month. We had gained a following from our years on the road. Faithful people who prayed and loved our music, but more importantly, loved us. As I kept refreshing my screen, more people were giving. I told Stoney, and the tears fell down his face. I don't know how to explain it, but when you know God is telling you to do something, you better do it. For me, and maybe to you as the reader, you think "Does God tell us to ask for money?" Well, the Bible says, "Ask and it shall be given.." We often forget the rest of that verse… "Seek, and ye shall find, knock and the door shall be open". I believe that by listening to the Holy Spirit, Seeking His will, asking for Him to deliver us from the financial pressures, and then watching Him open doors was about the most amazing thing I have ever witnessed in my life.

The day had come to go to Atlanta. One thing I forgot to mention, was when they set up our appointment, they paid for our airfare and hotel and gave us food credits upon arrival just to be there for the few days of testing. They even picked us up in a limo. I'm not talking a simple limo, I mean a stretched limo. You could easily seat 10 people in there. I was thinking to myself, this place is already looking and sounding better than anything Nashville has to offer!

March 17, 2019…

Prayers needed as I take Stoney to the Cancer Treatment Center of America in Atlanta today...We start tomorrow and for 3 days we will learn more about his cancer, the options for treatment and where to go next. We are so grateful for this opportunity to go to this place and get more information. We have not received all the funds yet to cover this adventure, but we know the Lord will provide. Please keep us in your prayers!

March 18, 2019…

Day one in Atlanta at the Cancer Treatment Center of America. They kept us moving pretty good today (and continuing). After meeting with several of the wonderful (most friendliest) staff, Stoney was sent to get a 4 hour infusion of potassium and sodium, which was extremely low. This will help with some tiredness and fatigue he's had. Tomorrow we start at 8:30am and will meet with several more staff members and dietitians to help with his overall daily life. Wednesday we will meet with the Dr and Oncologist to figure out what's next on this journey. Our Hopes and Faith are high! I'm so glad and thankful I know the GREAT Physician, but this place is making us feel a lot better about things.

March 21, 2019…

Stoney UPDATE:

Our visit to the Cancer Center Treatment of America in Atlanta was amazing!! They were nothing short of miraculous! Every person we met was just wonderful, kind and gracious. Due to the nature of Stoney's cancer, not everyone knows how to treat Neuroendocrine carcinoma. We met with 20 people over 3 days and became overwhelmed with all of the info that was given, but it was all GOOD!!! The oncologist seems to have a plan and we will go back again next week for the first of many injections Stoney will receive to help with the problematic symptoms that goes with this disease. This is the main reason he has not been able to work for 3 months. Then, each month we will make a trip to Atlanta for infusions and check-ups as well as talk about a "surgery" (or treatment) plan to specifically kill and remove these tumors over time. This is something that has NO cure, and he will have to live with this disease for the rest of his life, but it can be managed by injections and diet. The team we have on our side is there to give 100% of help to us and we are BLESSED!! Financially, it will be nothing short of a miracle to see how God continues to provide for us. Many have talked about hospital financial assistance, and we appreciate all the info you are sending and have gone through every door we can! We now wait for the Lord to show the rest of the way. I believe if HE wants Stoney here, HE will provide the way.... Thank you to all of you who have supported, and prayed in this matter! DO NOT GIVE UP!!! We need lots of prayers and encouragement as we continue to learn more about the disease and its plan of attack! Love to you all!

We came home from that first initial trip on cloud nine! We were so excited and thankful that there was a place that was going to treat Stoney with advanced actions that we did not have in Tennessee. The only complication was going to be the finances. In the past, that hasn't stopped me from asking or pushing doors open. I started applying for grants, making calls and trying to see what could be done. People, who were obviously concerned, had their own opinions on what we should do. I must admit when you open yourself up in asking for help, you will get help from all angles and not always the kind you hoped. We had so many incredible emails, calls, text and gifts; however, I allowed myself to be beaten up by the small number of people who were being negative and giving their own ideas. I already struggle with what people think of me, so some comments were hurtful and cutting me deep. I will never forget Stoney coming in my room and asking me why I was crying. When I told him why, he said this... "Beej (thats what he called me, not BJ, but BEEJ), how can you be upset at what is happening right now? You have put a need out there for me, and people are answering. God is working and showing up, and you are letting a couple of people rob you of your joy?" So, he had a point...I had worked so hard to find a way and make a provision, and now that God was working, the devil was working against me. The old devil had found a loophole in my brain, and was taking advantage of it. I finished my cry, wiped my eyes, and found a way out to the box of chocolates. In case you don't know, chocolate fixes everything, and it's always a good cure to stop the tears. Trust me, try it.

I was back on track and trying to listen to Gods voice, and no other. Side-note, when you let yourself become defeated by a voice in your head, try thinking about what voice it is. God doesn't want you to be defeated, He wants us to fight and win. Even now, when the gloom, darkness and tears come, I have to remember it's not God giving me those doubts and fears, it's the old devil. And quite frankly, I am getting really sick of him!

(2 Timothy 1:7 - For God hath not given us the spirit of fear; but of power, and of love, and of a sound mind. -NIV)

Through the month of April, Stoney struggled health wise. We couldn't seem to find anything that worked to help with his symptoms. Lots of ER visits, infusions, and bloodwork. I have never seen someone poked and prodded like Stoney, and this was just the beginning. The amount of grace he had still astounds me. He always kept his smile, sense of humor and love for his family and friends. He never wavered in his faith or trust in God from day one. Scared, yes, but who wouldn't be?

I am reminded of a sign we saw on the door at the Cancer Center the first time we arrived. It said this…

What Cancer Cannot Do: Cancer is SO limited…
It Cannot Cripple Love
It Cannot Shatter Hope
It Cannot Dissolve Faith
It Cannot Destroy Peace
It Cannot Kill Friendship
It Cannot Silence Courage
It Cannot Steal Eternal Life

There is so much truth to these words. We allow ourselves to be in bondage or crippled by fear, but Cancer can't separate us from God. Cancer is merely a word intended to drive the fear in us, but God is the Ultimate Driver, the GPS, and the Pilot, so reading these words reminded us to expand our faith and trust the One who is in charge…

April 3, 2019…

Stone Dartt UPDATE:

For those of you praying for Stoney, please continue! After several good days, he is having more issues with the cancer symptoms so we are headed to the ER today for bloodwork and potassium/sodium infusions. The Cancer Center feels like he is losing too much fluid. He was approved to have the injections he needs once a month (for the rest of his life and only $20,000 a pop!) but there are so many other needs and concerns right now! Please continue to pray and *if you feel led to give, I have set up a Go Fund Me page, a Facebook support page, and you can always send directly to him at home. He is trying to remain optimistic, and positive, but I am sure there are days he just feels defeat. Please keep praying and have your church family be praying for a miraculous healing! Thank you so much for being our Faithful Prayer Squad~*

On this visit to the Treatment Center, they approved lots of special needs. They gave me unlimited round trip air transportation that would last through our entire time of treatment. I never once paid for a flight to Atlanta, and neither did Stoney. They gave us discounted hotel benefits as low as $25 a night, and credit towards food. They supplemented his medical expenses with insurance, meaning what insurance didn't cover, they took care of. God truly covered every aspect of what we asked. Many people who gave towards our journey may read this and ask, "what did we give to?" Well, even though these medical procedures and treatments were covered, we did have upfront expenses for a few months before things began to be cleared. We also had an enormous amount of money in pills, supplements, and other necessities that were not covered and all out of pocket. We had deductibles, along with initial deposits on injections and shots. I would be glad to give figures to anyone who wanted to see them because there was nothing taken for granted. We were blessed each and every day by the many gifts and the prayers. If it had not been for that, we would not have survived as long as we did. God did not disappoint in my "listening" to His voice. I pray that for the rest of my life, I will be sensitive to His leading.

Claiming His promises daily and Calling on Him in prayer! As Psalm 46:1-3 says, "God is our refuge and strength, a very present help in trouble. 2 Therefore will not we fear, though the earth be removed, and though the mountains be carried into the midst of the sea; 3 Though the waters thereof roar and be troubled, though the mountains shake with the swelling thereof."-NIV

4

Loving Our Time

John 15:12: "My command is this: Love each other as I have loved you." -*NIV*

Things seem to get better once Stoney started his injections. These long acting Sandostatin shots were not cheap and had to be schedule every 28 days. It did not matter where we were, we needed to make plans to be at the center when those 28 days were up, or Stoney would start becoming symptomatic very quickly. The shots were never fun for Stoney, but they did seem to get easier. The needle was thicker than any needle I had seen before, and the technique had to be done right, or the shot would be wasted. They would shake the bottle with its gummy looking materials, and after it warmed for 30 minutes they would pull it up into a syringe and stick him good in the bum. He never complained. The only time he truly complained was when he had to have a potassium infusion. He would beg them to dilute it, even if it took 2-3 hours longer. He hated those infusions, and almost passed out after the first one due to the extreme pain it caused.

We celebrated his birthday on April 12th, and he was able to enjoy some cake, but we quickly found out that dairy would be something he would need to avoid for the remainder of his life. Ice cream was horrible for him, but he loved it. Sometimes he would choose to suffer the consequences just to enjoy the flavor. Our schedules to Atlanta had to start being planned out further in advance due to my traveling for business, because I was the caregiver. I was the only one that could go with Stoney once I was added to the flight vouchers through the Center, and I wanted to go with him. I believe that every person going through a medical crisis should have an advocate by their side. Someone who listens, and someone who can act responsibly and precisely when the time comes. It was an honor for me to travel with him. The nurses and care teams became our family. Little did we know at the time, CTCA would become our second home.

We were assigned a Neuroendocrine care manager when we initially arrived in Atlanta, and her name was Kristen, who knew her stuff. We were drawn to Kristen from day one, and we seemed to have an instant connection with her. Later, through our conversations, we found out that she and her husband, Todd, had a daughter who was tragically killed in an accident. She had experienced loss first hand, and she had such compassion to give toward others. I think we drove her insane over the course of 2 years. Well, maybe I drove her insane. She allowed me to call her any time, any day with questions about Stoney, the disease, concerns or if I just needed to talk. There aren't too many nurses who give you that personal connection. From talking with Kristen more about her daughter, we found she and her husband had a nonprofit organization called, "Ellie's Way". It was a website geared to those grieving, and looking back, another Godwink on our journey…

April 23, 2019…

Well, another successful trip to the Cancer Treatment Center of America!! The Dr and his team feel like the shots will help Stoney, and maintain symptom management. No other treatment will be necessary as of now, but there will be several kinds of surgeries and treatment options coming soon that were not available a few years ago. We feel blessed to have this team and hopefully Stoney can now go on with his normal activities!! Praise the Lord!!! (This Cancer is not cure-able but is manageable)

At the end of April, I had a very special group tour booked on a 12 night cruise from Honolulu to Vancouver. All of my tours were a concern for me, because I never knew if I was going to cancel them or be able to go. I also had mom and Stoney booked on all of my tours as my guests. The three of us enjoyed spending time together. My mom became another mother for Stoney, and she felt like she gained another son. Stoney had always been supportive in helping with my dad on the many years we toured together in ministry, and that carried over once we came off the road. Living next door to my mom, was fun for both Stoney and I because we could watch movies, visit, play games or do puzzles on almost any given night. We had the perfect set up. I always say, I got a maid and my mom got a cook. I love to cook, and she likes to clean. At least thats what I tell myself.

As the trip was drawing night, I asked Stoney if he truly felt up to going. His favorite place in the world was Hawaii, and we had planned to spend a few days on land with friends before going on the cruise, so his answer was YES! The injection seemed to hold him over, and give him some relief with his symptoms. I would also like to freely give some information to those who may wonder "You went on all these lavish trips while asking for money?" I know questions did arise, and I just want to say that at NO time did any money that came in for Stoney's expenses go toward any trips we took. All trips were taken from money I had made from my travel agency, as well as the comps that I earn through my business. These were all things that we dealt with on top of our health crisis. People thought it was terrible for Stoney to be traveling with me given his current health status. I agree to an extent, but it was also his decisions to go, and we had medical advice before every trip. I also know how much Stoney loved to travel. It was his life. As I said before, he had a list of places he wanted to go and now that his time was limited, he was taking every course of action to do what he could when he could! I have no regrets for taking him with me every chance I was given.

Stoney truly loved living.... He loved every aspect of life. He made the most of all of it, and always knew how to change a bad situation into a loving lasting memory. We toured the island of Oahu, Maui and sailed around Kauai before taking the 5 days at sea to Vancouver, Canada. Once we arrived in Vancouver, we drove down to Seattle and had lunch with some very dear friends that we met during our music ministry. What a wonderful time of sharing happy memories. When we arrived in Seattle, I had a surprise up my sleeve. I was flying mom home, but Stoney and I were actually turning around and flying back to Hawaii for a week to spend with his nephew, Nathan. I used my air miles, and condo points so that he could go back and enjoy time with his nephew, and that would end up being his last time to Hawaii.

We flew home from a trip where many wonderful memories were made. Stoney had a blast showing his nephew a place he loved so much, and told Nathan he had many plans to come back. We arrived in Nashville for just a couple of nights, and then returned to Atlanta for more appointments…

May 23, 2019…

Every time we visit the Cancer Treatment center of America in Atlanta, I thank the Lord for the people He placed in our lives to get us here and for the treatment Stoney has received. We went from hearing "you have just a few months to live", to a bright future for many years! God is so GOOD, and the Physicians/Staff at CTCA are amazing!! We still have a long way to go, but trusting the Lord each month to provide exactly what Stoney needs physically, spiritually, mentally and financially to continue his treatment and medicine at home. If you feel led to help...we have a few options! Thanks to all who pray daily and who have helped support his journey this far!

We had good days, and bad days. As with any life changing disease, you find ways to navigate all the ups and downs. He would go in for routine bloodwork, and often times have to take short acting shots to lighten his symptoms. He would give himself shots in his belly 2-3 times a day, and take as many as 20 pills 3 times a day. I watched him fight for his life, and to be honest I don't think I could have done it. The dedication it took was beyond anything I had witnessed, and we were just getting started.

May 30, 2019…

Bloodwork is normal...all flare-ups are due to stress and anxiety. The Dr said that financial stress and worry can cause lots of strange things. Stoney tried to go back to work today, but the Dr feels he is going to have to start gradually. He is under a great load of stress/pressure right now.

….EVENING UPDATE….Things can change in the matter of a few hours!

Please pray for Stoney. We are taking him to the ER in Nashville tonight for very high blood pressure and other symptoms that might be a side effect from his treatment. He is surrounded by loads of medical anxiety and is stressed about finances and the other details that come along with his diagnosis. Please pray we have the right medical team tonight and they can solve his issues quickly.

As Philippians 1:3 says. "I thank my God upon every remembrance of you". (NIV) I was so grateful for the support from people who never stopped praying. God laid us on their hearts for a purpose, and for that I will forever remain humbled and blessed.

May 31, 2019…

Well, as many of you read my post last night, and prayed for us...I am extremely grateful! Things could have been worse, but God was so good and allowed the Dr's to know exactly what was wrong with stoney very quickly. It has been a very difficult journey for him these last several months...learning he has a cancer that has no cure...not working for 5 months, and suffering from different side effects and symptoms each week. Yesterday, Stoney went back to work for the first time since January 9th. He had hoped that this would be ongoing, and that things were finally back to normal. He had been experiencing tension and headaches, and having to check his blood pressure each day, it had spiked to numbers that were extremely high for him. So, as a precaution, we went to the ER to find out that his blood levels were normal, and that he had experienced a minor panic attack, stress and anxiety. The Dr recommended he not rush back to work so quickly, but to take it a day at a time. Maybe start back slowly and work up to his longer hours. This creates a little more stress for Stoney as the giving has gone down, money resources are drained and he is back to the anxiety of "What am I going to do". We have looked into several options for funding, but have been denied and advised to be careful how we pursue things if he does indeed go back to work. So....I ask you to first, PRAY... Pray that God give Stoney wisdom what to do and how to proceed. He will have to continue his treatments in Atlanta every month for the rest of his life....The injections are expensive and there are lots of things that insurance will NOT cover, adding more pressure to his "career", and how he will be able to provide. I continue to work from home AND be a full time caregiver as much and often as I can, however, I am asking for help. If you would like to share a donation with/for Stoney, I know he would be so grateful and appreciative. I also know that this is NOT long term...He just needs to gradually work into his new schedule and pace himself. We are trusting the Lord in ALL things...Trusting Him to PROVIDE, to PROTECT and HEAL. God has us in the palm of His hand and it amazes me daily how strongly HE holds us. We continue to live in HOPE, and we THANK YOU for your prayers and support on this journey and ask for you to walk with us a little longer! :)

As things began to normalize, Stoney was able to go back to work. Life started to seem manageable and for a little while, we actually forgot he had cancer.

We were schedule to go back to Atlanta for Stoneys 6 month scans and we decided to take both our moms for a few days. It was hard for Stoneys mom, Sharon, to get away because she was a caregiver to her husband. We made plans for Tracy to have "care" so that she could go and enjoy a couple days with us. We thought we would make it fun and take them to Stone Mountain National Park. With all of the hype about Stoneys name, we thought it would be fun to go and see how things have changed, since both of us had not been since we were small kids. It was also a chance for our moms to see the Cancer Center, and meet some of the amazing people who were taking care of us. Stoney kept telling everyone who asked how he was managing at the center that it was the "Disneyland for the sick". He wasn't wrong! Everything was under one roof. In one or two days, we could have bloodwork, scans, meet with oncology, dietary, naturopath, chiropractic and pastoral care. It was just amazing the way they could keep things rolling with answers the next day, and we wanted our moms to see it in action.

We spent the first day getting scans, and then ventured off to Stone Mountain. We had some good laughs, but as Stoney said afterwards, "We don't need to do that again". haha!

The scans showed growth, and it was not the information we wanted to hear along with our moms. We know God has a plan, and we know that in the meantime, we will live life, enjoy it to the fullest and make memories. Stoney created saying earlier on in his diagnosis. "Each day I have now is a gravy day". Every day he had beyond the point of diagnosis was a day to enjoy, love and appreciate. And God gave him many great "gravy days".

June 23, 2019…

Well, 3am came early today!! We came to Atlanta for Stoneys monthly visit and injection. His bloodwork is perfect and he is doing very good!! We will be back July 22-25 for loads of tests, scans and appointments to see if the tumors are growing quickly or spreading. This will be the 6 month point. Please pray for miracles!! God is so good through the valleys of life. We have have seen our strength grow in and THROUGH the PROMISES of God!!!

July 24, 2019…

The report from CTCA was that his tumors have grown but that he is stable. We will have to come back in 3 months for more scans and reports. This is a long journey but we are thankful for God's grace and mercy!! Please pray Stoney as he continues to walk this journey. So much on his mind and overwhelming financial obligations. God is good through it all

The cancer journey can take you on so many emotional rollercoasters. I can't tell you how many times we laughed and cried. On good days, and bad days we tried to rejoice. Learning to love life despite knowing that tumors were growing, and taking over your body is a hard thing to accept. Through it all, there were all sorts of special moments to love. In August, Stoney's niece was getting married to the love of her life after a long courtship. We couldn't be happier for them, and Stoney was so excited to be alive and well enough to attend; however, he would have the honor of doing more than attending but officiating. Rachel came to her uncle Stoney and asked him if he perform their ceremony, and of course the answer was, yes. He was very intimidated and nervous because this would be his first! Not many people knew he was an ordained minister.

We all prayed Stoneys health would hold out long enough for him to partake in this special day, and sure enough it was a perfect day! Rachel and Kevin had asked Liz and myself to decorate and help plan their wedding. With only about 4 weeks to prepare, it came together beautifully and it will be a memory that I know she and Kevin will hold deeply in their hearts, as well as myself. Stoney was not feeling great the day of the wedding, but you would never know it. He made it through the ceremony with only one little slip, but it was funny and no one gave it a second thought. He had married his niece during this time that he was suffering, he was saying yes to things, and making memories to cherish because he knew time was running short.

The monthly injections that were working so well, had started showing signs of being less effective. Instead of 28 days, he was only getting about 21 days of relief. He would increase his short acting injections at home, leaving his belly purple and bruised. He pushed on to make plans for the future, and we didn't let this "breakthrough" cause us to change our schedule. He continued driving as much as he could for a source of income, while I continued working my travel agency, as well as tried to encourage folks to share a financial love gift if they could to help give Stoney a cushion. His hours were starting to become more limited again, and we began to become more concerned that if the tumors were growing, and injections weren't working, then what is happening with the cancer? We tried to be positive and not let our minds go down the aisle of self defeat, but it was evident at times and became our main topic in conversations. We would pray against it, and plead for Gods healing, but started to wonder if God chose a different path, would be willing to accept it moving forward...

5

Leaning on Time...

Jeremiah 29:11 - "For I know the plans I have for you," declares the LORD, "plans to prosper you and not to harm you, plans to give you hope and a future" -NIV

Fall of 2019 had arrived and we had plans made! I was headed to Maine with my mom to spend Labor Day weekend at a camp that we had ministered to for many years. I would see friends, and also spend a few days with my Aunt and Uncle in Canada. Checking on Stoney several times a day was part of my schedule. Again, I hated to leave home when he was having troubles, because I had become his voice when we went to the hospital and to the ER. He would get dehydrated, and nauseated that he could never really tell them all of the details, so I was the spokesperson. I didn't mind, and I was honored that he had chosen me to be his voice. However, being away for a week stressed me out more than being home taking care of him. I never knew when I was going to get a call, and need to change my plans to be home. All of his siblings worked, had families, and it was not the easiest for them to give him full time care. We both had an understatement that this was my place, my duty, and never an obligation.

I would fly home from Maine, and then jump on a plane to Florida. I had made plans to take Stoney and his niece, Marina, to Orlando for a few days for an art class and attend a party at Disney. Just days before we were to go, a hurricane had ripped though Florida, scaring many travelers from flying down. We, however, were in the perfect position to go as it had just passed the day we were scheduled to leave. The night we got there, we went to get some dinner, and there was no one around. To my surprise, I had never seen Disney so empty, and it was like we had the park all to ourselves. Stoney, being the Disney fan he was, enjoyed the time he had with Marina. He loved having an impact on his nieces and nephews, but never had the opportunity to truly do things with them when we were touring, so he was making his moments count. Marina is an artist, and a very good one at that. We enjoyed attending an art class together where she basically put us to shame with her painting. It was so much fun, as we enjoyed the good food, and entertainment.

Upon returning from Florida, we made the quick turnaround and headed out to Vancouver Washington with my mom. I had won a trip for selling Disney travel, and they were awarding me with a cruise to Alaska on Disney cruise line. My mom and I still look back to that cruise and think it was one of the most special memories we have with Stoney. He was very happy, and I had never seen him relax as much as he did on that cruise, taking in each and every moment. Every night he said to me, "Thank you Beej, this is the most amazing trip!" There was a part of me that wished I could take him to all the places on his list before time ran out. I began to lean on time, enjoying these moments while begging for more. I planned more trips in the Fall just so he could have some excitement. I tried including him on any and all excursions I was booking through my business. In our minds I think we somehow knew, these were "the last" of certain trips. We of course always talked about coming back, but at least in my mind, I was bracing myself.

I saw things not working like they should. I would hear the specialist say, "people live 15-20 plus years with these injections and there's always new trials coming out that will give more time." I began to get fed up with that each time I heard someone talk about it, because it was giving us more hope, and although the treatment might work on some people, it may do nothing for others....and I felt like we were falling into the category of "others".

September 20, 2019...

Prayer Request!! Stoney Dartt is having issues with his monthly cancer injection. They just aren't lasting long enough. They put him on an emergency *injection shot to give himself when he needs it, but it's $550 for a 3 month supply and really needs the help financially to pick them up. They are sitting at our pharmacy, but due to finances, he can't get them. If anyone would like to help him out, I know he would be grateful!! You can give through PayPal, go fund me, Apple Pay, or by mailing a personal gift. If you'd be interested in helping or want more information, please text or inbox me!! We go to Atlanta Monday for more info and another injection. More CT scans will follow in October*

September 24, 2019…

I got back from Atlanta last night from taking Stoney to the Cancer Treatment Center. The report went well... They do not believe at this point that any surgery should be done and that we should wait as long as we can before taking that step. They told him that unfortunately he would suffer through the symptoms of the cancer no matter how many injections he would receive. It's just the nature of the beast. They have started him on a new medication he will take 3 times a day that will work in conjunction with his monthly injection. He also has his emergency "self given" shots he can take as needed. Next month he will have several more scans and X-rays to see tumor growth and we are praying for a miracle. Please pray that the tumors will not have grown at all and possibly may have shrunk some...although we know the tumors will continue to grow, we are praying it will stop growing so quickly! We appreciate all of you who have supported us financially and have prayed daily! Please continue as we look to the Lord for HOPE and PEACE!

October 25, 2019…

Well today's visit to the Cancer Treatment Center was not as good as we hoped, but nothing to be too worried about. The doctors have decided to do a procedure on Stoney as early as January that was hoping to be put off for a year or two. The tumors are growing and they need to try something sooner than later to slow it down. He will continue to have his monthly injections, but this surgery will hopefully cut the blood supply to the tumors. He seems to be doing ok and hanging in there with the news...he's more worried about taking time off and not getting paid. Hahaha. I told him to not worry about that...God owns the cattle on a thousand hills, and nothing is too big for him to provide. We continue to trust the Lord each day for His perfect provision! Thank you for your prayers!!

Doesn't God promise to supply all of our needs if we ask? I love the scripture in Philippians (4:19) that says, "But my God shall supply all your need according to his riches in glory by Christ Jesus." (NIV) He was doing just that for us.

October 31, 2019…

UPDATE ON STONEY:

Well this is certainly not a treat today, but more of a trick. We are headed to the ER in Nashville to have tests run on stoney. Since his last visit to Atlanta, he hasn't responded to the injection like normal. He has missed 4 days of work and has felt weak and nauseated. His cancer symptoms are also in full bloom so he can't leave the house. Please pray that the medical team in Nashville can help him today. We normally always go to Atlanta for problems, but we can't really get there today...

I have so much going on as well, that this is not the best timing to spend an afternoon in a hospital, so please pray for the Lords timing, for quick results, for patience, for graciousness (I need a lot of it today) and overall good news and fixes.

UPDATE FROM STONEY….

October 31, 2019

Here I am in the ER again in Nashville after nearly passing out this morning at home. Because I am an oncology patient, they roomed me within five minutes of when we walked in the door. I am on an IV for fluids, they drew five vials of blood to do lab work with, and they took a chest x-ray. We are awaiting results while I get my fluids. Through it all, God is good! Thank you so much for your continued prayers and support, and a huge thanks to Bj Speer for being such a great caregiver and always going the extra mile to keep everyone updated!

UPDATE--- Before I could post the above, the nurse came in. Chest X-ray look good.... lab work looks good but shows low sodium & BiCarb... and they're going to finish putting this IV bag in me and send me home. I've had a lingering cough following an upper respiratory infection I had a few weeks ago, so it was also important to make sure I don't have pneumonia or some deeper respiratory infection.

It seemed as if the scan that was done in October had accelerated the growth of the tumors causing Stoney to become more sick. The stress was boiling not only in his mind, but also in mine. I had a huge trip coming around the corner to Israel. I would be taking a group on a cruise from Rome through the churches of Paul, and then spend 2 days on land in Israel with our friends, the DeYoung's. I had so much invested in this trip, and yes, once again Stoney was scheduled to go along. We had not mentioned too much about it in our facebook posts, because people would make snarky comments. I tried to avoid them at all cost, and then as Stoney says, "pray they get a rash!". Some days, I really dislike people! However, without people, there is no ministry. Come to think about it now, I wasn't in ministry at the time, so I am not sure why it bothered me so much. I guess we are always bothered by what people think, and their ability to cause more complications in our lives than they should. I had so many people give me suggestions, home remedies, health journals, youtube videos, etc… I am like, "if this is going to cure cancer, then why hasn't it?" Well, I really respect those people, and their kindness to help, but at times it was overwhelming to me mentally because I thought maybe I wasn't doing all I could. I was second guessing my abilities as a caregiver. Finally one night before this Holy Land trip, I fell on my knees and I begged God to forgive me for the things I felt in my mind and to restore me mentally giving me clarity in following His commands. It had worked up to this point, so why was I doubting again? Was it because Stoney was getting worse? Was it because of something I wasn't doing right? NO!!! It was cancer, and it was killing him.

All we can do when we can't do any more, is PRAY! Fall on our knees, and give it to Him. I had these moments on more than one occasion.

November 2, 2019…

UPDATE ON STONE DARTT:

The past few days have continued to be bad days for stoney. He has not been able to work, and has stayed in his pajamas close to the bathroom (sorry for the TMI). The ER seemed to think after getting fluids, and taking Imodium, that he would be ok. However, the cancer symptoms are really holding him down this week. Please pray he can get some relief. He is tired, weak and can't seem to make any progress this time around. He feels very discouraged and frustrated...

UPDATE FROM STONEY……

November 4, 2019

I can't thank all of you enough for the prayer support over the last week! Praise God, I had the best sleep last night that I've had in a week & I feel better today than I have in more than a week. I will go have more labs done here in Nashville tomorrow to make sure my potassium & sodium numbers are going back in the right direction. It has been the worst week I've had since February or March... quite miserable, complete with an ER visit to get labs & fluids on Oct 31 after nearly passing out very early that same day... and I lost a very much needed week of work in the meantime... not to mention a LOT of fluids... but God has provided a replacement for some of that lost income & I know He will be faithful to provide the rest. Sometimes your health leaves you no choice but come to a complete standstill... but ALL the time, God is good! Blessings to all!

November 7, 2019…

Still in the ER.... Some of Stoneys levels are good, while others dropped... it was not the results we were looking or hoping. They are conferencing with his care team in Atlanta to see what's next and what can be done. We continue to wait...ugh...

….EVENING UPDATE…

They released Stoney to go home and added MORE medication to his long roster of drugs.

They are hoping this will correct his bloodwork and relax some of the symptoms the is experiencing. I would explain, but its gross, so just imagine! hahaha! Thank you for your prayers!!

November 8, 2019…

UPDATE ON STONE DARTT:

Last night the cancer center called and consulted with the ER doctors in Nashville approving Stoney to travel and resume his daily schedules. He is on new medication and feeling better today...we PRAISE THE LORD!! We thank you for all the prayers!!

A trip was planned and booked a year ago where mom, Liz and Stoney were suppose to join me. The last couple of weeks put that trip in jeopardy, but we are thankful for HIS blessing and we pray for Stoney's continued healing as he is not totally back to normal yet. Poor guy is having to travel with 120 syringes, 60 glass ampules of super expensive cancer treatment injections, and is having to carry pedialyte with him everywhere he goes to keep drinking fluids to continually replenish his electrolytes. We are thankful to you who prayed, for you who have sacrificially given toward his medical and personal needs. We feel so incredibly blessed, thankful, and happy Where U Wanna Go Travel & Tours was able to host him on his first visit to the Holy Land!! Now I'm off to work!! :)

November 11, 2019…

Our first day in Rome was long, exhausting, adventurous and beyond exciting!! We toured Rome in a day...literally! Started at the Colosseum, then Piazza do Venezia, Spanish steps, Trevi Fountain, and ended in the Vatican City. We walked over 8 miles, ate true Italian Pizza (Alfredo for mom), gorged ourselves on gelato and enjoyed espresso! Weather was sunny and perfect just for us, as they've had rain the last several weeks...and as soon as we got back to the hotel, it started pouring so we remain blessed and thankful!! Met up with some of our group last night and today we begin 12 days through the Mediterranean with stops in Israel, Greece, Cypress, Turkey and southern Italy.

Well from reading this, you can see Stoney was able to tour The Holy Land with us! To God be the Glory! On our way over, we had a connection in Philadelphia and of course wouldn't you know, we ran into an Evangelist friend. He asked if he could take a picture of us with him, and of course I thought nothing of it. Within moments of him posting the picture, and tagging us, I had people messaging me wondering how Stoney could be so sick and yet be able to tour Israel. In my mind I was trying to think of ways to play damage control. How to put these fires out, while people were getting the wrong idea or misunderstanding the situation. Yes, it's true, he was sick. He had also received clearance from the cancer center to go the night prior to leaving with loads more medication. It was a choice he made to go, and looking back, I am so glad he did!!! Stoney fell in love with Israel, made me promise to take him back. Although that never happened, I am so thankful that Stoney got to experience it once. He shed tears in the Garden, trembled on the Mount of Olives, and we both wept on the Sea of Galilee (which is still my favorite spot on any tour). Why would anyone try to steal his joy (or mine) from experiencing the best that God has to offer.

Toward the end of this tour, Stoney began having "breakthrough" again. His numerous times to the bathrooms were creeping back to an all-time high. We would find ourselves returning home to make a trip to Atlanta for action.

November 26, 2019…

Here at CTCA and continuously amazed at how incredible the staff is and they never cease to amaze me even when we are a bundle of nerves. The care, the love, and respect they give is just top notch. We are refilling prescriptions that are not covered by insurance and getting set up for a surgery in January...I'll announce the date this evening when we get it scheduled so you all can pray! Stoney will have liver directed therapy which will keep him home for a week recovery and he will be uncomfortable for a couple of weeks. The doctor is hoping this will help for at least a year, so please pray!

….LONG DAY!! Pet scan completed, tests done, surgery scheduled and we are headed home!!!

Stoney will have liver directed therapy January 27th which will hopefully help his symptoms for a longer period of time! He will be unable to work for 10 days while he recovers to gain his strength and energy back. His tumors are stable and not growing as fast as they were, so that's good news!! Please pray that his injection today will take effect and work this month!! Last month was a dud! They said it could be the way it was given, as in not in the right spot. Thanks for the prayers!! Now to go home and celebrate a wonderful thankful time of year with family and friends!

As we left Atlanta on that trip, we were hoping for a better holiday season. Little did we know, life was about to get a little more chaotic and less kind to Stoney. It made me truly appreciate each day, and again, wish for many more good ones. I love Christmas, it's probably my favorite time of the year. Stoney loves when I decorate, and I really go all out. I have a 12ft tree I put up, along with about 4 other trees throughout the house. I decorate the fireplace, the dining room, and even the kitchen! We watch Christmas movies, drink hot chocolate, and play Christmas music on low through the evening. To have the holiday stolen from us was a nightmare, but to think that the previous year was his last at home was heartbreaking.

As I come back and re-live these moments, tracing my footsteps, and sharing memories from our past, I cant help but wish that God had given us more time. Us, meaning Stoneys family, myself, and our friends. Why was God allowing this to happen, and why was He allowing such pain to become a larger part of our lives? We had given our lives in Christian service, Stoney had given so much of himself to others, and now he has an incurable disease to suffer through, why? None of us are exempt, we live in a fallen world where bad things happen to good people. John 16:33 says, "I have told you these things, so that in me you may have peace. In this world you will have trouble. But take heart! I have overcome the world."-NIV

I believe it was during the holidays that I became more upset at what was going on in our lives because of the pure fact, I was selfish. I wanted to sit at home and enjoy what we always done. I didn't want to sit in a hospital or an ER. Now I wish we had taken little more advantage of the time we had in those places to pray more, to share Jesus a little more. Yes, we did that, but we should have done MORE....

December 10, 2019...

STONE DARTT UPDATE:

Prayers continued for Stoney. He came home from the ER last night very

tired and drained. Today he has no energy, very weak, no appetite and has begun vomiting. We are very concerned and are awaiting a call from the cancer center as to what our next move will be. Please pray for healing and new strength!

December 11, 2019…

Stoney Dartt update:

After much thought and prayer, we have decided to bump up Stoneys surgery date to December 27th. The symptoms are really controlling his life and they want to give him some relief, so they tried to schedule next week but could not make that happen so we will go December 26-30th for surgery and injections. Please pray he can hang on and get some relief until then...

December 14, 2019…

Update on Stone Dartt...

Thank you all for your prayers!! They are greatly appreciated!! He was seen by the ER staff right away and given 3 liters of fluids and potassium supplements. He got to bed around 2 this morning and had a rough night losing more fluids again. He is scheduled to have liquid infusions on Monday again and maybe more throughout the week as needed until his surgery date on the 27th. He is a trooper, but is just so frustrated as he continues to deal with all these issues. We are praying without ceasing and trusting God for a miracle. Two weeks seems so far away for him to have this surgery, but as of right now there are no openings for anything sooner. Please keep praying!! Thank you so much for all the kind words, thoughts and prayers sent my way as well. I'm tired, emotionally worn and yet so full of thankfulness to all who have lifted me up in prayer. Please don't stop! I'm counting on you! :)

December 18, 2019…

Update on Stone Dartt....

Stoney is back in the ER and being admitted for a couple days due to new X-ray findings of a shadow in his lungs which they believe is pneumonia. Pray they can treat him, get him well and this is not a new tumor from the cancer (which can spread). God knows!! Praying and Believing for a miracle!!

December 19, 2019…

Stoney was admitted to Centennial Hospital in Nashville for Pneumonia at this time. That's all we know while doctors continue to look at pathology reports. He is getting fluids and antibiotics. He is beginning to feel a little better, and at this point we not know how long they will keep him. Please continue to pray!!

More time off, more stress with regular bills and new medication. I know it's a very difficult time of the year to give extra, but if you can, we would greatly appreciate it!!! I will keep you updated!!

December 20, 2019…

Good morning prayer warriors! Stoneys Dr came in and said that somehow through the night his potassium dropped horribly low (2.2....cardiac arrest bad) They think what they gave him yesterday was diluted by the sodium they are giving him. I called the cancer center and our nurse there doesn't understand either how it could have changed so fast from being normal yesterday. He will stay at Centennial today and not go home, which may mean he stays through the weekend as well. We will keep you all updated but need major prayers that they figure this out. I have my doubts that the attending physician knows how to treat Stoney and they will not release info to cancer center now matter how many times I ask, which is very frustrating. Please pray and ask God to work it all out!!

UPDATE…

Sitting in the hospital with Stoney all day here at Centennial Tri-Star in Nashville has been so frustrating!! It surprises me how bad the care is in these places. It makes me incredibly grateful and thankful for the care and love we receive at the Cancer Center in Atlanta. You are not a "number or name" there, you are FAMILY!!! They treat you as if you are a part of them, and they love on you while they are giving the treatment. This experience today has been pathetic and ridiculous!! My claws have come out on more than one occasion, but it's only because I do truly CARE!!! We need to pray for a RISE UP of more nurses and Doctors who want to treat their patients as if they are a family member NOT a number... I am so thankful for my friends and family who are nurses who have reached out to me today with ways to help! You have been on my team and have blessed me with your words of encouragement!! Thank you for always being there for me.

Stoney had a horrible rough day! 6 bags of potassium, and more sodium... antibiotics and more! He is a trooper for sure. He is resting tonight...still with no dinner (yes after asking 3 times for food, he still has not received it- PATHETIC!!)

Please pray hard that he gets better results tomorrow and that he can go home for the weekend or at least by Christmas!! One week from today he will have his surgery!!!

Here is one of the rare posts from Stoney. I will notes that after this, he rarely posted about his situation, but merely shared my status. He seemed to draw further away from being informative about himself, and allowed me to be more of his voice.

UPDATE FROM STONEY....

December 22, 2019

PRAYER REQUESTED: As many of you know, I suffer with VIPoma - which is a rare subset of a rare cancer known as Neuroendocrine Cancer. I have a very large tumor in my pancreas & 10 tumors in my liver. I will post a Wikipedia link in a separate post for those interested in the specifics of the disease's diagnosis & symptoms, etc.

I've been at Centennial Medical Center in Nashville for 4 nights now. They're trying to get my potassium built up to a safe level before releasing me. At one point this stay it hit a critical & dangerous low of 2.2 which puts a person at high risk of going into cardiac arrest. And Friday & Saturday I spent much of the daytime literally writhing in excruciating (almost going unconscious type) pain during hours upon hours of potassium infusions and was only able to get about 4 hrs sleep Friday night. And hardly able to eat anything from pain & nausea. Uuuugh!!

THE PRAYER REQUEST:

I am scheduled with my care team in the Atlanta area this Friday at "Cancer Treatment Centers of America (CTCA)" to have my very first interventional procedure - a "liver-directed therapy" using a method called "bland embolization" which will attempt to deliver a non-radioactive substance right into the blood supplying arteries of the 2 largest tumors in my liver. They are very hopeful & confident that this procedure will yield drastic results for the better & that I should very quickly have relief from the symptoms. I' ll most likely be nauseated, in pain, & unable to work for up to a week or possibly more & will be unable to lift anything. PLEASE PRAY that my metabolic & electrolyte levels will stabilize enough by flight time on Thursday & continue into Friday so that a postpone won't be necessary- as my symptoms are only going to get worse without intervention & it will become more & more difficult to get the procedure done in a timely manner. Also I have a chest cough I need to get over ASAP - though the staff here don't believe it's actually pneumonia - which is the reason I was put in the hospital to begin with on Wednesday (they were concerned I might have it).

Thanks for your prayers & support. It is my hope to do a Facebook Live appearance from the hospital or perhaps from home sometime later today. I've never done that before & I look like a freshly thawed neanderthal right now, but I've been so ill lately & haven't felt strong enough to properly thank those who've given & prayed & shared my story with others. It might also be a time to answer questions some might have about my health situation or about how Mom & Dad & the rest of the family are doing, etc.

December 23, 2019…

PRAYERS NEEDED!!!

Today, Stoneys bloodwork did not show a huge increase in potassium levels. The cancer center will deny the procedure Friday that he needs so desperately if the potassium will not stabilize at 3.2. We need all of you to PRAY like never before!! We need a Christmas miracle!!! He will remain in the hospital and on fluids right up until the last moment on Thursday before our flight. We will make the final decision on Thursday based on his morning labs.

December 25, 2019….

We brought Christmas to the hospital last night. Stoney had a rough night with a bad reaction to a new medication they are trying... lost a LOT of fluids but this morning his labs are showing that his potassium number has hit 3.6!!! This is literally a Christmas miracle. This is God truly showing up and proving

Himself faithful once again. A lot can change in the next day or so, but we live in hope that God is going to continue to take care of this!! The surgery is in 49 hours from this moment!! PRAY PRAY PRAY!! We are in the final stretch!

...EVENING UPDATE...

Prayers tonight for Stone Dartt!! His potassium level dropped from 3.7 to 3.1 (which is still safe but not normal anymore) and we just need to get it up and remain before Friday morning!! We are at the finish line and need to just fight long enough to cross it!!

I like what Dr. David Jeremiah says about sickness, and having faith to overcome the trials when we feel our hope is gone. He says we must "Center our Minds", keeping it focused on the Lord. 2 Timothy 1:7 "God has not given us a spirit of fear, but of power and of love and of a sound mind." (NIV) He then tells us to "Count our Blessings", using 1 Thessalonians 5:18 as a reference. "In everything give thanks; for this is the will of God in Christ Jesus for you.(NIV) I was doing that. I was thanking God each and every day for the people praying, and the gifts provided, but I needed more of His presence. He then says to "Continue your Work". (Ephesians 2:10-NIV), and To "Claim your Promise" (which is my favorite) using John 11:4-NIV, "Jesus said, This sickness is not until death, but for the glory of God, that the Son of God may be glorified through it". (NIV) Can you imagine? God was using this sickness, this disease for something other than harm, but HIS glory! If I could just continue to claim His promise, and count my blessings, I might just see a way through the darkness. Lastly, he shares to "Consider the Future". How could I even see the future at this point? I was clouded and consumed with defeat, darkness and dread. Stoney was sick, he was dying ultimately, and I was trying to find solace. The scripture here is Romans 8:18... "I consider that the sufferings of this present time are not worthy to be compared with the glory which shall be revealed in us." (NIV) How could any glory be revealed in me at such time as this? I knew God was working...I knew God was pushing me to follow Him and in His leading, but I was fearful and doubt had crossed my mind.

6

Losing Time

John 16:22 - "So with you: Now is your time of grief, but I will see you again and you will rejoice, and no one will take away your joy." -NIV

Surviving Christmas was one thing, but knowing that Stoney would suffer like this even beyond this magnitude was beyond hard for me to process. I saw how sick he was in the hospital, the vomiting, the pain, and misery. How was I going to handle the days ahead? I guess God was preparing me for what was to come. GRACE…

The morning we left for Atlanta, I had a moment with God. I was getting ready at home, and would drive to Nashville to pick up Stoney and then off to the airport for the surgery. If all went well, it would be a miraculous few days. There was HOPE on the horizon, but we were also losing TIME. We knew that with every surgery, or procedure, it was cutting his time down. They could only perform these things so many times, and then we would be out of options.

Very few people know this, but that morning getting ready was one of the hardest moments I had ever experienced in my life. I had lost my dad, and that was difficult, but I seemed to know what to do and what was next. His funeral was a day I don't really remember all that well, because I had taken some medication to help me process and get through. I regret doing that, but I also know at the time it was needed for me to cope and to get to what was next. This moment now was surreal. I was about to do something nearly impossible. I was going to transport someone from Nashville to Atlanta via flying, when he hadn't been able to get out of bed for over a week. I was going to take him all by myself to a hotel, and then onto the hospital the next morning…ALONE! Did I need to take something? Should I take something for myself? Stoney had lots of medication, including Ativan and other things to help with anxiety and depression. I had medication to take from my own doctor for anxiety, but never took it. Would I need this to get through the next few days?

I vividly remember getting dressed, and becoming so emotional that I couldn't see straight. I fell on the floor, I wept, and I prayed a prayer that I can't remember today, but I know I had never prayed like that ever before, and probably never since. I begged God to heal Stoney, to remove the cancer, and to give him strength to be moved to Atlanta, but also I told him that I was giving Stoney to Him and if He had another plan, I would accept it and trust Him to see things for His glory. I told God that if He took Stoney home in the next few days, I would not understand why, but I would praise Him for His goodness, grace and love. I cried to the point that I wasn't sure I could even drive to Nashville to get him, and if I was being completely honest with you, I have no recollection whatsoever of getting from my home, to the hospital, to the airport in Nashville. I slightly remember that when I picked him up, his niece Rachel was there to see us off and give us hugs, but thats it. I know I prayed for about 36 hours without ceasing. I know that I told God a lot of things, but I was praying He would listen to me and heal Stoney through this surgery. Even though I told God I was giving Stoney to Him, I didn't have that to give! Stoney already belonged to God, and God already had a purpose, I just needed to be submissive and let God work. Sometimes we try to tell God what to do, instead of listening to what He wants us to do….

December 26, 2019…

We are just 25 hours from checking in at the Cancer Center for Stoneys Liver Bland Embolization procedure. The hospital and Nashville did bloodwork this morning and he was 3.4; however, that number can change up to 6/10 of a point within 6-7 hours so we are going and doing all the things we have been doing in hopes tomorrow morning when he gets his bloodwork, it will be 3.0 or higher!! Stepping out in faith as we have each day of this journey, and we are believing success for this surgery and a better 2020!! We are at the finish line y'all...just need your prayers to help us cross it!!

...AFTERNOON UPDATE...

Prayers needed. We are at the Nashville Airport and trying to get to Atlanta. Stoney is very weak, still a little dehydrated and very tired (and doped up). Please pray we can get to the hotel tonight safely and easily. That Stoney will feel peace, comfort, and get some needed rest. (And drink fluids!!)

...EVENING UPDATE...

It is 11:15 Thursday evening in Atlanta. Yes we made it here, which is the first of what we hope to be many miracles. Stoney is so tired, pure exhaustion from the hospital and has lost so much weight due to not having much of an appetite. He is nauseated almost 24 hours a day with small breaks when taking medication. He is getting ready for bed after eating a few bites and taking all his medicine for tonight. Our emotions run high, as we will not know until tomorrow morning if they will do the surgery. Lab numbers have to be in a good zone. If this works, surgery will be at 1:00 o'clock eastern time. I' ll update everyone as soon as I know!! We appreciate the prayers thus far and just need to cross this finish line tomorrow. I'm exhausted and trying to keep up on all the medicine, shots, food and drinks... it's A LOT!!! I'm continuing to believe for better days ahead and miracles. Hoping for a good night sleep!! I can feel the Power of prayer. I can feel the Lords arms wrapped around me, feeling blessed and thankful for all you faithful prayer warriors. Keep it up. Don't stop!!

December 27, 2019...

Hey Prayer Warriors!! We got our MIRACLE!!! He was just enough in the zone to move FORWARD with the surgery today!!! We bursted out into tears of joy, shock, rejoicing and thankfulness!! He is prepped and ready and they will start the procedure at 1:00!! He will be in surgery until 3:00 and go to recovery until 5:00! They may have to keep him in their special hotel, meaning I need to pay for my hotel to stay but that's ok. I need the rest, and he can get the care he needs. They said he will be in severe pain for at least 3 days and maybe longer, depending on how well he does. I will update y'all later, but in the meantime...THANK YOU for your prayers!!! God is so GOOD, and we have seen a TRUE MIRACLE OF GOD today!!

...STONE DARTT SURGERY UPDATE...

The surgeon just called me and said that the surgery was a huge success!! It's all done and he's in recovery. He was able to get all of the tumors (10) today so that he doesn't have to come back for another surgery next month. He will be in a little bit more pain, but the Dr felt worth it to relieve the horrible symptoms he's been experiencing. He should be good as new in 2 -3 weeks!! Keep praying for a successful recovery.

…EVENING UPDATE…

Well, it's 8:20 eastern time. I was able to spend a few hours with Stoney and he is...well.... very LOOPY! Hahaha! Anesthesia is NOT his friend (or maybe it is, depending on how you look at it).

He was able to eat an entire dinner, drink a decent amount of fluid tonight, get up to walk and use the bathroom. Very impressive first day they said! He is still in lots of pain, slightly nauseated but much better!! I am currently traveling back to the hotel to get medication they didn't have on hand that he takes, and then will go back to the center tonight to make sure he has it, THEN back to hotel for BED!!

All in all, it's been a great day! Just to be clear, and answer some questions.... the Dr cut the circulation off to the tumors so they will shrink and die. The tumors over time do indeed grow back, but this procedure can be done again. The cancer is not cured or gone... the large tumor in the pancreas can not be contained or treated and that is the "supplier" to the tumors in the liver.

It is extremely confusing and a different cancerous disease to most people. Neuroendocrine carcinoma is strange and more unique than most cancers. It can never be cured or go into remission like most other forms of cancer. (of course unless there is DIVINE HEALING from our Almighty God)

But it can be managed through procedures, like this one. There are a couple other things they can do if it gets this bad again.

Still...miracles happen like they did for us TODAY!!!

December 28, 2019…

Today is a pretty bad day for pain. Stoney is really uncomfortable and miserable. His sodium is still very low and they are giving him fluids, along with salt tablets and monitoring his kidneys now since he's got some bad numbers. They are keeping him in the cancer center all weekend to keep a close eye on him so continue to pray he can recover and heal quickly. The Dr said he will be in severe pain for 3 days so it's not a surprise. Just keep praying y'all!! The cancer center is taking incredible care of him!! I'm having to feed him and give him liquids cause he can't use his left arm for 3 days. This is the area where they did the surgery through the artery so no pressure can be applied. I'll update again tomorrow, but we are still on the right path I believe!!

December 29, 2019…

This morning, Stoneys pain is very bad once again. (All normal for this procedure according to Dr) His lab results are really weird and out of whack. Potassium is stable, sodium is moving in the right direction, and he has been getting fluids for 3 days! However, other numbers are all over the place. They are trying to find his new normal now since this procedure is done. The goal is to let him go back to the hotel tonight and see his Oncologist tomorrow, then get his lanreotide (injection) at 3 o'clock. Hopefully, we can head off to the airport and head home at 5!! We are aware that things may change, and to be honest, I'm ready for that! This whole ride has been a "is it gonna happen?" journey. God is good, and we are resting in His promises!! Keep those healing prayers coming!

…AFTERNOON UPDATE…

Look who is leaving the inpatient room at CTCA tonight!! He's still in pain, but headed to the hotel to get rested up for more testing and oncology tomorrow!! God is sooooo GOOD y'all!!! This IS only a miracle that God could do!! We are so BLESSED!! I stand amazed at the faithfulness of God. Pray him to Nashville tomorrow guys!!

December 30, 2019…

We are at Urgent Care (at the cancer center) now getting fluids because Stoneys sodium was critically low. This means, we don't get to see his Dr today, and we will end up staying in Atlanta longer which is making me so incredibly insane. I so wanted to go home, but this is more important, and I don't need people telling me "this is where you need to be" or sharing their instructions. I'm tired, I'm worn, I'm weak, and I just need people to pray that they can solve this problem! This is where we need to be for sure…but after almost 2 weeks living in the hospital, I just need more patience, strength and grace!! Gods got this!! I know that 100%!!! I just need the strength to finish the course... love to all!!

...EVENING UPDATE...

They are keeping us overnight, give stoney 2 liters of fluid and check labs in the morning. If his Sodium does not improve by morning, they will admit him again and begin new testing which could last several days based on the holidays. Prayers needed on many levels! We were almost home! I even had my boarding pass! :)

December 31, 2019....

GREAT NEWS!!! (Updates 12/31/19- 10:15am)

Stone Dartts bloodwork came back....he is within normal range to go home!!!! Flights were sold out until tonight, but between myself looking at airline back door sites (thanks to my travel agency) and working with CTCA, we are going home at 3:00 today!!! Lord willing we will be in Nashville at 3:15, (we gain an hour) and home this evening with friends and family!! God has once again showed up and shown us HE has a grip on us and is always ever interceding on our behalf!!!

The flight home from Atlanta was eventful. They gave him large doses of dilauded, a pain medicine that is very strong and he was having a hard time processing it. When we arrived at the airport, he seemed to be doing fine. We boarded the plane, and he started asking questions like "where are we going now?", and then as we took off, he was starting to get paranoid. Stoney never really liked talking to people on planes. He kept to himself for the most part, and only talked to others when they spoke to him. Both of us dreaded the airline passengers that wanted to have a conversation through the entire flight. You know the kind I'm talking about right? By the time you land, you've made a new friend, know all their kids, what they do for a living, and already planning a vacation together. We avoided eye contact all the time. However, this time, he was talking to everyone and it was actually embarrassing me. I grew up with a dad who thrived on embarrassing me, so you would think I was used to it. This precious lady, and her daughter were flying home from Atlanta as well and sat behind us. They boarded the plane behind us, and Stoney would not keep his mouth shut. This lady engaged him, almost as if she knew something was wrong with him. Her name was Wendy, and I am pretty sure Wendy knew everything that happened to Stoney for the past 12 months before we landed. As we were landing, Stoney grabbed my arm, and was scared. He said "Do you see it?" I'm like "see what?" "Do you see me floating outside of myself?" By this time, I was like, Lord Jesus land this plane and get us in the car, cause people gonna be thinking we are insane! I had to laugh at some of the things he was saying, because it was an out of body experience he was having. I don't remember everything he said, but after awhile, he said, "do you think I'm losing it Beej?" I said "yes, yes I do." He told me he felt like at that very moment, the tumors were fading away. He said he could feel them going away, and he was going to be cancer free and healed. Bless his heart… if only that were the truth. I tried to nod in agreement as not to disappoint him, plus people experience miracles, so why not now? I didn't want to undermine the Greatness of God.

When we got off the plane, Wendy told us a miracle that had happened to her. She couldn't walk, she had hip pain, and was crippled, but after people prayed for her and laid hands on her, she had been healed and was able to walk. She encouraged us to believe that God was in the miracle business and still able to heal. After we got home, Stoney said to me, "That lady, Wendy, she was an angel." I was like, ok… So, we had exchanged names and emails and I found her on facebook and began following her just to make sure I wasn't losing my mind.

After arriving home, which was a miracle in itself, we tried to celebrate Christmas with Stoney. All of a sudden while we were opening presents, he started to become very confused. He was asking questions like, "what is this?" (to a video game and case) He asked if he was at the right house, and so I began to become very concerned. I was exhausted from all the traveling we had done, not to mention the stressful past few days. I called his brother, Forrest, to come get him and take him to the ER so I could sleep. They spent the whole night at the Vanderbilt emergency room.

When Forrest brought him home the next morning he said to me, "good luck". Stoney had been awake for over 36 hours by this point and it was starting to show. I put him in bed and he just wanted to talk and talk and talk. He asked the same questions over and over again, and about drove me to the point of insanity. He went to the bathroom and came out and said, "Beej, tell me something. How was I just using the bathroom in your room, and came out of my bathroom? Did I teleport?" By this time, I was like, we need to get you some sleep fast. I tried getting him in bed again and played some music. Once he closed his eyes, I started to leave, and he would wake up and ask where he was again. It was nonstop. I called Liz over, and asked her to sit with him so I could go get coffee at my moms house. I was going out of my mind. Finally he fell asleep and he slept for several hours. When he woke up, he was much better. From then on, we never used dilauded again.

January 1, 2020…

First of all, Happy New Year!

Secondly, this journey is not over… last night, we started to open presents and have Christmas (since we missed it while he was in the hospital) Throughout the evening, Stoney became confused and disoriented so we got him to Vanderbilt hospital ER to make sure things were ok. I needed to be sure his sodium wasn't dropping or that there wasn't some other problem with his levels. He was there until 7am, and once home he was very anxious, confused and still slightly disoriented but all labs and vitals were normal. I believe Stoney experienced a panic attack or a little trauma, post surgery. He is also exhausted (me too) and was awake for 36 hours with no sleep, talking nonstop (and driving me insane, God love him). We are watching him closely and will keep you updated, but we are not out of the woods yet. We need God to cover us with protection, provision and PEACE!! We need to feel comfort right now!! Pray we can both rest and recover from a very busy, stressful couple weeks. Gods got this!!!!

January 2, 2020…

Hey guys, I've had a few people ask how they can share a gift for Stoney and I after the extra medical costs we were thrown the past 2 weeks. Stoney is doing much better today and feels more like himself!! He will not be able to work much for 2 weeks and will have another CT scan in February to seethe success of the surgery! We have high hopes for good things for 2020!! Thank you all who prayed for us!! You saw us through our miracle and were very much a part of it with all your prayers!! Thank you so much!!

January 3, 2020…

Happy Friday y'all!!

Stoney is doing so much better. Recovery is going well and we are so happy. Thank you all for praying so hard for him and for all of us!!! I am speechless when I think about the last couple weeks and how incredible this Facebook prayer warrior team has been!! Love you all and praying for an amazing 2020!!

Needless to say, ringing in the new year was another adventure. 2020 had arrived, and as you all know 2019 had its own idea of a rollercoaster ride! We were entering a new phase of life, one that would hopefully bring good news, but the cancer could only be contained for a short time before causing more hardships…

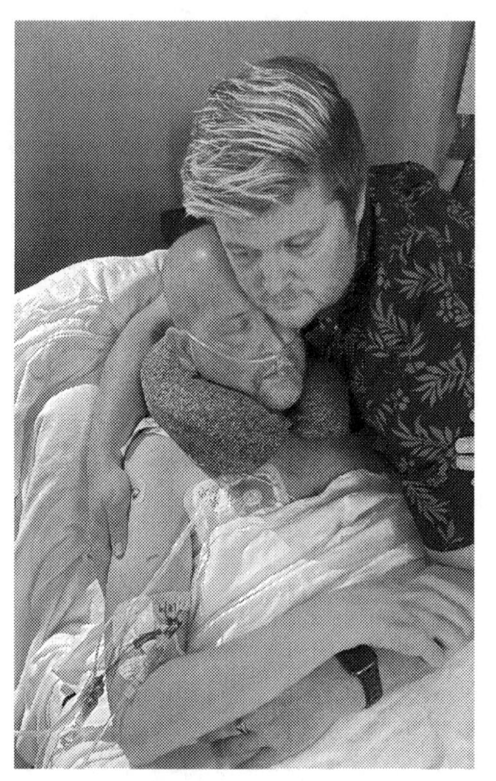

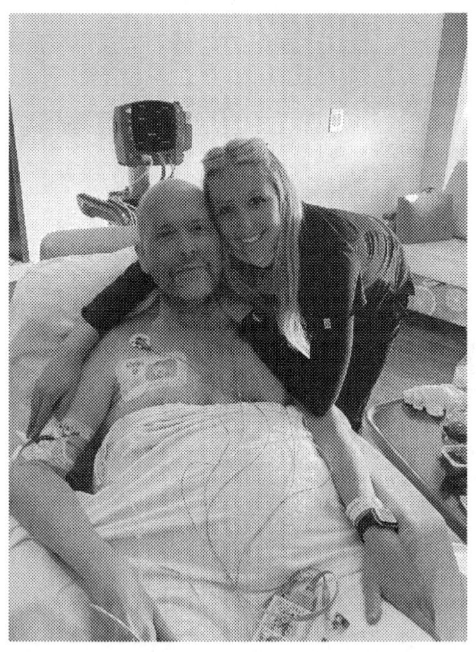

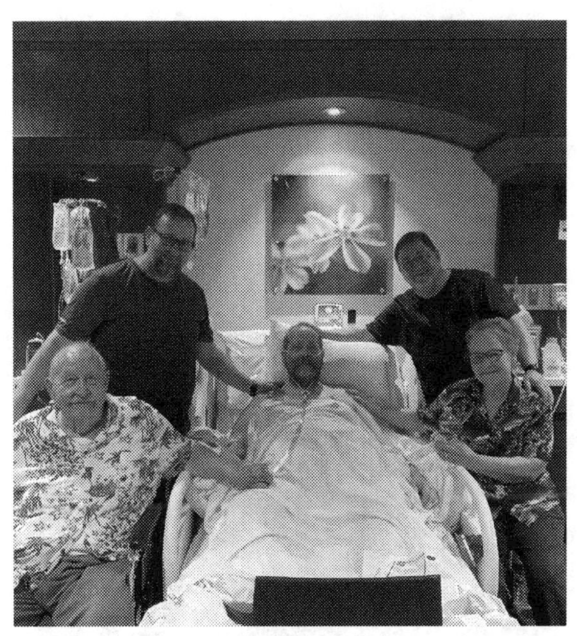

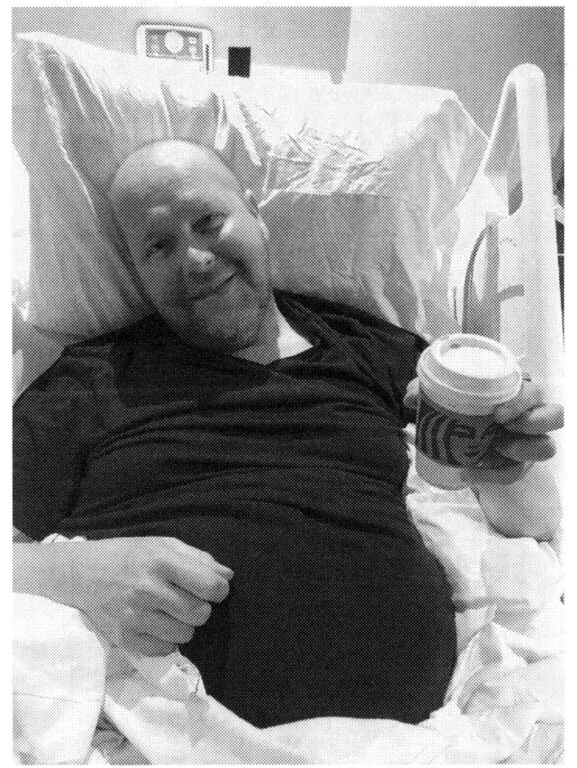

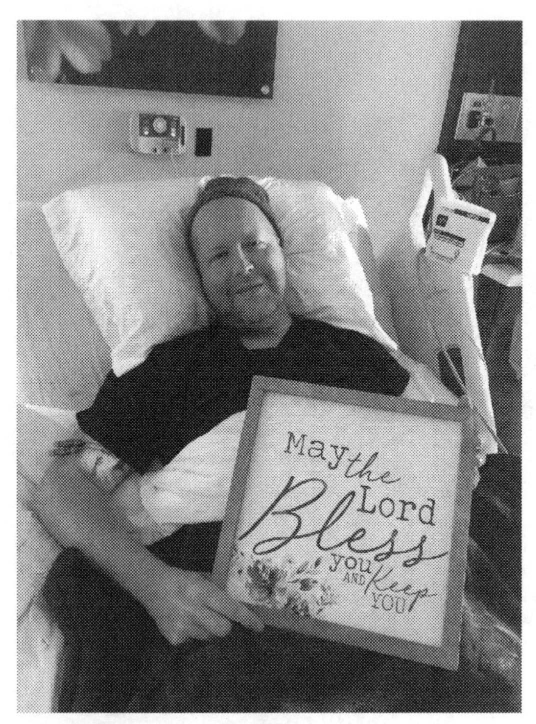
May the Lord Bless you and Keep you

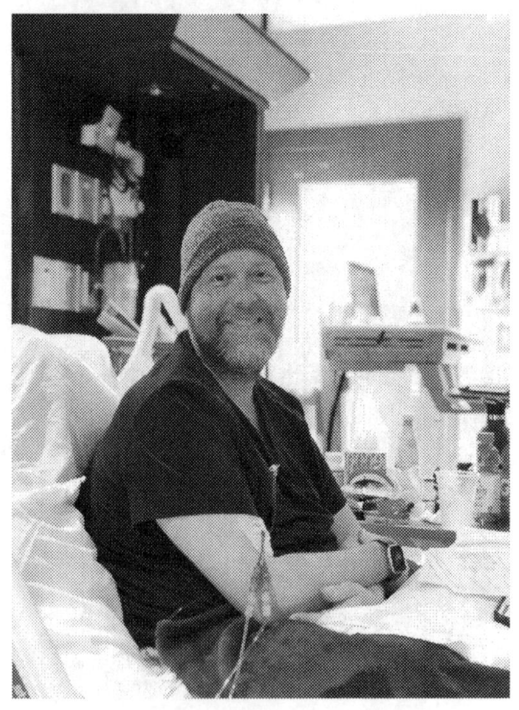

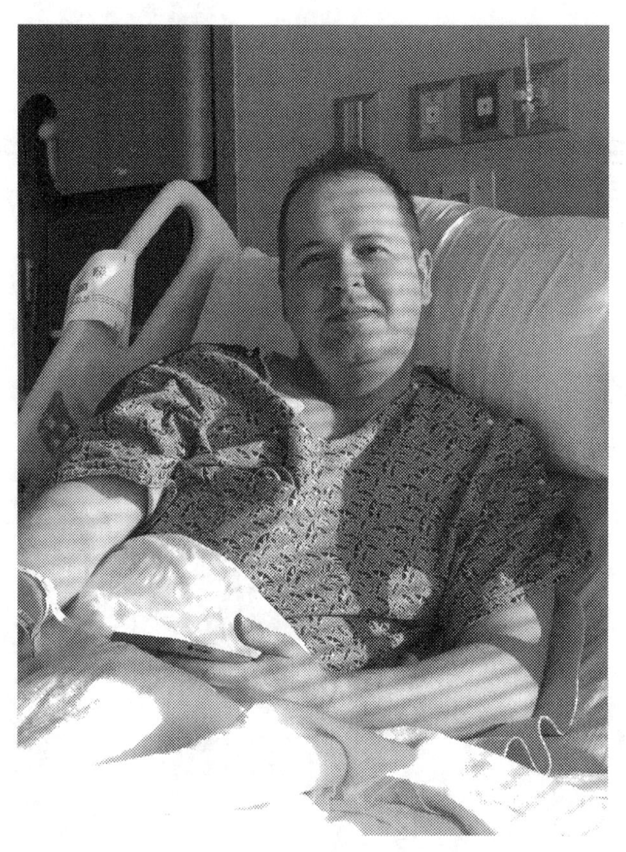

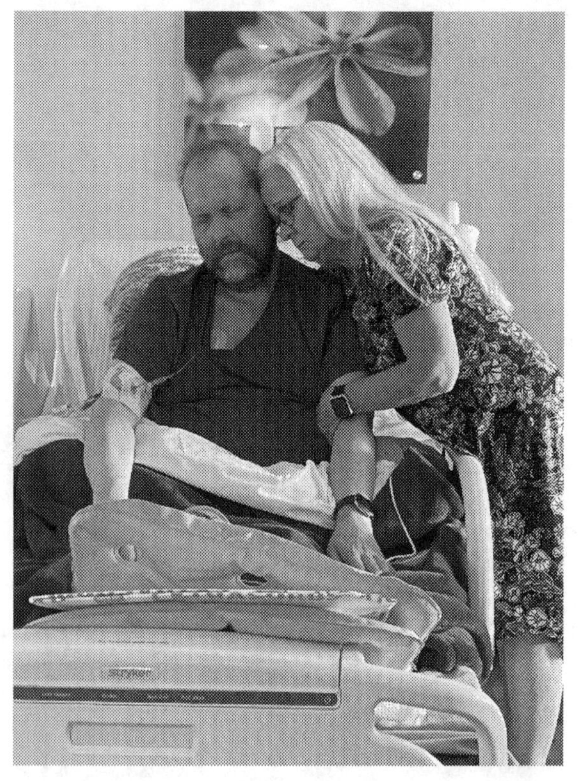

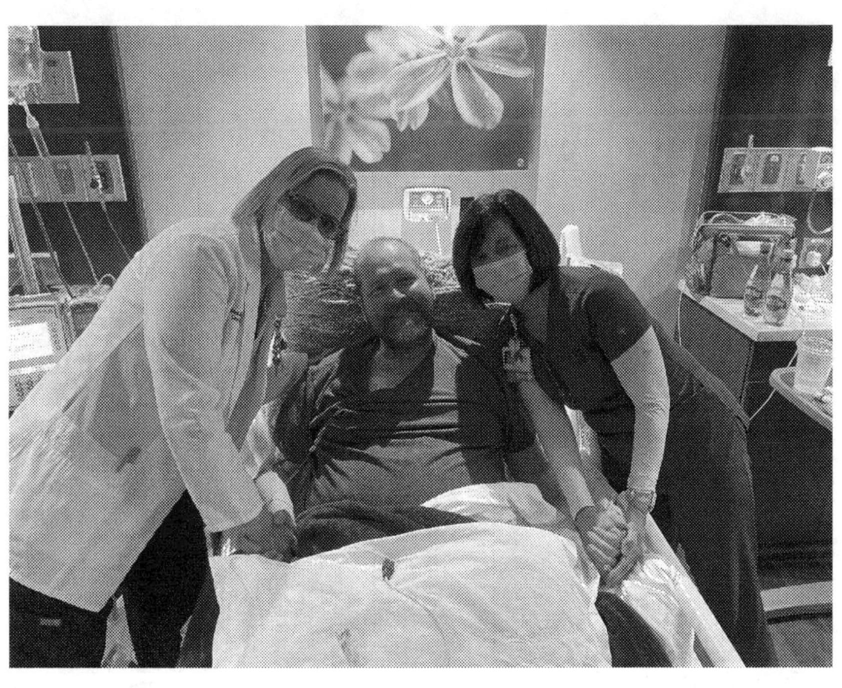

April 12, 1978 -
July 6, 2021
Stone Mountain Dartt

7

Laughing at Time

Proverbs 14 :13 - "Even in laughter the heart may ache, and rejoicing may end in grief." -NIV

The beginning of 2020 was off to a great start! Stoney was starting to feel the best he had felt in a long time. We were rejoicing daily at the positive effect this procedure had given him. I even booked a cruise to the Caribbean for him with his brother, Don and wife Debbie. We sailed to Puerto Rico, as well as a few other islands and Stoney did GREAT! He ate all the fancy dinners in the dining room, went swimming and took advantage of all the shows. He was laughing like he did before diagnosis. For 3 months we forgot he had cancer. No shots, not worries, no problems in the bathroom. Life was good. We were enjoying family activities and outings. Stoney was back to work and loving it. Meeting new people, and coming home to tell me all about his day. He met Nashville chefs, celebrities, including For King & Country, a guy from the TV show "Nashville" and many others. He was doing Instacart, and starting to make money again, and feeling really good about himself.

February 19, 2020….

Many of you have been praying for Stoney Dartt and he's doing GREAT!! We are so thankful for Gods goodness!!

We will be traveling to Atlanta for 3 days this next week for an MRI, Ct scan and several other tests (along with his monthly injection) to see how the tumors have either shrunk, grown or just plain disappeared! We do not know what to expect but are certainly trusting the Lord for His continued miracles!. God knows!! We are blessed for the support and prayers we have seen over the past year. We have watched and seen miracle after miracle!!

February 25, 2020…

Stoneys scans are back and the Dr said the tumors have shrunk and that they believe his procedure in December was a success. There is a new spot in the lungs that they are monitoring but are of no concern right now. Could be a past infection, a lesion from something in the past, etc... They are not concerned about that. He will maintain his monthly injections here in Atlanta and he is off ALL medication except for a simple probiotic and vitamins as per Dr orders. His bloodwork was EXCELLENT! Not one issue of concern there. So we are blessed and hopeful!! God is so good!! Thank you for the prayers!!

The reports from Atlanta were fantastic, and God was blessing. We could breathe a sigh of relief.

The news was giving reports of the coronavirus spreading in Asia. We weren't too concerned about it as we never dreamed it would become a problem for us here in the USA. My 40th birthday was approaching, and my life long dream was to go to Australia. Ever since I was a little kid, I just wanted to go there. I love kangaroos and koalas, so I just couldn't wait to visit. We had planned this trip over my birthday for some time, and I figured we were going to have to cancel it in December when Stoney fell ill. He encouraged me to keep it and wait. I am so glad we did. Then as the news continued to spread about the coronavirus, I was uncertain as what to do. At the time, it was still contained in Asia, with maybe one or two cases in California. We all prayed about it, and felt like we could do it and that God would take care of us. With Stoney feeling so well, we wanted to go since we weren't sure if we would ever have another chance. So, on March 6th, we flew from Nashville to Los Angeles and had dinner with Stoneys niece, Rachel, and her husband. They were out there working in California and were able to come to the hotel for dinner. The next morning we woke up, and both mom and Stoney were sick all night. Both had problems in the bathroom, and we had discussed cancelling our trip and going back home. I was so upset about it and thought it was disastrous, but would it be worse to get over there and be stuck in a foreign country. Fortunately, both of them thought it was something they ate, so we moved forward in getting to the airport. We travelled 18 hours on March 7th, leaving at 10:00am to Sydney, Australia and arrived at 8:00pm on March 8th. It was the longest flight I had ever been on, and I thought my mom was going to kill me for dragging her along. Liz, Stoney and I had made long flights before, but mom was not a fan of the long flights. I think she would tell you today it was well worth it. We all fell in love with Sydney, and there was nothing like waking up on the morning of the 9th, on my birthday to a view of the Sydney Harbour. We had a 2 bedroom airbnb in the middle of Sydney Harbour, where we could walk just about everywhere. We spent 2 full days touring the city, and traveling a couple hours down the coastline, visiting zoo's, aquariums and got to feed kangaroos! Stoney gave us so many laughs on that trip. He was so happy, and it was literally a breathe of fresh air for all of us to see the joy that was resonating from him. You could tell he was thrilled to have his life back. On March 12th, we boarded a cruise ship that would sail to New Zealand, making other stops along the way on a beautiful ship. I felt spoiled, and yet honored that God would allow me to enjoy this moment, as it would be one of the last magical memories with Stoney. None of us were watching the news, but the morning we were packing up, we saw Australias's version of the Today Show. Tom Hanks, and his wife Rita Wilson were filming and performing in Australia, and both had become ill with covid-19. We thought, wow, this is strange. It has made it to Australia, and there were more cases being reported in the States. Still, we headed to the cruise terminal with excitement to board our ship and celebrate my birthday!

3 days in and things were wonderful! We had so much fun, and we were all getting some rest, along with having a great time playing games, and watching movies. Then, as we headed to dinner, the announcement that shook the whole world happened while we were onboard a cruise ship thousands of miles from home. "Good evening ladies and gentleman…as you know the Covid-19 variant has caused impacts throughout Asia…" As he began to continue his announcement, my phone started making sounds notifying me of emails. I looked and opened it up, and the first email was from the cruise company notifying me of the global suspension. I showed

Stoney, and Liz. I was slightly afraid to show my mom, because I knew she would be upset and nervous about how we were going to get home. The captain was very calm, cool, and gracious in his speech. He made people feel at peace, and there was no alarm. He said, "we will monitor the situation, and keep you posted, but at this time the New Zealand Prime Minister has closed its borders, so we are trying to decide where to go next. We will make another announcement once we have received more information from our home office." I knew things weren't good, and in getting email from Stateside I was becoming more concerned. I received an email from the cruise line through my travel agent page notifying me what was happening before it was being announced on the ship. I quickly called the airlines, and had our flights re-routed before the captain had announced we were turning back to Sydney Harbour to send us all home. If if I had not received that email, we may not have gotten home in time, as the borders were closed the day after we landed back at LAX.

Stoney was scared that we would be stuck at sea like another cruise ship had been at the time. I reminded him how much we liked cruising, and it couldn't be that bad to be stuck on a ship for 40 days. The weather was beautiful, and the views were gorgeous; however, looking at some of the other videos I've seen online, it probably would not have been great. Stoneys nerves were starting to flare up, and he began getting symptomatic the last couple days of the trip. He started back on the self injections, and taking more medication after being off all of it since the procedure. We were all stressed out about getting home.

We arrived back home in Nashville, and was obviously in quarantine along with the rest of the world. Two days later, an email came from the cruise line informing us that people had tested positive on our ship, so we needed to be aware of symptoms. Never a dull moment. We were concerned about getting to Atlanta for Stoneys treatment since flights were grounded and mandates were in play. The stress and anxiety became more present, and this was not helping Stoneys cancer. We both noticed a change when we arrived back from Australia. It was as if a dark cloud had come back over him. Not only were we dealing with a pandemic with the whole country, we were dealing with a cancer possibly creeping back. Could his procedure have failed? Is the cancer growing even though scans showed improvement? We were once again asking God for answers, and having to wait longer than we wanted. If Stoney had any problems, we wanted to avoid the hospitals because they were full of covid patients and we didn't want to risk him getting sick with his compromised immune system. It seemed like we were being tested again.

April 3, 2020…

Well, we left home at 4:30am and are headed to Atlanta for Stoneys cancer treatment today. We weren't allowed to fly, so we are making the drive. Bloodwork is at 11, Oncology at 1:20 and injection at 2:30 then we will drive home tonight. Long day!! So thankful for the beautiful weather, gorgeous sunrise, and a nice change from looking at 4 walls. Lol. We are being careful... face masks, sanitizer, Clorox wipes and more. Well prepared for today! So blessed that the cancer center is willing to open its doors for us in the midst of turmoil and insanity. I am so grateful to all the nurses and doctors who have given their time and lives, safety and care!!

…EVENING UPDATE…

Dr Meiri is very happy with Stoneys bloodwork and last months Ct scans! He thinks that the symptoms he is having will ease up with the injection today. He was 10 days late due to this pandemic and getting here so hopefully he will be better after this! All in all, it was a good visit and we are thrilled with the good news. We are soon headed back to Nashville. Continue to pray for the 5 hour drive! Still quite a bit of traffic for the state mandated stay in place orders...

Even though Stoney had a good report at CTCA, he knew that something was not right. He wasn't able to work because of the pandemic, but thankfully was approved for unemployment. He noticed daily that things were not normalizing after his injection, and was becoming quite concerned. The staff at CTCA couldn't seem to understand why he was having so much trouble. They didn't want to do another procedure since he had just had one a few months ago. Having another procedure like he had in January would limit his chances in the future for another one.

May 1, 2020…

Stone Dartt Cancer Update:

BJ Speer

We met with the Dr this afternoon, and he has advised Stoney to try a couple new supplements and added a few things to his diet. He wants to run more scans on May 28 before making a final decision on the next step. There are 2 procedures that are options as well as changing the injection to a new one; however, the scans will tell him which direction to go. In the meantime, he needs to stay hydrated which is a problem for Stoney due to all the "symptoms" he has. His bloodwork was not great, and things need to change so we will be working on that... We are also hoping the injection he had today will take effect soon! Appreciate the prayers!! Don't stop! It's a long, critical and frustrating journey for Stoney. Just when things started looking so good, it turned so fast and back to where we started. We know Gods got this!! Trusting, Believing and Living in HIS promise!

May 19, 2020…

Stoney ended up in the ER, and is getting fluids and potassium infusions. Hoping they release him tonight... there is a chance he can go to Atlanta this Friday to be admitted at the Cancer Center.

May 20, 2020…

Asking prayer for Stone Mountain Dartt today!

His cancer symptoms are really bad and his electrolytes and blood levels are off!! We are headed to get labs done in Nashville, and then wait to see what the cancer center in Atlanta tell us to do next. Most likely IVF. He will have Ct scans and an MRI done next Thursday in Atlanta and we will await word on a possible surgery in the following days. He has lost 14 pounds in 18 days and constantly nauseated, loss of appetite and weak. We are praying for another miracle and that God will touch him and restore his body. The next 9 days are going to be extremely challenging for him as he waits to go to Atlanta so please pray hard they will fly by for him!

…EVENING UPDATE…

Still here at Vanderbilt Hospital in Nashville. Stoney has been hooked up to fluids all day!! They should be releasing him very soon for the night. The cancer center in Atlanta is trying to get us in this Friday, a whole week early for treatment. There are several "catches" with that since it's a holiday weekend and no one can be with him due to the "covid" rules. (Lord Jesus make Covid disappear! It's ruined enough lives!) anyway, I haven't been able to be in the hospital with him today either, just waiting... we know there is a plan, not sure what it is, but God has one! Please keep praying!! Love y'all!!

Covid changed everything in the medical field as you all know. It disrupted the lives of people wanting to be with their loved ones. People died alone, were left alone, and were cared for alone. It broke my heart to see so many people hurting from the effects of this pandemic. I was blessed to be with Stoney for almost 100% of the time at the Cancer Center. They had some limitations, but they were bended some (for us). We had become so close to so many of the people there. We became not just friends, but family. We were treated with such respect, and vice versa. I am so thankful that we had so many caring people looking out for us during this time, which was another Godwink that I knew He was looking over us through our valley.

May 26, 2020….

Well, we are in Atlanta and on the shuttle to the Cancer center! The airports were like ghost towns this morning and people all seem to be doing their own thing, no matter the rules and regulations. Lol.

Please pray we get some answers over the next few days here. That the scans (and MRI) will show the doctors what needs to be done...and that by some miracle they will have an opening for surgery ASAP!!

May 27, 2020…

It was not the news we wanted to hear. After seeing the surgeon, and looking at the scans, Stoney has new tumors in his liver but thankfully it has not spread anywhere else. Also, the tumors that the DR targeted in surgery back in December have grown again. They are trying to rush a pre-cert through for another liver directed therapy on him as soon as possible. Then they will follow that with a radiation procedure called Lutathera that is 6 months worth of treatment spread out. We are kind of discouraged, but know God is in control. Stoney is going to head to the urgent care unit here at CTCA to get fluids for dehydration. He has been vomiting and having other issues that are not normal, so losing lots of electrolytes. That's the news for today... please pray they can find an opening for surgery on the schedule immediately, and that we won't have to come back next week. That's our prayer!! There is HOPE... sometimes I get so overwhelmed with what's going on that I forget God has it all worked out. I end up worrying about something I can't control. This life we have is a gift, and I'm trying to appreciate the days we all have, enjoying it to the fullest, remembering that nothing is certain...other than the fact I know whom I have believed And received, and in Him I have everlasting life!! This life of pain, doom and gloom is just for a time... can't wait for Heaven!! No more sickness or pain!!!

…EVENING UPDATE….

The surgeons nurse (who calls us her "other sons" and is an angel and miracle in itself) just called while Stoney is getting fluids....she squeezed us in this coming Friday morning at 11:00am for a Liver Directed Therapy (embolization)!!! Recovery by 2:00 and back home in Nashville Monday night if all goes according to the Dr's plan! Y'all this is nothing short of Gods amazing grace and a miracle!! We were told yesterday it could be 7-10 days due to insurance and pre-certs. God is so Good!! We've been crying tears of joy!! God knew this before my last post!! :) Next prayer request, Is that Stoneys blood levels will remain normal after infusion today (and maybe tomorrow). He is losing potassium, sodium and co2 drastically and that is reason for all the fluids. The numbers need to be normal for surgery!! This is the same procedure as done in December and they may do back to back procedure with 3 weeks between. From there, they will go directly into the radiation procedure that will go From July through December (Once every other month). We stand amazed once again at how God continues to watch out for His children!! And we thank all of you for praying!!

May 28, 2020…

Just a Thursday morning update on Stone Dartt...

The last couple days has been a ride for sure. We are so thankful for all your prayers!! God has certainly showed Himself through this valley that He can still work miracles when there seems to be no way. Stoney is beyond amazed that he is getting this surgery tomorrow morning (Lord willing and his labs are ok) after we were told it could be 7-10 days on Tuesday. The team here in

Atlanta has been the most incredible hospital staff I have ever witnessed in my life. They are not doctors or nurses, but a family of heroes! We are so blessed to be here at a facility that cares for us as much as our own family. You have a pastoral staff that has church here everyday, prays with you, encourages you. The nurses and doctors are open about their personal faith and hope in Jesus... I'm telling you Stoney is right when he says this is the "DISNEYLAND of the medical world". Hahaha!! Only Stoney!! Everything under one roof, everyone fighting for you and your health. I can't say enough.

...AFTERNOON UPDATE...

Today, Stoney will be in infusions most of the day getting ready for tomorrow. He once again has a lot of odds against him with his numbers...he needs some huge miracles that those numbers not only come up, but remain up for tomorrow morning. The verse I read this morning talks about casting our burdens on the Lord, and I believe we so often do that, but then run back and pick them up. I'm trying to take some deep breaths, cast my cares and burdens on the Lord, and rest in His promises that He cares for me/us, His children. Things change, plans change, schedules change, that's ok... it might not be what we/I want, but there is a better plan, a better schedule in store. Leaning on Jesus is the security I need for today! A securing hand of safety in sinking waters!

Going through this brings back so many memories being in the hotel at the Holiday Inn across the street. How sick Stoney was. The sleepless nights, the sounds of nonstop vomiting, moaning and groaning, etc... I can literally place myself in each of these spots and play it out in my mind. It was so scary, so real, and yet Gods hand was in and over all of it. The fear Stoney was having never stopped him from laughing, smiling, and sharing his faith when he had an opportunity. He was such a light and inspiration even at his worst moments. I remember that so clearly. I also remember him telling me not to worry. Some days I hated hearing him say that, even though I knew it was true. It was like he was foretelling the future for us both. He had such grace through it all.

May 29, 2020...

Stoney is now out of surgery and in recovery. They want to keep him in house all weekend and monitor his numbers. They are trying to regulate it all before they release him. We should be home Monday night, but all that will depend on him and how he feels and responds. He is fighting the nausea real bad but they are working very hard to control that. The Doctor was able to be more aggressive with the liver, and there's a chance he may not need this Surgery again, but just the radiation procedure. We will know more Monday.

Thank you for your prayers!! Please keep them coming!! I am hoping to see him shortly for a few and then go to bed. I'm very tired and hoping I can sleep tonight!! Much love to everyone and again thanks so very much for the prayers!!

May 31, 2020…

Sunday update on Stone Dartt!!

Hey y'all. We appreciate the prayers of so many and overwhelmed by the support you've shown through kind words and prayers. Stoney is still admitted here at CTCA in-patient and making some good progress!! His numbers (electrolytes) are all starting to align and become more normal. He has eaten, and done all of the other "requirements" to be released :)

However, he is getting more fluids, including potassium, and magnesium today just to make sure he is stable and strong enough to leave tomorrow. They will draw blood at 5:00pm today and again in the morning before they will make the decision to discharge him, but so far all signs are looking good. Just keep praying!! His pain is being managed and he is hopeful things will get better!! Keep praying we can go home tomorrow night if it's the Lords Will and that Stoney will continue to make progress and get better. They will call us this week about the radiation treatment in the coming month(s). Thank you again so much!!

If only things had improved from here….

8

Lasting Through Time

I Corinthians 10:12-13 - "God is faithful, who will not allow you to be tempted above what you are able, but will with the temptation also make the way of escape, that you may be able to endure it." -NIV

If things had only moved in the right direction after Memorial Day Weekend. If the procedure had only worked. If only…BUT, God had different plans. Plans that were not ours. Plans that would leave us with more questions than answers. This time, the liver directed therapy only lasted about 5 days. A huge blow, and major disappointment to us all. For about 3 months life became quite uncertain…

June 5, 2020…

To our friends and prayer warriors!

Please pray for Stoney once again… After coming home and doing very well for a couple days, continuing his recovery, he has started having the same cancer symptoms once again, causing some alarm. We have a consult with the Nurse in Atlanta shortly, and hoping to get some answers. We know from reading the MRI report, that there are 2 new tumors, as well as growth in the bigger ones, which almost doubled in size. We are pushing and hoping for the radiation schedule to happen sooner than in July so stoney can have more relief. Given that this Neuroendocrine carcinoma is not curable, there are only so many times this radiation and embolization can be done, so please pray God will lay His mighty hand upon Stoney, and give him peace and healing.

June 18, 2020…

Good Morning Facebook family and prayer warriors! Please pray for Stone Mountain Dartt today!! He is headed in the direction of metabolic acidosis once again, and we are trying to figure out the next step. His first radiation treatment is June 30th and we need him well and strong enough for that!! He will need fluids and who knows what else right now so please pray for him... us... to make the right decisions and get the help he needs!! Our God knows all things, He understands and has a plan! Appreciate all the prayers you are sending!!

….Stoney is still in the ER at Vanderbilt hospital. His labs show low numbers and they have given him 3 liters of fluid and now beginning a potassium infusion. Hopefully they will release him around midnight to come home. Cancer treatment center of America in Georgia has approved us coming in early this Monday to be seen Tuesday. They will admit him there a week early before his radiation and treat him for fluids and electrolyte replacements. I will go, and stay close by as I am not allowed in the inpatient section of their facility. Please continue to pray for Stoney! He is beginning to feel discouraged and needs lots of prayer and encouragement to keep him going!!

June 22, 2020

Well, we are about to board our plane here in Nashville for Atlanta. Stoney will go in at 7:00am for bloodwork and based on how bad the numbers are, they will either give him a daily infusion until radiation next Tuesday, OR admit him until next Tuesday. Our prayer is that they will admit him so he can get the fluids and help he needs to be ready for his lutathera treatment. I will mention, other than a healing miracle from God, this is the LAST option and treatment method they have left for him to try. This treatment will span over 6 months in time, and will cause a very heavy burden on Stoneys physical health, causing fatigue, weakness, nausea, and other symptoms that go along with cancer treatments. They can only do 2 rounds of this Specific neuroendocrine radiation over the course of his life (until further testing is approved) so we ask for prayer as we enter into this new phase of his cancer journey. Today, he is very tired, very weak, and very dehydrated as his body will not allow him to contain and keep the electrolytes needed to stay well. He is frustrated, discouraged and ready to see improvement if God allows it. He will also be unable to work through the end of the year, which is causing him anxiety and nervousness.

We take one day at a time, we continue to trust in Jesus as we always have, and we remain committed to believing that in ALL things we give God the Glory, good or bad. We appreciate all your prayers and we ask you to continue to lift Stoney up in prayer, to share it on every church prayer list, bible study and prayer group... there is POWER in prayer and Healing in the precious name of JESUS!!

June 23, 2020….

Good Morning Facebook Family and Prayer Warriors...

So, here is the morning update and report from Atlanta... as Stoney struggled to get here this morning fighting weakness and nausea, his levels showed critically low potassium levels and Co2. His sodium was low but not critical. Most of his other vitals and levels are normal (this is good news as they need to be normal for his "lutathera" radiation treatment next week). They have indeed decided to admit him here in inpatient for several days to an IV, as well as octreotide drip (which we had hoped and prayed for) so that he can build his electrolytes up before Tuesday. I will be close by, since they may release him for a couple days to see how he manages without fluids, but must be close by in case we need to go back to Urgent care again. We are hoping and praying for better things. Stoney is feeling very weak and tired and needs prayers. Love y'all!! We live in Hope, and pray for continued healing, strength, peace and comfort!

June 24, 2020…

This morning, Stoneys potassium dropped again to critical levels even after infusions and oral intake. His body is just not holding the potassium like it should. His other numbers are normalizing, and they are confident they will get his numbers in line for his radiation treatment next Tuesday. He is also on a drip called, "octreotide", a form of treatment to help with his neuroendocrine cancer symptoms. He normally takes this as an injection 3 times daily, but they have him hooked up to a higher dose running all day long. They are highly considering a pump next week that he will live with to keep this medicine running through his body. (Similar to insulin)

Keep praying and I will keep you updated!!

June 25, 2020…

Today, we finally got the inpatient side of the hospital on the same page with his oncology team and they are trying to restore his potassium levels... He is unable to hold onto any potassium in his body. The cancer keeps flushing it out, making his level critical. They are not sure at this point how to manage that, but working on a plan to stabilize him until his radiation Tuesday. Lord willing they will find a way to maintain a healthy enough level to get the radiation and then monitor the potassium from home, by weekly labs and potassium infusions at Vanderbilt as necessary. There are still many unknowns, and many concerns, but we are pressing forward in hopes they will find a manageable solution to this problem. They will keep him over the weekend for observation and daily infusions... Stoney is doing ok, but it is so frustrating as diet has changed several times here, information has been confusing and contradicting at times, but he is trying to remain optimistic in the longterm solution to the problem.

Thank you for your continued prayers!! Until tomorrow….

June 26, 2020….

Today stoney was really fighting for good labs!! The Cancer Center tried a couple things and some failed and then some things worked!! As of tonight, his numbers have managed to stabilize. Keep in mind, things change daily!! They have started him on an opioid tincture to help slow his bowels down. He has literally lost a gallon and a half of fluids today, so they are replacing that through IV and more potassium infusions. They are doing so many things to try and help him maintain. My heart is so heavy for him. To watch this is painfully difficult, but I can't imagine being the one going through it. Please pray he can get through the weekend and that they are able to keep the numbers in the normal range for radiation Tuesday. From there, we will have a long road to find the best way to manage his symptoms until the second radiation treatment as he many not get relief until then. Thanks for your prayers!!

June 27, 2020

Today, Stoney needs immediate prayers! He was sick in the night vomiting and some of his symptoms are somewhat worsening. His CO2 and sodium are extremely low, and with more fluid loss, we are expecting the next round of blood work to be bad! They will continue to give him fluids, infusions and they do have time to try to get those numbers better before Tuesday, but it's super discouraging and he is getting very upset about it all. Even after the radiation, it could take weeks before he sees a change so we have to figure out just how to manage these symptoms and issues once he goes home... God knows!! Please PRAY!

Sunday, June 28, 2020

Good evening my extremely faithful prayer warriors!! It is after 9pm, and I'm exhausted... I'm leaving the center, headed to my hotel with a heavy heart and trying to rest in knowing God has this all figured out. Today, Stoneys numbers were moving in the right direction, however the weekend doctor is so fixated on controlling Stoneys diarrhea that he can't wrap his mind around the fact that it's due to the cancer. (number one side effect that Stoneys dealt with for 18 months) The diarrhea can't be corrected until he gets this lutathera treatment, but trying to get 2 doctors to agree on the same thing or way of treatment would be like getting the entire country to vote for the same president. Haha. It's just not gonna happen. They were threatening to postpone his Lutathera Tuesday to continue to work on the diarrhea treatment and infusions. Let's just say from a caregivers standpoint, I about lost it and might need to get saved again. Haha! They also tried forcing a pic-line on Stoney today, without consulting his care team, and he's not suppose to have that with the Lutathera he's getting. Let's just say, it's a mess and I'm tired and wish this was a bad dream. I know that God has this... I know we will all be ok and I know that tomorrow, no matter what happens there will be a plan and God will be in it one way or the other. The next 12 hours are critical for Stoneys labs to be in the normal range (after their horrible mistake of opioids which made him so sick) and in 36 hours, Lord willing, he will be receiving his first round of radiation!! I feel like I want to make sure everyone knows that we ARE ABSOLUTELY in the right place and have ZERE doubts of that. CTCA

Atlanta has been incredible. There will always be problems and issues in any and all facilities so I am in no way criticizing being here. The nurses have been just outstanding on every level and I know Stoney is getting the best care he possibly can. I would still rather be here than in any hospital back in Nashville.

Please continue to pray for good things. There is still time to fix it, and Stoney was feeling much better today after they got his CO2 back up. God knows and this is no surprise!! I know we have a prayer team that is constantly bringing him before the throne and there is power in that!!

June 29, 2020

Well, this evening Stoney was discharged from the hospital side of the Cancer Center! He has a long list of meds to take tonight and in the morning! We will be at the Cancer Center at 7:00am and his radiation will start at 8! (Lord willing....) He still has to clear blood work in the morning, but we are hoping for the best! We've gotten this far! We've had to pay $300 for meds at the pharmacy before we left and still have $500 more to get tomorrow before he can come back to hotel. Slightly overwhelmed, but we know God will take care of it.

Thanks so much for helping us get this far with your prayers...now help us get across the finish line!! I will make an update in the morning once he is officially in the radiation chair. They are keeping us here a little longer for extra infusions after radiation to restore his loss of electrolytes and will most likely have us bring in home health care 3 days a week for 2 months…

Long road ahead

June 30, 2020

Tuesday Morning Update on Stone Dartt....

I truly don't know where to start this morning... Do I dive in and share? build it up? It's an interesting time for me to be honest. I have tried being strong, supportive and steadfast the last week. In moments of doubt, I would try to ignore that negative and focus on keeping Stoney positive. When they discharged Stoney last night, I was scared that I wouldn't be able to handle the task of keeping his numbers stable, even though it truly wasn't my task to complete, but only that of the Lord! I nagged him to drink fluids, to take medicine, mixed his concoctions of meds to take, got him fed, we prayed, and I got very little sleep. For one, I was weak. I started to think about the what ifs? I had not allowed myself to really get there before then. As I have seen Stoney lose lots of weight, suffer pain, nausea, injections, surgeries, I didn't know what I would do personally if he couldn't have the Lutathera this morning. Alarms were set for 5:30am, but I woke at 4:30am when I heard Stoney having trouble in the bathroom... then again, before we left the hotel, and then again at the cancer center when we arrived. I pushed fluids, and he was getting so irritated with me, so I got angrier. hahaha! I pushed the meds, and he became anxious and so I wanted to give up. I sat on the floor at the cancer center and mixed his baking soda, potassium, phosphorus, etc... I was not letting him have bloodwork without it and I wasn't gonna let him tell me NO one more time. (I am an ONLY CHILD...what do you expect?) Anyway, his time came to get blood and from there, it was a waiting game. We had breakfast, and the more I pushed fluids, he would say "I am!!"... Ya'll, unless I need glasses or am going blind, he was NOT drinking fluids! LOL... We made our way to the appointment room, and waited. I can check his labs on my phone and they were not showing and the nurse was not coming to get us.... 25 minutes went by, and still NO labs and NO nurse. I knew in my heart this was not happening today. I tried to prepare myself, I thought I was going to get into Stoneys medical bag and pull out his anxiety meds for myself... I didn't, but I knew they were there! haha! Finally, his nurse came in from the outside (she had been running late to work) grabbed us and took us back. I had no idea what was happening... Maybe she hasn't see the labs yet? She brought us to this room with lots of "doggie pee pads" all over the place, and wondered if Stoney was being admitted to doggie daycare for a minute. She got him in the chair and started hooking things up and I kept praying that we wouldn't get this far, and then have the rug pulled out from under us when she finally looked at the labs. She told me to sit down, and I told her I was too anxious for that, and that I needed to pace (and pray). Our other nurse, who has walked literally every step of this journey with us, Kristen came in and said we were good to go, I asked about labs, and she said they were fine, nothing to worry about. I had a mild panic attack and was sure she was wrong. I still couldn't see the numbers on my phone... We had a GREAT visit with her, while Stoney was getting the preliminary fluids for Lutathera. They started with nausea meds, then amino acids before the actual radiation beads. We talked about faith, family, friends and how amazing God was to ordain this specific group of nurses to be tailor made to our needs, as well a firm love for Jesus Christ. Seriously, I still can't believe it all. Our nurse, Kristen and her husband, have an amazing story about losing their 6 year old daughter in a horrible accident and how the Lord brought them through and changed their lives... You can find their story at Elliesway.org and read more about it. It will make you cry, and connect you with the testimony of the incredible lady helping take care of Stoney (and me). But when I left the room, the other nurse who we love, Kim, gave me a hug goodbye before I took off and had tears in her eyes. She said, "I don't want to tell you this, and probably shouldn't, but I love you guys and I know you will pray for me. My dad was diagnosed with stage 4 pancreatic cancer Friday and I really don't want to be here today, but I knew you were coming, and I knew I could find some joy from being around you." She began to cry and again apologize for not being more fun (as usual) and involved in conversation, but it was a bad day for her. I told her that we, as Christians, need to help carry each others burdens and lift one another up in prayer. If you think of it, please pray for Kim Dunn's dad!!! (He is going to be getting treatment here at the center this week). ANYWAY, (lots of incredible little rabbit trails today) I get on the shuttle to go back to the hotel and I look at my phone and finally see Stoney's labs... I open the document, and I am NOT joking....Out of 33 numbers they report on, all but 2 were in the normal range!!!! HALLELUJAH!!! I pretty much fell apart and wept. I knew he was getting the treatment today when they hooked him up, BUT to see his labs NORMAL???? I KNOW it was ALL GOD!!! Period.... I talked to Sharon and then to my mom to give the update, and we all cried! haha! My mom told me about a post from a dear friend of ours (Jodi Renee) who has never met Stoney but shared in her devotional about him and for people to pray. When I opened the message and read, I began to cry again, because it sums it all up... "I fix my mind on ALL you have done" - Psalm 143:5 (NIV) … WOW!!! Doesn't that just bring it together? Lord God Almighty, I don't know how to thank or Praise you for ALL you have done, are doing, and will continue to do!!!

Thank you for praying, AND please don't stop!! They will monitor him here for 2 more days and then send us home. He will get weekly labs and go from there. The next Lutathera treatment will be the end of August, October and December!

I always found it difficult posting such good reports, because it almost never failed that after such a good report, came a negative one! Sometimes I wanted to wait a few days to post something when it was really good, because I just knew the next day I would be faced to write something sad. It literally almost never failed.

July 1, 2020

Good Morning Facebook Family!

I almost hate bringing this up after such a great day yesterday. However, Stoney had a horrible night. We were both up all night just trying to get to get to the center this morning to urgent care. We didn't want to call an ambulance last night because he would have ended up at a different hospital. He is trying to get himself dressed this morning without vomiting and will most likely be readmitted to inpatient. We need so much prayer y'all. Was suppose to go home tomorrow and who knows now. I'm so tired, and he's so sick. Yesterday went from great to horrible in an afternoon. Please don't give up praying!

afternoon update…

Stoney is at urgent care, he had a CT scan and is getting fluids right now. They are also admitting him into the inpatient side of the hospital for an undisclosed time. I will remain in Atlanta until I have further details. Thanks for your prayers!

July 2, 2020

Hey everyone, I apologize for taking so long to post, but we have been waiting for the Doctors to give us some news. Stoney was feeling much better today, and what they believe to have happened is tumor lyces...the tumors end up breaking down too quickly with the radiation causing the body have major metabolic issues and more. Stoney experienced acute kidney failure as well, but is doing better today and making some progress. They believe the Lutathera was a success, and is doing its job, but these things can happen in the process. They will keep him through the weekend for observation and to make sure his numbers remain stable. When I left today, they told me that due to Covid increases in the state, the Governor has reversed the orders for hospitals to have no visitors. I will not be able to see him at for a few days, and that makes me nervous since I have been his advocate, and doing most of the speaking with the doctors and nurses the last 10 days!! We will do some FaceTime and Skype in the meantime, but this Covid junk really needs to go away soon!

They may release him Monday, and we will see the Oncologist Tuesday and then come home Lord willing if he has a good report and ALL goes smoothly through the weekend. So far, his symptoms (diarrhea) from the cancer has improved, and we are seeing some GREAT signs that this treatment process is going to work!! From here, he will have the Lutathera radiation treatments August, October and December, with his injections on the in-between months. A long road ahead, but God is so GOOD and we are so thankful for His blessings and ALL OF YOU who have been praying!! We need you to continue. Stoney has been feeling blue....a little down and discouraged just from the incredible painful experience he has gone through in the last 10 days!! He needs a boost, a hug, lots of love sent from you all to get through... I appreciate those who have messaged, given, sent us texts, calls, etc.... It has meant the world and I apologize if I haven't responded to each personally, but its been a little overwhelming here. I am so thankful that we are FOREVER IN HIS CARE!!

July 3, 2020

Stoney is feeling good today, but his bloodwork is not so good. Both his CBC panel and metabolic panel are showing really bad numbers today. They are giving some infusions, and trying to get them stable but he has a long way to go. I sure hope they can figure it out soon. We've been here 12 days, and I am ready to go home. Trying to enforce him to drink fluids, walk the halls and eat his food on top of making sure the nurses are doing what they are suppose to (trust me, I've caught many slip ups and have had to speak up!) all from my hotel room, is NOT EASY!! I am so irritated over this covid junk consuming everyone's life, causing separations, vacation cancelations, job losses, etc.

As we celebrate our country this weekend, it's independence, our founding fathers, our freedoms...we are so FAR away from where we should be as an American people and it's SCARY!! I can't watch the news or read it right now, because I can't tolerate the anxiety on top of what I'm going through here. Here's what I do know...There is nothing that is taking God by surprise. Stoneys health issues, covid, protests, politics, literally...none of it!! As we celebrate this weekend with family and friends (or alone in a hotel room) let's remember to

LOVE one another, to be POSITIVE to one another, to APPRECIATE our freedoms and the men & woman who fought for it!

Thank you for your prayers, for your concerns, for your kind words. I am learning each day how to navigate this medical nightmare!

Praying for Stoney to have better numbers tomorrow!! Progress in Prayer!!

July 5, 2020

Good morning friends! I hope everyone had an amazing day yesterday, and continuing to enjoy this holiday weekend.

Stoney remains in the hospital, with numbers beginning to normalize slowly. They have now had to add calcium to the infusions as well as phosphorus, but they believe it starting to align. The radiation has caused his creatnine, red and white blood count and hematocrit to drop as it normally does with any chemo or radiation. He will be on something for that at home as well. Hahaha. He is as close to a walking pharmacy as anyone I know. We calculated last night his new prescriptions are at about $900 out of pocket for what he's having to take. We are unsure at this point if that's a month, or through the radiation process, or just a few weeks after each treatment. There is much to learn!! There are talks he could be discharged tomorrow evening and see the oncologist Tuesday for an update, BUT....who knows?! Things have taken wild turns everyday so as I sit in the hotel room trying to relax and catch up on some rest. I have also indulged in some donuts compliments of Dunkin Donuts (and thanks to my friend Elizabeth Kieser). I do NOT NEED these donuts but I must be honest...they are helping with emotional support. Hahaha!! We continue to take it a day at a time, trusting the Lord. I am incredibly GRATEFUL for the prayers and financial support that has poured out during this time. The expenses have grown beyond what we had imagined, but so thankful to all of you who have come to our rescue during this time. It brings many tears just to think and even write about it. Gods faithfulness has been overwhelming!!! I We thank you from the bottom of our hearts!! Here is to a better week, and to going HOME!!!

...EVENING UPDATE....

Good evening Facebook world... Tonight, I come to you with anxiety, transparency and disappointment. After talking with Stoney today, I feel like I need to put on my superhero cape and fly over there and just burst through the walls and rescue Stoney myself. I typed out a whole message, and afterwards reading it back realized it wasn't right to post.... there is no need to disrespect anyone. I just feel bad that he is not getting the care I wish he was getting, or that I could help with. I guess being a spokesperson from a hotel room is not easy at all and I have no purpose. Pray for me tonight, that I will let things go, that I will trust the Lord and continue to believe He has a plan that is greater than anything I can imagine. That even if His plan is NOT mine, that both Stoney and I will learn to live in HOPE and Trust Him, no matter the outcome. Its hard for me to not take charge and do something, I have never been a patient person...(Everyone that knows me would tell you that, and I admit it).

Pray for Stoney tonight, that he will find comfort. His symptoms are coming back....more diarrhea, more discomfort. He hasn't slept more than a few hours each night due to the prednisone that they have him on (as well as a hundred other things), his legs and ankles are swelling, the nurses are not fast at helping him or getting answers. There is just A LOT I cant even tell you right now that breaks my heart...Praying for PEACE tonight, and ANSWERS tomorrow!! I just want to go HOME!!!! SO very badly! I am praying tomorrow we will have a direction on which way we are going to go here... Love you all!

July 6, 2020

Not much news today. Stoney still has low numbers and they are continuing to keep him for another few days. I think he is going slightly insane (to those who have seen his last Facebook picture post) but at least keeping his sense of humor through it all. He is set up on an Octreotide drip to help with his diarrhea symptoms. On a positive note, his kidneys are doing very well! The Oncologist will be in to see him in the morning, and make some decisions. Just keep praying that he will be able to absorb all the nutrients and not lose them. I appreciate all the kind words, prayers and encouragement. Gods got this... He's got me, He's got Stoney, and I think we are gonna be ok!

July 7, 2020

Today, I got a free pass up to the room with Stoney!! I was very thankful to get in a visit and see what's going on! I got to speak with the nephrologist, the oncologist and floor Dr!! I was very thankful! Today's news was more positive, but no word on discharge. Stoneys symptoms are most likely going to be something he lives with for another couple months until he gets a second round of radiation. He is bruised all over from the shots, heparin shots, pic lines, etc. poor guy looks awful! He is starting a new chemo pill next Friday that will be added to the roster of medications. He is managing to keep things stable orally instead of intravenously, which is very positive since he was on IV for so long. There are more changes to come, but remaining optimistic. I told the Dr I was forgetting what home looked like, and asked if I should start moving my furniture down here and naming a room after him (the "Stone Mountain" room) afterall we are in Atlanta!

I am praying for news tomorrow that will allow us to make plans to come home, but we will just keep trusting the Lord!! I feel the peace from all your prayers and the Lord pouring over me, and Stoney does as well. We love you!! We appreciate you all so much!!

July 8, 2020

Well, today has been a very eventful day!! Stoney was discharged at 2:00 today and since we couldn't get a flight home until Friday, we decided to rent a car and drive one way home to Nashville and surprise the parents!!

Stoney did very well, but has been fighting his symptoms heavy today. He will have to deal with this for awhile, maybe 3-4 more months!! He will start a chemo pill Friday that will attack the tumors along with the radiation. In the meantime, he will do his best to stay hydrated, keep his electrolytes maintained with lots of supplements, and get blood work every Monday to make sure he is not going backwards. He will need your prayers daily!! We go back to Atlanta July 28th for an injection and then August 25th will be his next radiation treatment. Hopefully he won't have to be admitted this long each time!! This was an adventure, and I couldn't have made it without the Lord and all of you faithful prayer warriors and supporters!! I feel so honored and blessed!! Please don't stop those prayers....we are going to need them!

Love y'all and goodnight from Nashville!

Once again, back at the hotel I was listening to songs when I was alone and finding comfort in them. The Lord brought to my mind a song by Randall Dennis that was probably first recorded in the 80's, but I had heard a more recent recording by another of my favorite groups. The song was "Forever in His Care". It goes like this…

There was a time that I would fret, About the time that lies ahead
Until the time my Savior said, "You are mine, never forget" - so
Why should I worry if it shines or rains, I'm safe and warm under His wing
I'm in no hurry for an earthly king, I'm forever in His care

Honestly, with everything going on, the easiest thing to do was to worry and fret, but why? I knew my shelter was under His wings. I had posted about it, I had testified about it, but why was I doubting it? I love the line that says, "I'm kissing goodbye to all my worldly woes, I'm forever in His care". I wanted so badly to just kiss all my heartache and worldly woes away, but I struggled with holding onto them I found myself laying my burdens down, then racing back to pick them up. Being in His care, resting safely under His wings is the most precious place to be. It's a place of calm, a place of refuge, and a place to be restored. I knew all I had to do was to "let go" of all my cares and worldly woes and trust Him.

July 9, 2020

Prayers are needed right now. It was so nice to get home last night, but today has ushered in new challenges. Stoney was feeling weak, and nauseated, so we were on our way to get bloodwork in Nashville to make sure numbers were stable. On the way, he began vomiting in the car so we headed to the ER at Vanderbilt. Due to COVID, I cannot stay, so he is waiting to be seen by a Doctor. In the meantime, CTCA is working on Home Health Care approval. Until then, we will take it a day at a time. It comes as no surprise to the one who hears us pray (a good Dartt song, by the way) THANK YOU so much for your continued prayers.

July 10, 2020

Good morning Facebook world! Well yesterday was an eventful day. After dropping Stoney off at Vanderbilt, he waited for 4 hours in a waiting room of an infected cesspool of Covid carriers, without being seen. I drove back to Nashville and picked him up and took him to our local hospital here in town (which we aren't a fan of) and that brought back a load of memories!! Rewind 19 months ago when a nurse practitioner told us he had 5 months to live with no biopsy or Dr approval. Stoney was not thrilled to be there, but at 9pm, we walked in and he was seen right away. The staff was friendly as could be and they got bloodwork and fluids started!! We got home at 2:00 this morning and me, being out of my mind, decided to make Homemade chicken noodle soup... you know...cause that's what you do at 2am after being in the ER. Haha!

This morning, home health care called and they are working with insurance and CTCA to get things started Monday morning. They will have to insert another pic-line which Stoney is not happy with since his arms are purple from the last one as well as a failed attempt in the other arm. He is anxious and concerned, as anyone would be in this situation. Praying we can get through the weekend!!

The adventure continues!! Keep praying! Love you all!!

Stoney is headed back to the emergency room tonight for more fluids and issues with vomiting and dizziness. Prayers appreciated. I really don't like this and feel horrible for him. I don't understand Gods plan sometimes, but I know there is one, and I know if we trust Him, He will draw us close under His wings.

Here we go again... CANCER STINKS!!!

July 11, 2020

They have admitted Stoney into our local hospital for observation and care. They will monitor him closely and get him fluids to fight the dehydration. They will also be working on putting in a picc-line so that home health care can do their job at home. We are praying that we can get this under control, get him home, and find a way to manage these issues. We go back to Atlanta July 28, and really need to be doing a lot better than this!

Appreciate your prayers!!

July 13, 2020

Well, it has been a weird weekend with Stoney. I didn't report much, because we have been trying to figure life out...He was admitted into our local hospital in Springfield Friday night, and he is still there. They are hoping to *release him tomorrow afternoon and will move him to Vanderbilt to have a Picc-line placed on Wednesday. His Potassium has been critical everyday, and they have been giving him infusions, but he loses so much in the output of stools. He is also losing lots of bicarb and sodium, so they need to figure out how to manage that. We are faced with many issues right now, and some very hard decisions. One VERY difficult decision is, relocating to Newnan Georgia for the next 3 months while he continues his radiation therapy and can be supervised daily with infusions in which is cancer care team can closely monitor instead of a "hodge-podge" situation here in Nashville where he is moving from hospital to hospital. His cancer team feels this is for the best as we move forward in getting him better and stronger. His nutrition is lacking, and he has lost 40 pounds in the past 2 1/3 months. Home healthcare is NOT going to be an option now, because of the loss of electrolytes his body is dealing with. He needs bloodwork everyday, followed by infusions to fix the problem of the day. This is a HUGE and MASSIVE expense, and yes we have thought of several details, but feel it is the best case scenario for Stoney at this time. The Cancer center feels confident that once he receives another treatment he will be able to come home, but in the meantime we need to be in Georgia for the next few months. This brings me to the financial part of things. We are going to need to raise $6,000 over the course of the next 3 months. This seems like an astronomical amount of money, but GOD CAN AND WILL DO IT!!! I am stepping out in faith, trusting the Lord to support our endeavor in the next step in Stoneys cancer treatment journey and I am asking YOU to help us with this high ordered prayer request!! I don't know how it will all come together, or how long it will take but if this is where God wants us, He will provide for all the details needed. You can give through facebook, PayPal, through love gifts sent to his home....If you would like to help us, we would appreciate any support you can give. The PRAYERS will be greatly appreciated as well. No gift is too small....*

Many people may have questions and concerns....You can direct them to me personally, and I would be glad to answer them. I know that so many of you care deeply for both of us and will have STRONG OPINIONS and personal feedback you would like to share and offer, but I trust that you understand we have chosen a path that we feel is best for this specific journey. We are believing the Lord for a miracle...trusting HIM to provide, trusting Him for HEALING, and asking God to do the IMPOSSIBLE!! Thank you all for your prayers....we have a LONG ROAD ahead and I am asking for peace, comfort, grace, mercy and lots of LOVE!

July 16, 2020

We are headed to Vanderbilt this morning to meet with Stone's PCP and also to run more bloodwork. Home Health Care cancelled on us yesterday, but they are coming tonight to set everything up. Stoney is trying to remain positive and hanging in there. He will certainly need fluids tonight. We are just praying we can keep him out of the ER in the meantime! He is doing better with nutrition at the moment, and we seem to have the nausea slightly under control. Praying for a good weekend, and more information from Atlanta to follow on Monday! Thank you fo praying!!! Don't stop!

Well, I learned how to run fluids tonight!! Stoneys labs today were somewhat stable. A few numbers were off, but he is hanging in there. We are hoping that running these fluids at home will keep him out of the ER for the weekend. We have plans to go to Atlanta July 26th and we are hoping this will work until then!! God is GOOD, and we are so thankful to all of you faithful supporters and prayer warriors!! Keep it going!!

July 19, 2020

Well, today, we share a PRAISE!!! After a challenging few weeks of Stoney feeling bad, horrible bloodwork results, IV fluids, nausea, poor eating habits, I am THRILLED to report that the last couple days Stoney has been doing GREAT!!!! 2 rounds of labs have looked great, his appetite is getting stronger (to the point I'm in the grocery store a lot and cooking a lot!) and feeling stronger than he has in weeks. I am so happy today to see this change and positive result. I KNOW it's because thousands of people are praying for us and with us. God is so good, and we are BLESSED!!

We get bloodwork again tomorrow, we continue to run fluids from home and leave for Atlanta as as planned on July 27th!!! (NOT EARLY ANYMORE!!!)

Thank you Thank you Thank you!!! Do NOT stop these prayers!! Please!!! We are seeing God work every day, through the storms and in the sunshine... safely sheltered under His wings!!

July 23, 2020

It has been a few days since I put a detailed post on here about Stoney and figured it was time!! I was actually hesitating, because I felt like things were too good to be true, and I was scared I was goin to jinx it. Lol. Stoney is doing remarkably well!! Home health care showed me how to give him fluids at home, which we did for a few days, but then he became strong enough to go without for a few days!! The cancer center told us not to do fluids unless needed, and since he was doing so well, we held off. He continues to get stronger day by day, his appetite may break the bank as it is growing each day, (he's gained 6 pounds this week which was needed after losing 42!) and his color and attitude is back to normal. I don't know why we act surprised when we ask God to do the impossible and He does, and we look/act shocked. Hahaha. We go to Atlanta on Tuesday, for injections, oncology report, and many other appointments through the day. We will have a better understanding for what's next, but with him doing so well, we are hoping for ALL good things! His chemo pill has showed zero side effects for which we are grateful!! We are so humbled, blessed and appreciative to all those who have prayed, given in support, and shared encouragement. We had some very rough and brutal weeks, and we are now seeing some light at the end of the tunnel. Please do not stop praying!! We have 5 more months of a rollercoaster ride with radiation and treatments, so the prayer and financial help will be needed!! God is soooo GOOD!! ALL THE TIME!!

July 28, 2020

Today, stoney had a GREAT report in Atlanta at the cancer center. His platelets are down, but they can correct it with supplements and he is scheduled for his next radiation treatment August 25!! We will be there for 5 days while they sort through things.

They do not need us to move down to Atlanta right now, but we will stand by, and wait for the next treatment. His levels can drop again and become critical after the next treatment. We are so thankful for the care team in Atlanta and the love and support they've been through this journey. Please continue to pray for Stoney as he works through medication changes and we await the next treatment. Thanks so much for all your prayers and support!!

As you can see, our June and July 2020 came with its own nightmare. We fought almost everyday to survive. Stoney certainly climbed many mountains that stood in his way, and he refused to give up. Over the course of the next few months, we had many good days and found some time to enjoy once again. The days were few and far behind, but we did have them. This was a turning point for us in where the time would take us. If the Lutathera was going to work, he would have success and have many wonderful days ahead, maybe even years. If these treatments were to fail, we would be facing the difficult decision to give in and let the cancer take its course. We wanted it to work. We were told it was going to work. Now we had to wait and see… Waiting and watching are not only the worst, but the hardest!!….

August 24, 2020

Headed to Atlanta for round 2 of radiation!! We begin at 7am eastern time tomorrow Morning. Praying for good things, and no problems!

August 26, 2020

Good Morning!! Just a PRAISE REPORT!!! Stoneys Lutathera Radiation Treatment #2 was a success and there were ZERO side effects!! He slept great, feeling good and has a great appetite! This is a complete change from the last time when he went into tumor lyces. They are keeping us in Atlanta today just for extra precaution and we will go home tomorrow. Thank you for your prayers!!! Keep it up!!

September 1, 2020

Yesterday was a bit stressful for me. I have not been to the Dr in a very long time...Stoney went for his weekly labs, and I went to the Dr for a checkup and bloodwork. The suspense in waiting for results as they drew 8 vials of blood was overwhelming! My tests all came back good and normal and no ultrasounds were necessary as thought were once needed. I'll go back in November for a follow up to make sure it's all good. I was just told my cholesterol was high and I'm overweight. Duh!!

So, today I rested in the kitchen and made a little surprise for our pastor and his wife, as well as the rest of us. Lol. 3 mini Strawberry cheesecakes, and 3 Coffee Heathbar crunch cheesecakes. Baking and cooking help my mind relax and destress.

Stoney also had the best bloodwork results he has had in 18 months!! Just a miracle!!! The doctor took him off 3 meds and reduced the rest for now. It's just a blessing and a miracle. We are so thankful!! Don't stop PRAYING!!! 2 more treatments left...

September 19, 2020

I would ask you all to pray for Stoney... he is having lots of trouble with his symptoms this weekend. Actually the last 10 days have been really bad, but has been manageable until now. He's getting very anxious and nervous... we leave for Atlanta Tuesday for his monthly injection and more bloodwork. Praying we can get this under control. Stress levels are rising. Cancer stinks!! It's so easy to forget when things are going well...

Life seemed to be status quo. We were trying to be careful in protecting ourselves from covid, and yet trying to enjoy life. We stayed close to home, other than a quick trip to Florida for a few days. Staying close to home doesn't mean you can escape the insanity thats still out there in the world. One day, mom, Stoney and I decided to go into Nashville and walk around our outlet shopping mall. Neither Stoney or myself had gone back to work since the shut down. I was still booking travel for some, but cancelling trips as fast as people booked them. The travel business was at a standstill, and those who wanted to travel didn't need me booking their weekend getaways. When Stoney was feeling good, we liked to get out, so here we were in Nashville and gunshots go off while we are shopping. Talk about fear and anxiety! Stoney ran into the store yelling "there's a shooter" where mom and I were shopping and the worker rushed us into the back room and locked the doors. He then helped us get out the back entrance to the covered lot where we hid and waited for security to clear us. We watched helicopters circle, and checked the phones for updates. I am telling you, never a dull moment! I told Stoney you can have and incurable cancer you spend your whole life being treated for, and yet get shot by some lunatic who is mad he didn't get the sale price on a pair of shoes! Life is but a flicker, and we never know from day to day if today will be our last.

September 30, 2020

Stoney, mom and I stopped at Opry Mills today on the way back from getting Stoneys labs. We had lunch and walked around before getting coffee in the food court. We went into the Disney Store for a few minutes and as we walked out Stoney heard gun shots...we ran through the Samsonite store next to the Disney store, and into the middle employee section, ran down a ramp and hid in the path outside. We heard helicopters and saw over 20 police cars and ambulances. We quickly ran to our car and got out safely but we are all quite shaken. Each day is so precious, you never know what's going to happen and when. Our lives could be taken in a flash... I'm glad I know where I'm going, but these events are scary. This weird world we are living in is not for the faint of heart... people are unpredictable and frustrating!!

October had arrived. Fall was in the air and we were itching to go somewhere! My cousin Kristin and her husband had been wanting us to go with them to the Grand Canyon, so we thought about it and thought it would be fun to go out west and see them, and tour the canyons. Our friend, Liz, joined us and we had a nice time. While we were with them, Stoney once again started having problems. It is strange how stress, and anxiety seemed to bring on his symptoms faster than normal. We came back from the West, and went to Atlanta hoping the lutathera treatment would work and give him some relief, but change was once again around the corner, and this time…we were headed down another low, a low we would not rise up from…

October 20, 2020

It's early y'all!! Here in Atlanta with Stoney for round three of radiation (Lutathera). He is hanging in there. Feeling tired, and wishing things were better with his treatment and cancer progression. Every day is a new day, a day to rejoice and a day to be thankful that he is doing this well...considering where he was!

Lord willing his labs will be good this morning, his treatment will go smoothly, and we will be home tomorrow night!!

God knows the way through the wilderness, all we have to do is FOLLOW

October 21, 2020

Prayers needed today!

I know so many people are dealing with so much, that my problems feel minimal... I'm trying to be the best caregiver I can be, to listen and to make the right decisions for Stoney, but it's draining and overwhelming and frustrating at times. Some days I want to hit him over the head, and it's NOT even his fault!! CANCER STINKS!! I'm just trying to learn daily how to understand it, how to be better at dealing with it and to be selfless in doing so. I've never been patient, and I've honestly just stopped praying for it cause I'm tired of God testing me with it. I figure if I don't ask, then poof...I' ll be patient. I know that's not the way it works tho.

I'm also trying to operate my Travel Agency in the middle of a pandemic where not many people are traveling, or still too scared; or, things like cruises, theme parks and international travel is still locked down. I have lost 99% or my tours and vacation packages this year which has killed my commissions and finances...however, I have seen God provide in miraculous ways once again. He showed up, He delivered, and yet I continuously doubt.

October 23, 2020

Stoney has had a few bad days after radiation, but we are praying that he is turning a corner today. He is trying to stay on top of his fluids and take all of his meds. He is mainly exhausted and we are noticing that this third treatment is really kicking his bum!! We also pray that means it's working!!! We go back for an injection November 17 and his last radiation for now will be December 22nd. Thank you for your prayers!!

November 11, 2020

Stone Dartt Update...

Stoney had a rough night... Vomiting in the night and dealing with low blood pressure. We are getting ready to go back to the ER again. I'm so tired of this and hate seeing him suffer, but God has a plan! Trying to be hopeful in a gloomy circumstance. Prayers needed for both of us today!

As we come up on another Holiday season, there will be more updates and posts to read, as this was the way I kept people informed about our lives. As we look at the hands on a clock, we are approaching the midnight hour…So the time of our lives does the same. Maybe you've noticed the chapters in this book are all about time, and there are 12 chapters. We were entering into a new phase, a new era so to speak in the cancer journey. A phase that had us running out of options, ideas, and time….

9

Longing For Time

Psalm 84:2 - "My soul longs, yes, even faints For the courts of the Lord; My heart and my flesh cry out for the living God." -NIV

Time...I just want more time! It is so easy to be selfish with time, but it is worth it? I was having dinner with my mom last night (current day), and we were discussing the events that went on with Stoneys cancer journey. I wondered if I hadn't pushed so hard, or encouraged him to fight, if he really would have done as much as he did. Was I a driving force behind it? I think there is a limit as a caregiver at how hard we must push the person, and we must be careful that it's not out of selfishness. Of course we all want our loved ones around and we want them on this earth as long as possible, but I am sure those that are suffering find it difficult to go, and guilt from the those that love them on how much they should fight. I often tried putting myself in Stoneys shoes as hard as that was. He was the patient, he was sick, he was the one getting fluids and fighting. It's easy to be a coach and to make someone do what YOU want them to do, but it's a different story for the patient who barely has enough energy to stand up, or lift a fork to eat.

As we stepped into another season of this journey, we both tried to be positive and sensitive to each others needs. The patient/caregiver roles can become quite emotional, but it can also put the other on edge and cause anger and punishment towards one another. I won't lie and say everything was perfect through the whole process, but we did well navigating each others feelings. I am sure there were many times Stoney wanted me to go as far away as possible because I was driving him insane, but thats only because I cared. Again, at what point do we step back and let them (the patient) make the choices they are comfortable with, without thinking they are giving up.

During our time in Atlanta, I had the opportunity to invite two other friends to the cancer center for treatment. One, some very dear friends of our that we toured with earlier in my years with my family. Robert and Joyce Hayes were wonderful musicians, and they were the music directors at America's Keswick in New Jersey. It was a Bible conference, as well as restoration and rehab facility for recovering addicts. They were wonderful people with hearts of gold and we had not seen each other in over 17 years. I saw on facebook that Robert was diagnosed with stage 4 pancreatic cancer and requesting prayer. I immediately called messaged Joyce and told her about our time at the cancer center and said if she was interested, I would put her in touch with the right people and get them in for a second opinion. She agreed, and within a couple of weeks, they were already in their treatment plan. Through the following months, I would have many wonderful moments with them at the center, and sweet fellowship. They would even encourage me to sing, which is something I had not done in 2 years and had lost my voice through this journey. I had become less confident in myself and felt like the life I once knew on the stage was something of the past, and I couldn't find my musical voice. They would invite me to the chapel at the center, and encourage me to sing with them, or sometimes just listen, and pray with them. They became a great blessing and spiritual resource to me in the coming days.

Another, was a new friend. Ashley Britt was our Pastors niece. On one Sunday, while meeting outdoors, our pastor mentioned that his niece was sick. She had been tested in her local hospital and they found a mass in her colon, liver, and other areas. Her belly was swollen from the tumors and they were uncertain anything could be done. I talked with Terri, our pastors wife after church and gave her the information needed to contact the center. Within a few weeks, Ashley had also contacted the center and was beginning treatment. After doctors at home gave her a death sentence, the cancer center had given her hope, and within just a few months the tumors had shrunk and she was well on her way to a better tomorrow. Same with Robert I might add. He was given 5 months from diagnosis and as of today, it's been a year, and he is doing very well with the treatment plan at CTCA. You never know what God is going to do… Our time at the cancer center may have only been to share with others to receive care. God may have used Stoneys cancer journey to provide a way for others to get care and a possible cure. Even though the treatments didn't work for him, we were seeing others benefit from this wonderful place we loved so much. There is always a purpose, even when we aren't sure what it is.

I must say that I was becoming upset at the fact that these people we were bringing to the cancer center were getting such a great help with the worst of diagnosis, and yet Stoney was told this was the best cancer he had and they could treat him for a very long time. I will admit, I was jealous. I remember having coffee with Joyce Hayes one day, and confiding in her how I felt. I knew it was wrong, and it just kind of slipped out without me thinking, "this is her husband" I was talking about. I am thankful for those people, like Joyce, who love us unconditionally and aren't afraid of what others may say. She looked at me with glossy eyes, and nodding her head and said, "I wondered". At that time I told her I was sorry. That I didn't mean to say that, but that I just didn't understand Gods plan. We both had other friends struggling with cancer that were doing great and God was healing them, restoring them, and here I was feeling like my prayers weren't getting through. Joyce never judged me for my feelings, she never criticized me for my thoughts, but loved me through my hurt. We were able to pray together and talk about our deepest fears of our loved ones fighting this horrible disease. Joyce actually encouraged me through this process to write music again, and I did. My favorite quote she would write in her blogs was, "He sees, He knows, He cares…" Even knowing that first hand is still hard to process when you are going through a valley. You struggle with emptiness, loneliness and wonder if Jesus cares. It was a constant struggle to stay grounded in my faith. I believed the more I shared our faith, allowed others to see Jesus in me, that I could stand firmly on the rock of my foundation. Was it easy all the time? NO! I had many days and nights fighting with God, wanting to know His time line. Wanting Him to show up and DO WHAT I WANTED! What if through all this time, God wasn't planning on healing Stoney, but teaching me about a greater purpose? Scary isn't it? Sometimes the trials we face are actually tests for His higher calling….

November 18, 2020

During our visit to CTCA Atlanta today, I was able to see my longtime friends, and musicians, Robert and Joyce Hayes!! Robert is being treated here at the center for 2 kinds of Cancer, and they both need your prayers!! It has been 17 years since I've seen them and it's like we never skipped a beat!! Reminiscing about the years my family toured together in music, to dealing with cancer management and all the things involved along the journey!! What a great morning! For me....it's just what I needed today!! So encouraging!! I'm so thankful and blessed we have Jesus to walk with us and care for us. I don't know what people do without Him. Please pray for Robert, Joyce, and the many people who are fighting cancer here!! As Joyce says, "Our God sees, He knows, He cares!" I love it, and I believe it!!

Stoney is doing well, and seeing some improvement. We are on our way home, and so very grateful for the prayers and support you've shown!! Please don't stop!

November 23, 2020

So many people have prayed for Stoney over the past year and a half on his cancer journey. I am so grateful and appreciative. TODAY, I would ask you to pray for me... I am hitting a very deep low that I am struggling to rebound from. With covid rearing its ugly head worse than ever, I am so angry at life in general. I am exhausted....My business is sinking further behind and becoming non-existent as the days go on, cancelling plans left and right and the holidays seem to be going to the pits each day. I am so grateful for so many things, yet struggling to find words and feel more depressed than thankful. Stoney seems to be having more bad days than good, and more people I know and love are hurting, sick and dying. I know we are't suppose to really look ahead, but live today and in the moment, but its so hard to find any positive in the current environment. I am not asking for sympathy, for critique, for verses of wisdom and strength... I am just asking people to PRAY... I need an uplifting, I need peace, I need strength, I need GRACE, and I need financial miracles in my own life since being a full time caregiver and (basically) unemployed right now has impacted my life. I don't know when things will change, or if they will.... But I know God told us to "ask" and He wants us to be transparent and honest... I am just begging for prayer that I will find a way out of this darkness. I pray for a HEALING on so many people, including myself... May God be ever so present in these horrible days of uncertainty...

During the Thanksgiving weekend, I fell into the lowest point of my life. I have never felt so depressed, and I even wondered if I could rise above this darkness. I can tell you that what it stemmed from was carelessness of staying in communication with God, as well as allowing people to push me over the edge. Covid-19 had been raging now for about 9 months. Peoples lives were changed because of it. People had experienced loss of loved ones, and separation anxiety had become a real issue with people.

I have always loved to cook as long as I can remember and entertaining/hosting dinners and parties are what I do best. I not only enjoy it, but I excel at it. I like to give my parties themes, and decorate over the top. Well, for Thanksgiving I had planned to cook for the Dartt family which I normally do. I would cook for around 25 if everyone showed up. I had prepared the meal and prepped everything and was all ready to go. Then it all boiled up into a showdown of covid fear. While we were being careful throughout the year, there was still fear among some in the family, and so plans changed at the last minute. I took it as a personal punch, and just fell deep into despair, anger and hurt. It would be the first among many of these feelings from close personal friends through this journey. Some that I thought were my closest allies would soon hurt me with comments and careless words and actions.

I allowed myself to become so full of sorrow and anger that I trapped myself in my room for days. I did not eat, rarely drank, and just wanted to die. Honesty 101...We have firearms in our house, and I was so bad off, that as a precaution to me, Stoney had them taken from the house. He knew this was the worst I had ever been, and the worst he had ever seen me. He was worried, and even shed tears in my room praying that I would find light and hope. He was concerned that I was in a pit that I would not be able to crawl out of. I, personally, was worried about myself. I had the most evil thoughts in my head. All put there by the devil of course. I told God that I wanted to die and that there was no more purpose for me. That I didn't want to live. I prayed that God would heal Stoney and take me instead, because he wanted to live and I didn't. I am telling you for 3-4 days I fought a battle I had never fought before. I turned away my mom, my best friend, Liz, and never took and calls and barely texted. I allowed hurt to control me, instead of Gods love. I can't say I remember exactly how things turned around, but I do remember this voice saying, "BJ, I love you. I have great things for you. Trust me, and follow me." I remember crawling out of bed and going to the living room to find Stoney there with tears in his eyes, arms wide open ready to give me the biggest and warmest hug. I knew that I was being tricked into feeling worthless and unloved. I had an army of people praying for me, who were following us and lifting us up. I knew that if I made a post on Facebook, people would pray. If I sent a text to a group of people I keep on speed dial, they would call to lift me up. I had to remember who's I was, and keep my head up and my eyes on HIM. I could not allow myself to be distracted by people, or their opinions. I could not allow myself to fall and break because of words and actions. God was the creator of my life, the giver of my gladness and joy. I had to choose to accept what He had, and trust the "still small voice" he had placed in my heart and mind.

Looking back at that time, I know it was ONLY God Himself who pulled me out of that pit, because moving forward I would face many hard days, and I never felt the depression come over me like it did during those days in November.

November 25, 2020

For those who have been praying for me, I sincerely thank you from the bottom of my heart. I ask you not to stop. I hit the most serious low of my life, and I'm still trying to find my way out a little each day. Ive wanted to be alone, and I needed it, to be honest; however, as a caregiver it's difficult to get that complete silence. Please pray for Stone Mountain Dartt, as he is in the ER getting fluids and being checked out at our local hospital. My mom took him, and is staying with him right now. We are not sure how long it will be since it's the holidays. He has been there for 2-3 hours and still hasn't gotten into a room yet. We need some serious prayers!!

December 1, 2020

We arrived at the cancer center in Atlanta at noon, they got us into urgent care, drew blood, and are already running fluids. The Dr's are consulting to see what the next step is, and waiting to see about a room to be admitted to, on the hospital side of the center. I can honestly breathe a sigh of relief because we are HERE!! Thank you for your prayers!! His potassium is very low, along with sodium and co2... thank God we are where we need to be!!

Feel free to share a gift on this "giving Tuesday" to help us on this unexpected trip down here

It's been a long day!! A day that started at 3:30 this morning for us. Stoney is settled in his room with fluids running and the Dr will be in to see him in the morning. He ate dinner and is feeling better now that fluids are going. The next big step is to figure out how to stop the electrolyte loss. They will start working on it in the morning. I'm checked in and snuggled into my bed about 1/2 a mile away. Got some groceries and dinner and now ready to sleep. Thank you all so much for your continued prayers!!! I have felt them and am truly grateful. I shed a few tears today just reading comments. To those who have shared a gift, I am speechless. I am thankful. I am blessed! This trip was not planned and we had added expenses involved so I appreciate the extra help!! God bless you and here's to a good night sleep!

December 2, 2020….

This morning the Dr came in and updated us on the labs from this morning. His electrolytes were actually lower today than yesterday but because he was so dehydrated, all the extra fluids they've given him diluted some of his numbers. They are working on getting him stable but it will take a week, maybe 2. We are planning on being here through December 20th at this point. Things can change and we hope they do, but for now this is home. They are also considering TPN or PPN which would give him nourishment through IV and bypass his stomach to see if that helps with his "dumping syndrome". So much to discuss and consider. It's a daily process, but we are so happy we are here and he's getting checked out and cared for. Some have said "nice room" and indeed it is. The cancer center here in Atlanta is top of the line and they are doing everything they can to make both of us comfortable during this difficult time. I got stoney a pillow and blanket today so he feels more at home since we will be here awhile, and I grabbed my small table tree from home as I left yesterday morning so I could keep it in the hotel, to help me feel like I wasn't missing too much of the holidays. I left the lights on the tree on all night and when I woke up, I felt like a little boy at Christmas. It was comforting to me at this time. It's amazing how God allows us to channel some of those memories when we need them. I am much more at peace now that we are here and stoney is getting top notch care. It's true it's not what we planned, it's not what we wanted, but God is with us, and we are where we need to be.

We have no idea what's next... after the radiation, will all of this work for stoney?? Who knows??!! I do know that one day at a time we will be shown the next step on the journey. Until then, we will continue to thank God for His many blessings, we will play Christmas music here in the hospital room, and we will continue to pray that God provides our needs and supplies us with peace and comfort, because that's all we can do in this moment at this time!!! Love you all so much and I pray that in some strange way our testimony will be a blessing to many knowing we have a GREAT GOD who is faithful, merciful and just. Keep praying!!!!

December 3, 2020

After getting Stoneys potassium to 3.2 last night, he tanked back down to 2.4 this morning. However on a positive note, his CBC panel (which is red/white blood count, platelets and hematocrit/hemoglobin) is normal now and his other metabolic levels are improving. Co2 and sodium is up (not normal by any means, and no longer critical, but moving in the right direction) keep praying they know what to do next. His body is just rejecting the potassium so they will keep trying new things and continue with infusions and oral potassium today. The possibility of a new Picc-line where they can give him food/nutrients is being discussed, but the concern is it would have to be pulled after his radiation on the 15th and a new on one placed 3-4 days after that. They are trying to be sensitive to his veins right now. There are literally so many negatives to the positives with his condition at the moment, so please keep praying. We have a long road ahead of us!! God already knows, He's already there...we just need to keep moving forward and praising Him in the center of it all!!

December 4,2020…

Where to begin? After yesterday, I had honestly lost hope and was bracing myself for bad news. And before I share the praises, I must inform you that with any sickness or disease, there are good days and bad. Yesterday was certainly a very BAD DAY!

People have asked how I've been, and to be honest I'm exhausted and emotional! Hahaha! Last night I sat at Stoneys bedside and claimed the promises we have in Christ. I opened my hands, and I cried to the Lord for His blessings to be poured out onto us, for a Healing that only He can give, for Mercy on this journey. I prayed for the mountain to be moved, miracles to prevail and for minds to be blown in a miraculous healing! Proof that only God had showed up! Lots of tears flowed from my eyes.

Today, I arrived early to meet with the doctors, to see stoney sitting up eating his breakfast! I teared up seeing a small answer to prayer. After not eating anything yesterday and throwing up I didn't think he would feel the best, but he was eating! No nausea today (as of this post) and he just finished his entire lunch! I got him up to walk around the hall twice and even though they are still adjusting his blood pressure, (it's very low) things are looking up today. His oncology team will be in later today to discuss some options to keep him on track for radiation on the 15th. Our wonderful and incredible nurse, Kristen, who has been with us from the beginning, (she is an angel sent from God) told us that Stoneys NET test results taken last month had come back. In July his test was 80 showing the tumors were aggressive and high grade. Today, the report given to us from last months test was 40!!!! And we still have one treatment to go! This means the tumor activity is shrinking and blood supply is being cut off. It's great news and something to praise the Lord for! So why he is struggling so bad? His tumors are angry! Lol. They don't like what's happening and they are causing a problem with symptom management, which is crucial we get to the radiation treatment on the 15th. It doesn't mean they will be gone but means he could have relief for awhile. Unfortunately things could get worse, for it to get better. We are thankful for this little bit of good news! It gives us some positive fuel to run on today. Stoney got behind with his levels yesterday so today we are catching up. He has already done every single thing he has needed to do today so far so progress is being made in the right direction. We do not know what tomorrow will hold for him, but today is a good day, and we will praise Jesus for it!!

Pray with us that mountains are moved, miracles will be seen and minds will be blown!! DON'T STOP PRAYING!!!

December 5, 2020…

URGENT PRAYER NEEDED!!

Stoney is once again vomiting and losing lots of fluids... we need MASSIVE PRAYER that they can get this under control. And also figure out a way to get his levels back up. Things are really looking bad right now, and stoney is struggling with maintaining his good spirits. I continue to fight this battle with nonstop praying. Again, for this medical mountain to be moved, miracles seen and minds to blown that this is something ONLY GOD could do. Please stand with me in pleading for Gods healing, that the devil and his forces would stand down and stay behind, and that our God would be glorified. Jesus, I beg you for a miracle that only you can give!! Make me a stronger warrior through this, and not to be weak!!

If we all flood the throne, and lift our prayer and praise not just for Stoney but others in need, then other will see the POWER OF THE ALMIGHTY!!!

December 6,2020…

Well, today has been a stressful day watching Stoney go from bad to worse. With crashing electrolytes, vomiting, refusing to eat, nonstop nausea, it's been a hard day. However, after the doctors pretty much told us we would need to give in to the Picc line idea. They had it done around 6:00 and let me watch! It's absolutely incredible what they can do.... I have a new respect for health care professionals! Stoney was very nervous after a bad experience in the past, and truly had wanted to wait another couple of weeks and get it done at Vanderbilt with their technology. The funny thing was, the girl that did the procedure not only trained at Vanderbilt, but taught the staff at Vanderbilt and brought the same kind of machinery tonight!! Go figure?! Oh wait...that's right, GOD DID THAT!!! Just a special gift in all the ups and downs today. They have also started running the bicarbonate and potassium, and they are giving him meds for nausea and hoping they are on a new track to get Stoneys levels back to normal. We have 1 week left before treatment so the clock is ticking!! Continue to pray for the medical mountains to be moved!! Pray that miracles will be seen and minds blown at the amazing things God can do!! We Press on!!!

I also had a special blessing tonight by being able to go out to dinner with my special friends, Robert and Joyce Hayes (who we toured with for many years) who is being treated here as well. It was a break for me and a nice relief to have a laugh and share stories. I went back to the center to check on stoney and as I was leaving, I snapped this picture it the center tonight. This place saves lives and cares for people. We are blessed to be here!! Please keep praying!!

December 7, 2020

This morning I came into the center, and it looks like the Picc Line was a success and did what they wanted! Stoney was able to gain some ground with electrolytes and his bicarb was up to 16 (from 9 yesterday). Potassium is still critical and has a ways to go, but he has so far eaten all his food with no nausea today. Tonight they are beginning TPN for 1 week to give his bowels a rest. Trying to stop the loss. He may need to go home with it, but for now it's temporary. It's not the best news, but praying after his radiation he will do well enough to go back to eating again. There are praises to sing here today. No, it's not everything we wanted all at once, but that's seldom how God works. I had to go out and get a few necessities this afternoon since we will be here for another 10-14 days. Feeling more peaceful today and trusting the Lord for all our needs!! Wishing I was home and with my mom celebrating the holidays right now, but I'm praising God for what He's doing here!! Thank you for your prayers!!! Keep them pouring out!!!

December 8, 2020

Well today has been a bit of a poop storm in the sense of really bad medical care. Basically the Dr and nurse assigned to us today were "on call" people, so not from here necessarily, and not very efficient, and did not know our case AT ALL!! CTCA is also reeling from a new system change, which has literally made everyone who works here completely insane. They all feel so bad for not being trained properly before it rolled out, so not the nurses fault. So it was like starting over from scratch for a day. I have made some requests, made some remarks, and we now have a new nurse from here on out and a wonderful new floor doctor that is very smart! Hopefully tomorrow they will catch up with the oncology team and agree to be on the same page!! There was many hours stoney went without fluids that he needed, so we lost some ground; however, the labs that were drawn earlier were wrong and the news ones that came in did in fact show progress was being made!! Things are moving in the right direction and his co2 that was 9 Sunday is now 21!! Only 1 point from normal now. He is getting his second bag of TPN (food in a bag) at 8:00pm and that seems to be working well so far. Tomorrow should show more signs of improvement and his care team said today they would move forward with radiation if labs looked like they did today! So all in all, a good day, but more frustrating than anything!! Stoney still looks good, in fact the bets I've seen him since we got here, and feels decent (not as good as this morning but certainly not bad) and is way more optimistic today.

One issue today I caught was his bicarbonate bag was being sent through his hand IV and not the picc line. That is very dangerous so I am very thankful I caught it and was able to get it fixed ASAP. That's the main reason he has the picc in the first place!! So lots of little (and some big) things that we needed to work out.

Keep praying!!!

Praying for incredible labs tomorrow!

This stay is getting costly and people have been so generous in helping! If you would like to share a love gift, you can donate through the link below! Much love to you all!!

December 9, 2020…

Today seemed liked a yo-yo. Stoney started very frustrated with everything. We've been here 9 days, and it just seemed to be one of those days you just wanted to pull your hair out (not much for Stoney! Hahaha!). We had one of the best nurses we've had today and she was just an answer to my prayer!! The Dr wanted to do a CT scan to make sure there was no other problems, and let me just say that for a few hours we were on pins and needles praying for no new problems. Results came back, and showed clear! Nothing new, tumors stable, no problems to be concerned about. His labs showed things were improving in most areas but potassium is still quite critical at 2.3. He's been losing roughly

2 gallons of fluid a day, so they have to replace that plus keep current. It's a process for sure but he's doing fine and trying to keep his spirits up. Praying they can continue to make progress, even if it is slowly.

On a plus, I was thrilled that my friends Robert and Joyce Hayes (who are being treated here as well) was able to visit with Stoney and share some joy!! I also got to visit and have lunch with a new friend, Ashley Britt and her friend Kristen as she is here being treated as well. So, I was busy today and wouldn't trade it for the world!! God is pouring out His blessings through the valleys of life and I stand amazed!! God, continue to work, to move the medical mountains that are before us all, and blow the minds of these doctors!! Keep praying, and if you feel like sharing a gift to help with the overload of expenses, you can give through this link below! Love you all and please keep praying!!

December 10, 2020…

Today, Stoney is doing well considering his lack of sleep. The Ct scan yesterday showed no evidence of anything new or concerning. His MRI that he had in November had showed multiple tears in his shoulder, and so now it is beginning to really cause him some major pain. This IS something NEW in the management of his care now. So, the doctors are trying to find something to give him that won't interfere with his current treatment as well as his liver enzymes. It's a delicate balance I tell you!! His metabolic panel is beginning to align, but the potassium is still critical for now. His CBC panel is taking some hits with the extra fluids so it's diluting some numbers. They are giving him some things to fix his platelets and blood counts so he can be ready for radiation Tuesday. He still has not had any solid food since Monday as everything is through a bag (TPN) and will continue through the month most likely.

We ask you to pray for continuous direction in his care, his metabolic levels, and his new pain he's experiencing in shoulders. For the lack of sleep he's had today, he is talking a lot!!! I might have to bring in my earplugs later. Lol!!

God is working!! We are seeing things happen, and feeling His presence!

December 11, 2020….

Today, on top of having all the nurses enjoy the candy, we've had the entire care team come by today... nephrologist, nutrition, oncology, naturopath, and ICU Dr. Stoneys radiation treatment, Lutathera, on Tuesday has been officially CANCELLED! (Or should I say postponed) They are concerned with the low platelets, and not being able to control the diarrhea (TMI) yet. So our Oncologist looked deeper into Stoneys ct scan from the other day, and sees that the colon wall/intestine is inflamed which is causing a lot of the "fluid loss". So, they have begun a new steroid today to slow the bowel down and heal the intestines. They are hopeful they will see results by the end of the weekend, maybe Sunday. They will hopefully discontinue the TPN (food in a bag IV) and send him home to get strong and enjoy the holidays and then do lutathera in January or maybe even February. It is not uncommon to push the last treatment out up to 16 weeks so they feel like it is a good option for Stoney right now and to not have the stress of pushing to Tuesday and the "what if's". Obviously, things need to slow down in the intestines, and stabilize electrolytes before we can leave. We still have lots of unknowns, and obviously things could change again especially if nothing slows down, but it's the next bit of information for now!! We will still be here another week, but until we know more, we press on!! We will share the love of God, continue to praise Him, and watch what He does next!!

December 12, 2020…

Today Stoney was feeling the effects of his new steroid, which has kept him awake for a couple days. His lack of sleep has increased his ability to talk, tell stories and give me more ideas than my mind has comprehension for. Hahaha!! The positive in this, is that his issues are somewhat reversing. That means, because he is not losing as much fluid, he is holding it and his electrolytes are now going the other direction. He started to show signs of swelling in his legs and feet, so they are watching him closely! Tomorrow they will pull him off the TPN and introduce real food again. We are praying his intestines can process it normally and he won't go backwards. He will receive his injection as scheduled on Tuesday, and reschedule radiation in January (probably the 12-13). They are considering letting us go home Wednesday, but again, it all depends on Stoney and how his body responds to all the new changes. 10 more days of steroids...so that should be interesting. Hahaha! Pray for me!! Lol!!

His Octreotide drip that is changed every 2 hours is costing $2500 per bag. We found that out today and I think I nearly passed out! Hahaha!!

We are surrounded by an incredible care team, an amazing outstanding staff of nurses who we have become friends (family) with and feel blessed by the care received. God is working, God is using them and us! I just can't believe this place that God has allowed us to be!! Please pray for all the doctors, nurses, patients and those involved here at cancer treatment centers of America!! (Newnan, Ga).

December 14, 2020….

Well, tonight I was expecting to have a really great update, which is why I'm kind of glad I waited until tonight, since things change. I'm even hesitant to write anything anymore because things change so quickly. This morning Stoneys labs were picture perfect to be honest. It was a good day...no TPN, no octreotide, no running of fluids, it was just great. He had physical therapy, he had visits from nutritionalist and others, including discharge operators!! We were all ready to make plans to leave tomorrow and head home.. then things changed like a breeze on a summer day. Stoneys afternoon labs showed his potassium had dropped (not critical but low enough to be a problem) and other numbers fell as well. The steroid he has been on which has stopped the diarrhea (to the point of going the other way) has caused him to be completely not right in the head. He was acting strange, shaking, feeling suspicious and anxious of everything and just not himself. So when I left tonight, he basically accused me of some things (that I know aren't true and I know it's the meds) which really hurt my feelings. I'm still pulling myself together from that, because no matter if he didn't know, it just feels like a knife in my heart since I've been here for 2 weeks sacrificing my days and being an advocate. Trust me, I'm working through in my own way and praying to forgive. Hahaha! I stayed so late at the hospital that everything was closed for food, and I could not even grab dinner! McDonald's even closed at 9 here! Haha! As I sit here in the hotel room tonight, I'm frustrated and slightly anxious, but yet somehow peaceful. I know that this is a test. A test of how I'm (we are) going to handle this news and a test of faith as to what I believe God is going to do. As I told my mom on the phone tonight, I almost started crying when we got the results and knew we had to stay longer, but yet I know that this is NO SURPRISE to God. Things could change in the morning. Things may not go as we had planned, but we will always be in the center of where He wants us to be. It's a test of surrendering my Will to Him. Accepting the things I can't change, and Trusting Him to provide what we need and when to give it.

I would covet your prayers tonight as I am in a battle with myself. I'm exhausted, I'm emotionally frustrated and spiritually conflicted, but also strangely confident in knowing that when the morning comes, I will have the strength, grace and ability to confront it and face it with the Lord by my side. I'm so thankful for all the prayers, and I would just beg you to continue to pray us home!! Pray us through the holidays, pray us through the next treatment, and pray that we will come forth as gold through it all. I have had some amazing thoughts, songs I've written, and ideas for the future that have come to mind in the past few days and I absolutely can't wait to share them all with you!! God is working even when we can't see the next step ahead... love you all!!

December 15, 2020

Stoney had a very rough night. His steroids are getting the best of him I think. His resting heart rate was 150 in the night so they did an EKG and it showed some irregularities. They drew blood that showed he was a candidate for a blood clot so they just took him down for an angiogram. We were supposed to be discharged today but we will now be here a lot longer, so that's fun...

Prayers needed as Im feeling the pressures of all of this, and Stoneys mind is foggy in some ways and we just need a lot of prayer coverage right now! We have been witnessing and testifying so the devil is attacking! Fighting like a warrior to stay strong!!

December 16,2020...

This is a post that I thought would be more difficult after last nights post. Yesterday, the Dr came in and told us there was a new tumor inside the right valve of the heart. There were also 2 lymph nodes that looked cancerous and could have been the culprit of spreading the cancer to his heart. Things were dark and stoney began to become paranoid and scared, as that news can destroy you inside and out. We sat in disbelief, and I began praying...for several hours we just remained silent and prayed. Everything we were doing here, testifying, sharing our faith, talking openly about Christ, giving candy with the Christmas story on it, we were having church and the devil didn't like it. To me it was like the story of job. The devil asked God to take away everything from him to see where his praises would go. We were being tested...I left the hospital shaking, heart pounding, and wondering how we would move forward and all the decisions ahead. I made calls and had peace talking with some family and my mom. The oncologist came in last night just before I left and said we need to look further into these scans because I'm just not convinced that the treatment we are doing isn't working since the NET tests were showing improvement. He seemed baffled and wanted to dig deeper. He called it pseudo progression meaning when the body receives radiation, the tumors can grow 2-3 times the size during the course of 3-4 months until the radiation is complete which is why they don't like to do scans right away. He was holding on to the fact this was not new but inflammation and that the steroids were not helping the "looks" of the spots. He scheduled an echocardiogram which was done last night. So much info y'all. Anyway, stoney called me a couple times scared last night wondering if he was going to wake up today. We prayed...I set a timer every hour all night to wake up and pray, to plead the blood and believe in medical miracles! This morning stoney texted and said, "I woke up!" Hahaha. I got ready and met with doctors this morning and they stabilized him enough to come back to the hotel tonight. The doctor addressed some questions and when I asked him about the echo report, he said "they haven't read it yet?". I said no. He said I read it this morning and your heart is great. There is no blockage and the spot in the valve isn't there. Talk about tears!! There is a mass behind the heart that is of concern but again the oncologist thinks it's swelling of dead tumors. There is fluid on the lungs which they believe could be from all the fluid they gave him here and then just sitting in bed for 2 weeks with no activity. So tomorrow we begin tests and appointment and biopsy's and go from there. It's not as dark as it seemed and there is some hope in the midst of a new prognosis but God is STILL God!! We feel encouraged for now and thankful stoney can go to the hotel for a couple of good nights sleeps before we get more info. We will meet with pulmonary and cardiologist in the morning and our oncologist Friday to discuss what's happening next. If there is new cells, they will start chemo ASAP...if it's the pseudo progression which is expected, they will resume radiation in January as planned. For now, we claim victory in this information that the heart is clear and strong!! The steroid is causing jumps and arrhythmia so we press on with that news. We are here until Saturday for now, and maybe Tuesday if needed.

Listen to this song that is a favorite of mine that just causes us to stop and listen...

December 17, 2020

It's 6:40am and we are headed to the center for blood work and appointments with pulmonary, cardiologist and a possible biopsy today or tomorrow morning. Oncologist tomorrow for the final verdict on what's next. Stoney feels weak and exhausted and also had an increase with symptoms last night so he's very worried things are coming back (since lowering the steroid) and he will be readmitted so please pray for Gods perfect peace in all of this and in Him. We are hoping maybe a new picc line Monday in Nashville with temporary fluids done at home as I administered to him in august. We shall see what the Lord says, and what the days hold!! Keep praying!! God is up to something. He's teaching, He's leading, He's providing through people like you, He's proving Himself daily to me, and in HIM will I continue to trust and follow! Love y'all! I'm fighting like a warrior today!! Got my shield and sword, let's DO THIS!!

(Here is a photo from yesterday with Stoney getting his picc-line out by one of our favorite nurses at CTCA these last 2 weeks, and then last night of stoney back in the hotel room. He was tired, as I just made him walk about a mile, so he's trying to smile even though he may have wanted to kill me! Hey, physical therapy told me to make him move!)

December 18, 2020

Good morning people!! It's another bright and early morning in Newnan, Ga! Back at the center for bloodwork, and a biopsy this morning. Stoney is feeling ok, just nervous and anxious as anyone would be right now. He lost what was equivalent to 3 3/4 gallons of fluids (poop) within a 24 hour period so we are interested to see how that looks in his bloodwork today. We are preparing to go home tomorrow, but also bracing for the possibility of staying for infusions and possibly being readmitted to the center. The whole purpose we came down for on December 1st, was fluid loss and it seems we are right back where we started!! So, we need your prayers!! We are hoping and praying that we could go home, have another picc line placed and give fluids at home, but obviously there are many unknowns right now in the situation. Your prayers are appreciated, welcomed and needed!!

It's been 18 days in Newnan now, with the chance of more on the way so we would like have peace in accepting whatever God has, comfort in knowing we are where we need to be, and wisdom in all the decisions to be made! God hasn't left us, He isn't surprised, and He's here with us!! Let's ARMOR UP, and prepare for the day ahead!! One way or the other, I have a bed to lay my head, food to eat, and love from so many people, so I' d say I'm blessed!!

...UPDATE...

Labs today are excellent. Better than yesterday. I don't understand at all but I'm so glad God does! He loses 4 gallons of fluid in 24 hours and has perfect labs. That's ONLY God!! I continue to stand amazed and blown away by what God is doing. Medical mountains are being moved, and God is working overtime, thousands are praying, and blessing are pouring. I stand amazed each day and wonder what new thing we will see, endure, have to walk through, praise Him for, pray for....this journey has been interesting for all of us, but God is showing up, even when we don't get what we want, He gives us exactly what we need. He is with us and near us. Thank you all for the prayers!! We meet with Our oncologist at 4:15 and then will make a decision on what's next for going home...tonight or tomorrow!

December 19,2020..

After the appointment yesterday with the oncologist we were allowed to go home. Stoney was not able to drive due to the anesthesia he had earlier in the day so I'm not sure who was more scared, him in the passenger seat or me driving. Hahaha! It was a longer drive with the weekend and holiday traffic, but we made it home around 10:00 central. The Dr increased the steroids to try and help with fluid loss so Stoney will have to deal with the awful side effects from that for just a while longer. It's not working yet, as he is still going through the "dumping syndrome" so it's extremely important for us to stay on top of fluids, electrolytes replacements and all the billion pills he's on! We are just praying to stay out of the hospital for the weekend (and longer). Waiting for PICC line orders to show up and then we can do extra fluids at home.

We are still not 100% sure of the biopsy results which should come in Monday or Tuesday so we need you all to pray the results are negative!! Pray super hard with all you have to pray!! Otherwise treatment will look different for Stoney in the upcoming months, so we are still asking and begging for the miracle!!!!

I would like to say being home is wonderful, exciting and all I wanted, but with the new challenges he is facing here, I am just asking for peace and comfort as we WAIT, and deal with the unexpected!! God has us already wrapped in His arms and He knows what we need and what's next, so why is it so hard to just let go?! I'm blessed and thankful for all the prayers of people to get us through and get us home! The plan now is to try to enjoy family and friends, enjoy the holidays and trust the Lord for what's next!! Much love to all of you!!

As you can see, getting through the holidays were always rough for some reason. We came home from a long visit in Atlanta, and yet we were finding ourselves right back in the hospital at home. Home health care had to come out to the house and teach me how to give him fluids, as well as TPN (Temporary Parenteral Nutrition) at home to help keep us out of the local hospitals. I would mix vials of formula into a large bag that would run anywhere from 12-18 hours. He would carry a pole around with him, or stick the bag in a backpack.

Stoney just wanted to go back to Atlanta. He trusted them, and he knew what they were doing. Our Christmas this year was spent at Vanderbilt hospital in Nashville, and on Christmas Eve, they nearly killed him. They thought they were trying to help, but in doing so, they made so many mistakes that by withholding fluids, it nearly took his life. They would spend the next few days trying to get him stable enough to go back to Atlanta. He would then have to begin chemo treatments that would make things much worse....

December 20, 2020

Well, we are back in the ER at Vanderbilt. I called ahead, pleaded my case, and drove Stoney down here as fast as I could. Had the staff waiting when we got here, started bloodwork and already roomed and fluids going. The plan is to admit him tonight, place a picc line tonight or tomorrow morning and if labs are decent enough to run fluids from home, they will let him go home tomorrow night. Lots of steps involved in this process though. Your prayers are greatly appreciated as I am tired and feel overwhelmed. I knew this was Gods perfect timing because the lights were green, the traffic was clear, and the ER was empty and waiting just for us. Valeted my car and got a wheelchair to get him inside and the whole thing happened without a hiccup! Such a blessing!! We are still praying to be home for Christmas!! Lord willing!! More trials, but more opportunity for God to pour out blessings!! "In the eye of the storm when you're confused and torn, just look to me I' ll help you see I' ll give you what you need."- if I only knew when I wrote that song 21 years ago I' d be living it today

He is our Rock and Shelter, our Pilot, our Captain, our Physician. Oh how I love Him and oh how I trust His Holy Name!!

December 21, 2020

Well, we are still here in the hospital! Stoneys co2 levels are still low and today they gave him his first co2 boosters, which is normally used in the ER for emergency. His other numbers are in the close range to go home tomorrow (Lord willing!!) but we will have lots to do at home. I have been on the phone all day with home health care, providers, and physicians to make it possible to have fluids done at home. Stoney will get bloodwork 3 times a week at home and I will give fluids everyday as well as bicarb infused potassium 3-4 days a week. We will push through to his next radiation treatment (until we hear otherwise. Still no biopsy results yet. Tomorrow hopefully) and then see what's next. Hopefully this new plan will keep him out of the hospital. We will have some costs involved, and have no idea where it will come from, but as I work on all that, I am so glad that we may be able to handle some of this from home!! Please keep praying that numbers will stabilize tonight and we can manage things at home through the holidays!! We still need plenty of miracles, but I'm so very grateful I know the ONE who not only rides on the wings of the wind, but who calms the storms and still has the power to heal!! Thank you for your prayers and support and I ask you to keep it up!! I'm so glad God is with us ALWAYS!! What a comfort!!

December 22, 2020...

Today, we received the news from the biopsy that was done in Atlanta on Friday. The results came back positive for spreading... this was not the news we wanted, but we have a plan in place thanks to our fantastic care team in Atlanta. They are baffled by what they are seeing, and truly aren't ready to call it, but they feel Stoney needs to press on with chemo. They have scheduled us to arrive in Atlanta on January 4th, and begin treatment immediately. It will be 4 rounds with scans done afterwards. They are hopeful and confident that this new treatment will do what is needed and may even stop the diarrhea symptoms completely. That's their hope! Stoney remains at Vanderbilt hospital for his electrolyte imbalance, and when they increased the bicarb, it pulled his potassium down in the danger zone. They are now working hard and finding a balance, so will be keeping him longer for now. In the meantime, I have home healthcare ready to when he gets home, I have all the plans in place for going to Atlanta in 12 days, and I am continuing to believe for a miracle in the midst of the madness!! Please pray for these things....1. For Stoney to feel better, and be encouraged, and to have the fight needed to proceed!! He's so tired of it all, stressed, anxious and wanting relief, so we must PRAY for Gods comfort and peace. 2. That the treatment will take effect ASAP and he will have no further symptoms or side effects from chemo...3. For financial help as we now go back to Atlanta for this treatment not knowing the days we will need to stay. I'm hoping my mom will even come with me to help carry the burden and give me a day off or 2 as needed.

My takeaway...God has not changed, He has not left us, He has not changed any plan that was already in place before this news. He IS STILL GOD THE ALMIGHTY! He has the power to change and move mountains!! Let's NOT be defeated, let's STAND together in prayer, and let's be warriors in this fight and not allow the devil to get any victory in this! I'm pointing fingers at myself as well. We must be strong and courageous!!

Keep praying for us!! I really want Stoney to be home for Christmas!!

December 23, 2020...

Today, Stoney is struggling with his shoulder pain once again and is having to take some pain meds which aren't the best for his liver enzymes but it's needed today. The floor Dr has changed for the holidays, and she is bringing in a team of specialist including a nephrologist to help with Stoneys electrolytes. They are still the same, and not changing. Staying low.... they are not releasing him anytime soon unfortunately, but hopefully he will be getting better. The home health care supplies have arrived and I am willing and able to give fluids as soon as he gets home. In the meantime, trying to remain cool, calm and collected and trust the Lord for His leading. This holiday season is not at all what we had planned, had expected or wanted, but it is what God has allowed. Yesterday, Stoneys brother sat with him all day so I could have a much needed rest and today I'm taking care of all the business side of things and medical calls, and consults before going down to spend the evening in the hospital. I'm trying to find a way to split me in half and be in 2 places at once and finding it challenging, but Im finding the joy and peace around every corner which you all have been praying for and I'm so grateful!! God is so good, and I feel as if He is working in me more than ever before. Encouragement in cards, texts, gifts and strength like never before, along with HOPE in my heart!! Pray these things upon Stoney. He needs an uplifting, not just physically but mentally and spiritually! Oh for God to be glorified through this situation!! May I continue to look towards the hills which comes help and never doubt that Emmanuel is with ME everyday!!! You are all blessing my heart and giving me so much strength to push forward!! I love you all and ask you to keep praying!!!

For those of you who have shared gifts already, my heart explodes with gratitude, thankfulness and love from the bottom of my heart!!

December 24, 2020

Today has been a rough day for Stoney. Last night at 10:30pm they decided to move stoney to a different floor and different room. He was not happy and very anxious which caused his symptoms to flare. This morning his numbers were not great but not as bad as they've been. Co2 still low. They also threw him a bombshell and told him they were taking all food and liquids away and starting TPN without consulting with the cancer center in Atlanta. Another anxious and stressful moment. I've done my best to communicate with the doctors and staff about our needs and it seems this is the only direction they are willing to go and might let him come home Monday or Tuesday on TPN. The cancer center is closed until Monday so it's hard to accomplish much until then anyway. He will remain at Vanderbilt through the weekend and we will see what next week holds. They believe the cancer needs the chemo badly to help with this issue so we will pray that January 6th will quickly fall upon us, without missing all the blessings that may come in between! He was moved *to a bigger room, he can have 1 person visit at a time, he is feeling better and less pain....these are all BLESSINGS and reasons to give thanks and praise. We will not allow ourselves to be defeated or back down. We will stand strong and courageous and not fear. Christmas is different for everyone this year, and while it really stinks (hahaha!), I feel we are learning more THROUGH HIS LEADING. We are learning to rest in HIS promises and find comfort in knowing HE is still in control. There are truly no surprises here to our Father, so we will do our best to take a deep breath and enjoy what we can, while we can and where we can!! Please say a prayer for us this Christmas Eve. I'll be sharing my night at the hospital with Stoney and then back at home late with my mom. Tomorrow will be the same, as if it were me, I would not want to be alone on Christmas Day, so I will move Heaven and earth to be in 2 places at once because God said I can do it!!!*

and yes, I'm still working out those details. Hahaha! I firmly believe in cloning now. Hahahaha!!

God bless y'all and merry Christmas!!

Consider sharing a gift this holiday season to help with current and upcoming medical expenses

Stone Dartt Update...December 25...Christmas Day...

I started getting text messages from Stoney at 5:45 this morning upset and concerned. The night staff had pulled his oral intake of fluids, which caused him to become severely dehydrated, nauseated, dizzy and light headed. They said it was Dr orders, and nothing they could do. Stoney was so upset. I finally got him calmed down and we prayed and waited until nephrology and doctors came in to discuss the issue. After arguing with an extremely pig headed, egotistical doctor, I was able to share and express the concerns and have orders reversed. The major problem is that Stoneys cancer is so specific, rare and uncommon (less than 140,000 cases) that people want to reinvent the wheel and solve the problem on their own. It's a very delicate metabolic balance. So we had a great nephrologist join us on the team and I was able to connect him with our Atlanta nephrologist (that's a miracle in itself being a holiday and he worked privately for us) and we have a plan in place. They blew 3 veins trying to get blood due to dehydration (worse than when he went in on Sunday) and doctor wouldn't even admit she was wrong. Her associate called and apologized after the labs proved it. (I still think the Dr should be apologizing for the major setback, but God will forgive her).

They now have to replace the single lumen picc line with a double and increase the rate of fluids to get him hydrated. The new nephrologist seems optimistic about getting things leveled out now with fluids and his TPN (food in a bag) and get him home where we can handle things here before going to Atlanta. We are dealing with a major setback so praying hard they can now move forward. I've also made sure Dr "loser" is no longer with us!! (Not trying to be disrespectful, but it honestly would be helpful for healthcare professionals to actually LISTEN to their patients and learn from their history and past issues. And not try to reinvent or fix it on their own and be a hero)

I believe things are on the right path for now, but we do need miracles and prayer that God will continue to lead and direct.

In the meantime, Stoneys 2 brothers spent some time with him today and mom and I were able to have a nice Christmas together at home. (In between my medical phone calls!) I was able to fulfill my moms wish and make her a peppermint cheesecake, and enjoy a very basic Christmas dinner.

Add the Nashville bombing/explosion into this equation and it made for a very interesting day. Stoney is just a couple miles away from the explosion and new curfews are in place for downtown which make things harder on me to get there. Life is full of complications, but I'm so thankful that God has it worked out. I have no idea what each day holds but I'm glad I truly don't have to worry about that, because my steps are already ordained and planned out. We are BLESSED!! I would ask for a little extra prayer for myself right now... some high blood pressure, tense shoulders and headaches have me a little down today but I'm pushing through!! All in all, it's not the day I wanted, BUT the day that God has made. We can literally celebrate Christmas any and every day because of Gods goodness!!

Merry Christmas everyone!!!

December 27, 2020...

I did not get an update on yesterday because I spent the day in the hospital, and was too tired when I got home. Stoney was still struggling yesterday with hydration and trying to feel better. After giving him over 10 liters of fluids, he is feeling some better today and sounds like himself. Even got to FaceTime this morning and open my Christmas present!

The bad news is mixed with good news I guess. Depends on how we look at it. I will not be able to give stoney fluids at home. The amount he needs is just too much right now, and I would not be able to handle it. The plan is to discharge him Tuesday morning and drive directly to Atlanta and have him readmitted there in the cancer center. From there they may be able to begin the chemo treatment and watch his vitals better than Vanderbilt. They are much more equipped to handle Stoneys condition.

We need major prayer and miracles that this will be expedited and the right team in Atlanta will be able to handle it during the holidays since his care team technically isn't there until January 4th. Vanderbilt just doesn't really know what to do with his situation and they don't want to start over. We have no idea how long this trip to Atlanta will be. I'm guessing at least 2 and a half weeks but maybe more depending how stable they can keep stoney after his first treatment of chemo.

I will admit that we are anxious and nervous, but yet we believe it's the best decision and we know God is in control. The expenses will be around $1200 for the month, but I am once again trusting God to supply as HE always does, through His people... you have prayed with us and for us. You have supported us from all around the globe, and now I'm asking you to stand with us and once again join us for another adventure. As I take today to pack, and prepare my mind for what's next, I feel a Peace in following our Savior down these topsy turvy roads. Not knowing what scary or exciting thing is around the corner, we will walk forward and continue trusting Him as we've done all year. Each day I wonder how we are going to manage the day, week or the month, but somehow here we are with HIS miraculous provision. So...here we go!!

Please pray for more medical mountains to be moved and that we will continue to praise Jesus through the good and bad as hard as it gets!! We love you all so much, and are full of so much gratefulness!!

December 29, 2020...

Good morning!! I am soon to be out the door, headed to Nashville to pick up stoney and drive straight to Atlanta with few stops as possible. They are discharging him only for a transfer to CTCA. They will be waiting for him and to arrive, and admit him to their care. The oncologist will either be in tonight or tomorrow to assess Stoney, and then decide whether they can move the chemo forward or if they need to wait and try to figure out a different solution. Lots of unknowns are before us, and yet I feel a peace and comfort about it all and I pray stoney does too. I am so excited that my mom is coming with us!! Mainly to help me out, and give me a break when we get there and sit with stoney a couple days while I can turn everything off and rest. I'm reaching my limit for pure exhaustion and need to rest!! The car is packed for about a 3 week stay, and we are remaining optimistic that God has a plan, and look forward to see what exactly He is going to do. I'm going to miss my bed, my home (that I've barely seen this month), my friends here and so many activities I enjoy this time of year....BUT, it's worth it! I know I'm doing what God wants me to do, and I can feel the prayers from all of you which is why I'm asking that you not stop, but increase!! Share with friends, church families, pray that Stoney will feel the love and support and that we will all get through this stronger than ever and giving God the glory for all of it!! We know He is working!! Faithful we must continue to be!!

Here is the link if you would like to help with the extra expenses we are faced with…

December 30, 2020...

Sorry for missing a day in posting, but things have been chaotic! We arrived in Atlanta yesterday afternoon at 3:40 and went right up to the urgent care where they closed the doors about 20 minutes after we arrived! It was close! I drove the whole way and to say I was stressed would be an understatement. Stoney was sharing his thoughts on my driving and giving "unwanted advice", but it wasn't until we got about 45 minutes away when we stopped at Chick-fil-A for lunch that I became super concerned when stoney was not able to compose a sentence, and began slurring his words. I had no idea what was going on, but I got him some food and he seemed to be ok. They told us today it could be from the extreme lack of sleep as well as protein deficiency mixed with metabolic losses. I kept looking for stroke like symptoms. From then on, I think I drove faster than the millennium falcon could fly! (The only star wars reference I will probably ever use. Haha) Upon arrival, Stoneys labs were what I had expected, perfect...ugh. Vanderbilt had tanked him up so high that his numbers looked good, which caused them to wonder why he was there. Long story short, they are unable to do direct admit to CTCA unless it's a medical emergency transfer (ambulance) and we didn't want the cost of that! They ended up getting stoney a room at 9:30pm and started getting him settled, however his TPN was on hold, so that caused a new world of issues. Today, stoney looked good, and is relieved to be here and getting outstanding care by the nurses and doctors who all welcomed us warmly!! They know us here by name and we have grown to love so many of them and feel like family!!

As the oncologist is still making his decisions on treatment, they are working on tweaking the TPN so we can live with it at home and find a way to stay out of the hospitals! If the plan still goes as follows, stoney will receive chemo next week and remain here for observation for several days.

I am showing mom the beautiful town of Newnan so she can do what she wants when I'm in the hospital and not feel like a prisoner here. The center has so graciously allowed us to swap out as needed, which is something they normally don't do, but they feel so bad for stoney and have appreciated our positive attitudes and upbeat spirits. God is so good!!

Please pray that Stoney will continue to feel good, that the TPN will be managed and approved for home, and that the right chemo treatment will be chosen and no side effects. We will have some extra expenses here and we are so grateful for those who have contributed already, and we are trusting the Lord for the remainder! We are so thankful to be here and know that God is showing us daily the next step! I am so very happy my mom is here. Coming back to the hotel after being in the hospital and having her with me to eat with and talk to is a huge blessing to me after many lonely nights. Reading all the kind words and those sharing prayers is so encouraging to me!! I am still believing for miracles!! God is doing too many incredible things for me to stop believing now, so I will continue to follow HIM each day, and allow HIM to speak!

Love y'all so much!!!

December 31, 2020...

Well, 2020, in a way you've stunk to the high heavens and you've made life miserable for many people, but in fairness you've showed us how to slow down (when not fighting cancer). I am certainly ready to kick 2020 out and welcome 2021 with open arms in hopes that God blesses immensely!! As stoney and I talked about today, God's faithfulness through this insane year has been something extraordinary! We've seen Him provide for us all year long when we were unsure how we would survive each week. We've seen Him get us the care needed to fight cancer, and continuously find ourselves amazed at how He leads and paves the way when it looks dark and cloudy. I've met more friends, and have been more open with my faith then when we traveled in ministry...I've listened to others with compassion more because I know what it's like to want to be heard. I've found truth in waiting and being patient, and I've seen God pour out blessings when I thought they were dried up.

God has been GOOD!! Even in the struggle!

Today, our oncologist came in and shared his plan of attack and here it is...this weekend they will focus on adjusting the TPN to meet Stoneys needs. It takes time, and they are working on the perfect formula that we can go home on and live some normal days until he's improved enough to be off of it. Monday, they will place a port in Stoney, and begin a 46 hour chemo plan as an inpatient procedure so they will have eyes on him around the clock (which makes me more peaceful since we were told that normally doesn't happen-another God thing) and then they will keep him until Tuesday January 12th to receive his monthly injection. If everything runs smoothly, we will go home and come back every 2 weeks for 6 rounds of chemo treatments and then scans to follow. They believe this will make his symptoms easier to deal with and allow him to enjoy life once again AND hopefully without TPN!! We are so thankful for an amazing staff and team of doctors that work together to develop a plan Thats tailor made for stoney. We feel so blessed here, and are so thankful to be here!! Tonight, mom and I are going to celebrate New Year's Eve with Italian food in our hotel room and FaceTime with Stoney! I doubt I will be awake at midnight since I haven't been able to make it much past 11 these days. Haha!

We look forward to what God is going to do!! Stay tuned for more information!! Here is a link of you feel led to help with our extended expenses!!

God bless and HAPPY NEW YEAR EVERYONE!! Let's make 2021 the BEST YET!!

Closing out the New Year was in way a blessing! I was DONE with 2020, and ready for a new start. What that start would be, I had no idea. Were we running out of time? We were we headed for new blessings and miracles with chemo? Was a miraculous healing ahead? All I knew was that we were in Gods hands and He was preparing each of us for what was ahead. I was so thankful to have my mom with me for the New Year. I was thankful that Stoney had hope to look forward to, and to be able to press on. I was thankful we still had each other and that our life was still one to live, and love. We had friends and family surrounding us in prayer, supporting us financially spiritually. We had everything we needed for this time in our life.

That night at the hotel while mom and I ate our Italian dinner, and watched the New Year brought in on TV, we talked about Gods goodness through this time. She asked me what I thought was going to happen, and if I thought Stoney would come through this. She asked me if I was ok with the next forms of treatment. So many questions, and at the time I didn't know the answers to any of them. I thought I did. I had hoped that what I expected in my heart was the right answer, but would later come to realize that God had other plans for us.....

10

Loneliness of Time

Deuteronomy 31:6. "It lets you know that you should be courageous and know you are not alone, since the Lord God is always with you" -NIV

As we entered into a New Year, it would be one that would bring many surprises. We would once again see Gods faithfulness, but experience great love, loss, and loneliness.

It is interesting that in times of emptiness there is a fulness of Gods love. For those of us who are believers in Christ, God gives us something that the unbeliever does not have…comfort in sorrow. As we struggled through months of hardship, God was what I believe preparing us. He knew Stoney could no longer live like this, and He had a better place for him. When the radiation and chemotherapy methods were failing, I started searching for other options. I was not going to settle for what the cancer center had been telling us. I knew there had to be other options.

January, February and March was a struggle. It became more difficult to care for Stoney. I took a step back from my travel agency, because I was slipping on deadlines for bookings, and could not keep up with the daily organization and skills needed to run the agency. Stoney was needing more care, and I was feeling more pressure. I found solace in music. I listened to many gospel groups I grew up listening too and found myself singing around the house more than normal. I began to step up my prayer routine because I was feeling defeated on a daily basis. I became lonely. I was losing my best friend before my very eyes, and yet I had to be strong for him and keep him running for the finish line. The Cancer center kept giving us goals to reach for. If we can get to this date…If we can just take a few more pills…If we just add more medicine to the TPN… Stoney was getting tired, and I was exhausted. Another year ahead of more testing, more trials and more effort on both of us. I was doing this alone. I was juggling the emotional, physical and spiritual angles of caregiving and I was failing on all thrusters.

We tried taking a trip to Florida with Stoneys brother and family in February, but ended up in the hospital down there for infusions. We tried going out to dinner in Nashville but he ended up nauseated and tired so we gave up on that. We seemed to slowly grow further apart if thats even possible in the same house as patient/caregiver. I was more lonely than ever, and I tired to give Stoney all I could. I tried encouraging him, watch movies, fix his favorite foods, but all of that was falling short. I can't even think about what was going through his mind. How was he feeling through all of this? If I was feeling like this, surely he was dying inside as well. The devil played mind games with each of us. I know that it is only by the grace of God that we both kept fighting.

I could not bear losing my best friend, and I was not going to be the one blamed for any of it. I was going to fight the toughest battle of my life, and drag him along for it!

January 1, 2020…

Well first of all, Happy New Year!! There is not a lot of news today as they are still trying to get Stoney stable. His electrolytes are just not an easy fix, so it's taking lots of time. This weekend they plan on adding whatever they can to find a formula that works to keep his labs normal. They are still hoping to proceed with chemo on Monday, but obviously that will be contingent on his numbers. We have had a wonderful time chatting with the nurses, and continuing to get to know them as friends. We are so blessed with an incredible staff, it's just mind blowing how quickly they have become a large part of our extended family!! As we look to Monday, please pray that God give us peace and comfort at what is ahead and that Stoney will be strong enough to face the chemo with no challenges!! God is so good and so GREAT, and we are learning each day to follow Him and standing on His promises! I'm looking forward to my first day off tomorrow, staying in my pajamas and allowing my mom to spend the first full day with stoney. I can't wait!!! Praying for no frustrating issues to deal with.

January 4, 2020....

Today has been a rough day for stoney. He is feeling low, tired, and discouraged. After worrying all night for the chemo today, he was informed that the chemo was suspended by insurance and could take 5-15 days to be approved. I got on the phone with the insurance company and pleaded my case, as well as his care team manager. We were able to get it approved, but still unsure if it will be tonight or tomorrow before it starts. There are many concerns, obviously, that come with chemo but trying to have faith that this will work as it's kind of the last option. Stoneys nerves have been hard on him today, and he's losing so much fluid that he just feels exhausted all the time and losing energy. I am believing for a miracle and trusting the Lord that if we all just flood the throne with prayers, God would touch him and give him some encouragement!! Keep praying for the mountains ahead to be moved!!

Love y'all!!

January 5, 2020....

Today, Stoney was feeling very well after his first night/day with chemo. The chemo will run through a pump for 46 hours. He is having mild side effects like numb fingers and toes and slight sensitivity to cold drinks, but other than that he is doing very well. He ate better and his labs were surprisingly better, so we are praising the Lord for this wonderful day!! We know that the days will be harder, but we will take today as a victory! God is so good!! We appreciate so many praying for us, it just feels so good to know that you are holding us up in prayer!! Please don't stop, because it's going to carry us all the way through!! We need the extra prayer for the rough days we will have

We have extended our stay through January 13th for now as we will wait until after they give him his injection before we head home. Things can always change, but that is the plan for now! After several busy days of news and ups and downs, it's kind of nice to have some calmness. I am looking forward to a good nights sleep after a restless night. We will continue to trust God each day and fight this cancer as hard as we can!!! Giving God the GLORY for the Great day we have had, and the ones that lay ahead!!

January 7, 2020...

Now interrupting your political mayhem report to bring you some positive information!

Last night at midnight stoney finished his first round of chemo! He is feeling great with minimal side effects so far, and even had to test the barriers of the "no ice" rule. If someone says "no, absolutely not", what do you do? You try it. Haha. While it was not as bad as they had said, he does realize with every treatment things will progress and be harder but for now he is back drinking his cold fizzy water and chewing on ice when he can

The numbness in his fingers and toes is subsiding, and thus far no nausea has been present so we rejoice in that for today!!

His metabolic levels were stable this morning, and although discharge was discussed for today, they are going to keep him and monitor him for 24 more hours to make sure his potassium does not drop again. At that point, he will stay at the hotel with mom and I until Tuesday when he gets his injection. Home health will come to the hotel and show me how to give TPN there for the weekend. He will also have TPN at home for the next month to make sure he's getting all his electrolytes for the day. Next round of chemo is scheduled for January 18th.

We thank God for His provision over us here, and TRUST Him to continue to supply the needs as we walk by faith each day. As we are surrounded by political unrest, fear, anger and concern in our country, may I just encourage you all to count your blessings in life! Love on those who think differently, live for the Lord in all areas of your life, and take time to laugh and find joy in what's around us. Life is way too short to live in anger. As a child of God, we are gonna live forever with the ONE who created us!! So, why worry or concern yourself with the mess going on... Let's be so grateful for Gods blessings in our lives and love one another, sharing HIS love for others to see!! I' ll start.... I'm so thankful, and grateful for ALL OF YOU who have stood with us during this cancer battle for stone. You've given sacrificially, you've prayed continuously and you've loved unconditionally!! I stand amazed at your love and gratitude!!

Please never stop praying, and we'll never stop fighting!! Stand strong, and warrior on!!! Let's pray for MORE GOOD DAYS!!!!!

I had decided after watching some news at the hotel, that I would change the channel and start watching HGTV. Probably not the greatest option, since I wanted to go home and change everything in my house. I think I even had plans to build some great feature in my back yard, and I'm no architect nor can I hammer a nail straight. I would go to the Cancer center and sit with Stoney and show him the shows I was watching, and he would roll his eyes. We watched so much TV during our days at the center because, well, there was nothing else to do. We met so many wonderful nurses who became our friends. I reached out and brought them cupcakes, Starbucks gift cards when I could, and before we left from our longest stay, I wrote 88 Thank you cards to the staff thanking them for their service and kindness. They had given up their lives to help others. Some nurses were single mothers who barely have time to see their kids just so they can work to provide. Some were working 3 jobs to pay off students loans, and even going to night school to further their education. Stoney and I became obsessed with these wonderful care providers. I think I am getting ahead of myself, so lets go back to the journal in January and re-live our emotional journey of chemotherapy!

January 9, 2020...

Yesterday, Stoneys numbers were not as good as they needed to be to go to the hotel for the weekend. If home health couldn't get to hotel last night, they would need to keep him until Monday, which is what happened. I was so upset and irritated...not at stoney necessarily, but this journey that has worn on me, family members, and even prayer Warriors. As I sat out the window yesterday and shed a few tears, I looked outside and saw God in the sky (so to speak). It has been raining here in Atlanta, stressful, and kind of depressing lately with world news and our medical fiasco. But as I looked at the window and began thanking God for so many small things (an amazing place of treatment, incredible workers, life, financial needs have been met, LIFE, safety, etc...) the sun peaked out to give me this gift, then it clouded over and began to rain again. It reminded me that through the storms of life, God is there, pouring down His blessings. I began to think that God was protecting us from something worse, maybe stoney wasn't meant to be at the hotel for his own medical protection. That God has our days ordained and orchestrated. That we put too much hope in doctors and their ideas, instead of God and His divine direction.

I am remaining hopeful that Stoneys labs will continue to improve and he will be discharged and able to go home as planned on Tuesday. His numbers this morning were stable, and the Co2 that dropped to 15 came up to 18 and we just need to get it to 22 by Monday, with the other numbers stable in the process. His blood pressure is back up and not down in the 80's/40's, It's not impossible!! I continue to be in prayer for not only our situation, but hundreds of our friends who are experiencing health issues, and deep sadness and despair in their lives. God is so good and so big, we must hold on to Him during these days, and find peace trusting and looking to Him. "If the Clouds are the dust at His feet, just imagine how GREAT HE MUST BE!" (A line from one of my new favorite songs)

Be blessed, Be encouraged, and Behold the Love of God!

January 11,2021....

Well, this morning is not a happy post.... I will start by sharing the positive tho. Mom and I had a great evening with our friends Robert and Joyce Hayes, catching up 12 years and sharing special memories together. It was great to get out of the cancer center and enjoy time with our dear friends!!

We thought Stoney would be discharged today and sent home on TPN tomorrow after his injection, but his levels are struggling. His metabolic look decent and controllable, which is GREAT, but his blood panel was taking a huge hit. Red, white blood cells, along with hemoglobin and hematocrit numbers plummeted. They also gave him a steroid yesterday to help with low adrenal gland issues, but it drove other numbers down. His fluid losses are cut in half, which is great, but with that comes other issues. It was as if they didn't allow the chemo to do it's thing before trying several new "other things". They are also running a sepsis culture for bacteria that we must wait 48 hours to get results. Patience is not my friend right now. Haha.

Stoney is so frustrated, and I'm just in a holding pattern not knowing where to go next so to speak. I will be making plans to stay longer in Atlanta while we make plans to send mom home since she has been here for 2 weeks with me already. I have no idea how long we will stay at this point and I have no idea what's next. Stoneys next chemo is a week from today, but A LOT must happen between now and then to move forward. God knows... today, I am resting in Hope. I am casting all our cares upon the Lord, preparing to march into a new battle, and wait to see what's next. While this is not the news we wanted, it is the news we were meant to receive today. Stoney is swollen from the steroids and extra fluid buildup, so we are praying we can get that under control as well. Praying for no more new obstacles!!!! We need some good news, need some sunshine.... but also this is more time to reflect, rejoice and count our many blessings! Please continue to pray as we struggle to find direction on this health journey. God is still in control!

January 14, 2020

Good morning! First of all, I am sorry for not posting for a couple days and I do appreciate many of you asking what's going on. It's been a little chaotic with changing news throughout the day!

Stoneys sepsis tests came back negative which was a huge blessing! Other blood tests came back with wacky numbers and things all over the place. His volumes and frequency came down for a few days, but that was due to a steroid he was on. Since coming off the steroid, he is overly swollen, uncomfortable and things are moving back in the wrong direction. The good news is... we sprung him loose from the center yesterday afternoon so that he could come back to the hotel and stay here until his chemo starts Monday. I learned how to hook up the TPN, which is super overwhelming, but I think I can handle it. We have appointments at the cancer center today and tomorrow for blood draw and to make sure everything is stable for now. Stoney has major shoulder pain which is from a torn ligament and so he was up in pain most of the night. He can't take many things for pain with all of the other meds he is taking so it's a timing issue. The swelling is also very painful but he is doing everything they tell him to do so keep praying!!! We are trying to stay out of the hospital!!! Please keep praying!!! As nice as it is to be free from a hospital room, we just want to make sure we are doing what's best and that he can have relief. I am working on flying my mom out Saturday night so she can be back at home. Today, I am doing laundry and trying to pay bills from the room, as well as stay on top of all the medicine. I am very tired, and trying to be at peace with it all and have a clear mind. It's been 48 days total that we started this full time hospital visit/journey. Praying so hard for some light, fun, good times!!! We all need it!!

The sun is shining outside though, Gods blessings are new and exciting each day, and we were able to see some wonderful friends the last few days. "Looking unto the hills where comes my help AND HOPE!)"

January 15, 2020

Ok...here we go! I'm gonna try to hit all the details!

Since yesterday, your prayers have been ever so appreciated and important. Yesterday when we went to the center, Stoneys labs were just shy of what was normal. His blood cells came into good range, hemoglobin hit high for the first time since first chemo, his metabolic panel were almost normal! Potassium was just a tad low, but we are working on it!! It was a good day!! I finished my second night of giving him TPN and had no problems!! It was like making a science experiment and I am actually slightly considering taking a medical class for fun because I am finding it all fascinating. My heart is growing so big for the nurses these days and I admire all of them so much for what they do and the care they give (most of them. Haha. Not at Vanderbilt! Hahaha)

Today, we are headed over to get more labs and have a meeting with nutrition to make sure everything lines up with their goals. Stoney is still completely swollen, but the fluid drainage is getting better and I bought some soothing gel pads for his shoulder and that seems to be helping. He had a much better night!! We know this can change on a daily basis, but again, a victory for the day!! He feels good and has been laughing and we've enjoyed watching old movies with mom in the room here. I bought her ticket to fly her home tomorrow night so please pray she has a safe flight and remains covid free. This will be her first time flying since the pandemic started so she's a little nervous but I told her to just be overly safe and cautious!!

For me, I'm ok. Finding my new normal, and learning to find a scheduled pill time for stoney. I am weary, but can feel the power prayer that is poured over me so I will not worry but continue to press on and look up!

Our needs? Being here an extra week meant another week of hotel. Many have offered for us to stay in their homes within the area here, but as you know with medical issues, it's easier to have the flexibility of coming and going as *needed, and being on your own schedule. We have extra food cost here in town but I just made an Instacart order this morning. It's nice being across the street from the cancer center so not a lot of extra in fuel. I have spent $500 in just medications alone that are not covered with the center and since this is a new year, insurance has rolled over. Our daily out of pocket cost for the TPN is $130 a day and this will be carried out through the end of January for now. Insurance will pay 80% once we reach the deductible but for now we will be billed weekly.*

I have no fear!! God has walked with us through this entire journey and has provided beyond means of what I could have imagined. I know that He will continue to cover it all, bless those who continue to give, and bring us comfort in what is ahead! Why?? Because HE IS GOD! Yesterday on our way out, the chaplain saw us, and prayed with us. My eyes filled with tears because where on earth could you find a place like this that people just stop and pray with one another? God is protecting, providing and prevailing over us and I am grateful for all of you who have been praying and a part of our family through this!! We keep on keeping on!! Please don't stop praying!!!! We've come this far by faith leaning on the Lord...and we will continue on!! Love you all!!

January 17, 2021...

Yesterday, we took mom to the airport then came back to the hotel and watched some old vintage movies here at the hotel. Stoney is doing well, but had a slight fever last night that was better this morning. He is still struggling with the extreme shoulder pain but is doing better. Lab Levels were good again for 2 days in a row with TPN at the hotel so it seems to be going well for now. Tonight he will have to hold all food and liquid for about 16 hours because they decided to put his port in tomorrow afternoon. They were going to wait until February, but an opening came available so they wanted to get it done! He is nervous about that which could be the cause of a few extra symptoms he's having but praying tomorrow will go smoothly and no problems getting behind on supplements and pills. His appetite is good, but still has the continuous shaking due from chemo. They will resume chemo Tuesday now instead of tomorrow which will keep us here an extra day but we are ok with that.

I must admit, I am so excited to think we could go home this week (Thursday or Friday) but at the same time, I'm trying not to get my hopes up!!

God is so good getting us this far along, and I have no doubt He will continue to provide for us. I miss having my mom with here with me, but I'm staying super busy constantly getting pills together and keeping up with his schedule. We keep praying that this next treatment will go as smooth as the first, that God will continue giving us strength and peace, and provision we need to be here!! I stand amazed!! Thank you for praying with us, and please don't stop. Pray that we don't get sick!!! There is so much sickness going around, and covid spikes that we just pray we can stay well!! They won't treat stoney if he has a temperature this week. This week will be very interesting as there are some issues we have to work out with some appointments so we need your prayers!! Be blessed and stay tuned for updates this week!

January 19, 2021....

Good morning! Yesterday, Stoney had his port placed and did great!! His labs yesterday were great, and all the nurses commented on how great he looked. An improvement from when we arrived December 29!

We rested well, and started round #2 of chemo this morning at 8! He has wires going everywhere. His arm for TPN, port for chemo, a wire for blood draws, etc... He is doing well and his attitude is outstanding!! Now we ask you all to PRAY that this round will be as good as the first! No symptoms or side effects, and that we will be able to go home Thursday afternoon as is the plan for now!

I woke up this morning with this song in my head...my mom & dad used to sing it, but it was written by Henry Slaughter. "Children of God don't have to worry, they always have Gods promises to lean on. Children of God know Gods mercy, whenever there's a problem, there's a Father in heaven who cares. His Grace is sufficient to meet our every need, with Him we find security, in Him we find real peace!" I am so thankful that God hears us, meets us where we are, provides our every need and loves us unconditionally.

Keep praying!! For those going through trials, May God meet you where you are, fill you with peace, and provide for you in ways that you don't understand!! That's God!!!

January 20, 2021...

Today, we will stay in the hotel room and rest as much as possible. The chemo pump is hooked up and his TPN runs through the night. So far he is doing very well. He struggles with the cold sensitivity, and neuropathy in his fingers and toes, and slightly shaky, but other that that he is feeling good. Such a blessing!!!! Tomorrow morning we will head to the center at 10:30 and they will remove the chemo pump at 10:45. Lord willing after that, we will head home. Please pray for safety as we travel home, and the finances to continue to cover the needs we have. God knows all about it!!

Last night we had the great privilege of having dinner in the hotel lobby with our pastors niece and good friend, Ashley Britt . I was able to help Ashley get into CTCA back in October where her treatments are going well. Please pray for her as she gets her scans in 2 weeks. Ashley is struggling with colon cancer so please pray for her and her journey here. We enjoyed pizza in the lobby, and a 3 hour visit that Stoney was glad to have after being stuck in the hospital for 45 days! We are praying so hard that nothing stops us from going home tomorrow and being able to actually have Christmas with family and friends this weekend. We still haven't even had Christmas yet!!

Thank you for all your prayers!! God is still working. He is still showing us His faithfulness daily and we are so blessed!! Praying for continued peace, comfort, strength and grace, as well as all our needs to continue to be met.

January 21, 2021...

Well, the chemo pump was disconnected and we were set free!! Stoneys labs this morning showed a normal metabolic panel (1/10 pt loss on potassium but we can fix it) and they sent us home!! I drove up to pick him up at the entrance, and he said "move over!!" I was apprehensive but he hasn't been able to drive much or do anything so I couldn't say no. We are an hour north, and he is doing good and I am ready to jump in when needed. For now, today is a victory day!! We hope to celebrate his dads (Tracy) birthday this weekend, as well as have Christmas! We praise Jesus for what HE has done!! We give HIM the Glory for allowing us to come this far, to see Him work, to see Progress. I don't think either of us thought this day would come...we had hoped, but doubted many times. Thank you all who have prayed, who have given, who have loved on us!! These past 8 weeks have been hard, but have been a growing experience and we know this is only the beginning!! Keep praying for us!!! We will continue chemo treatments Feb 8-10! We still have many needs, but for now...we lift our hands up to God and say THANK YOU!!!

January 24, 2021....

Stoney is doing very well, and we PRAISE GOD for it! We were able to celebrate his dads 77th Bday yesterday and we both enjoyed visiting with the family, since we hadn't seen anyone in quite awhile!!

His appetite is coming back, and in fact he's enjoying some cookies made by our good friend, Liz, tonight!

Home healthcare will be here in the morning to draw blood and change his picc line dressing. Overall, he is feeling really good! The TPN is going well, and no major problems there....

Me?? I'm ok. I had a doctors appointment scheduled tomorrow for an ultrasound on a lump I found on my neck but my doctors father died yesterday with covid, so I've been rescheduled. I'm nervous, but also trusting the Lord that everything will be ok, and God will give me peace

I'm catching up on laundry, cleaning up the house, and repacking for the next trip! Taking care of all the financial records, bills and business I've been behind on. Thankful for my mom and others who have provided food since I haven't been grocery shopping yet.

I just want to thank all of you for continuing to pray for us. We have felt it, and we are so grateful. Please keep praying, and if led, your love gifts/ contributions allow us to keep on this journey with less stress!

I am amazed each day how God supplies our needs, and let me tell you... we have so many! We serve an Almighty God, and as I sit on my couch staring at my Christmas tree (which should be put away by now), I feel blessed and shed tears of joy over how GOOD He has been to us!!

THANK YOU THANK YOU THANK YOU!!!

Please keep praying!! We go back to Atlanta Feb 7-10 for round 3 of chemo!!

January 28, 2021

The last few days at home have been so nice!! We finally had Christmas with family and friends. We even got to try a new restaurant in Nashville (Paula Deen's), we've enjoyed watching old movies and eating junk food.

Stoney is doing exceptionally well with the exception of his painful torn shoulder. The TPN is allowing his numbers to remain in tact, and we are grateful. Tomorrow home health care will teach me how to change his picc line dressing which has me nervous but I'm ready for the challenge!

We have some upcoming needs with medical supplies but God is good, and we trust Him to supply what we need.

Keep praying as we travel back to Atlanta next week for round 3 of chemo!

February 3, 2021…

Good Morning Facebook world!... I have been putting off posting mainly because I felt like I had over saturated Facebook over the past 8 weeks, but I know people have been asking about Stoney and my situation with my neck. I guess you could say I've just been overwhelmed and so busy being a caregiver that by the time I sit down, I just want to sleep. I have been exhausted lately. Stoneys care is a lot to be honest. There are so many pills, and schedules and things that have to be in a sterile environment, etc... I have learned to change his Picc line dressing, give the TPN, I've made calls to doctors/nurses nearly everyday, etc... he has been in extreme pain with his shoulder, which is a torn labrum. We finally got pain killers yesterday that don't even seem to be working...he does have an appointment with pain management Tuesday in Atlanta during his chemo treatment. That also leads me to the request for prayer...we leave Sunday for Atlanta and will be there until Wednesday. Pray that this third treatment will go well and no side effects will take place. The weather is giving snow and freezing temps, so safety as we travel! We will have about $500 of medicine to pick up while there that is out of pocket, and should last through March. With both of us not working, it has been amazing to see how God has provided through all of you folks sharing your support, love and sacrificial giving. I just don't even know how to thank you enough. I keep getting scared when I look at the bills each month, but I have to remember God is in control and He will provide, and HE DOES!! People have asked why we *don't file for disability, but doing that effects our financing at the cancer center, which is way more effective than disability!!*

I still do not have an appointment (reschedule)with my Dr about the lump on my neck, but have something Feb 25th to move toward for now. I'm trying not to stress about that, and trusting the Lord for whatever He has next. I still have my Christmas decorations up, and what I wouldn't give to have someone take them all down for me, cause Lord knows I don't have time for that!! Maybe I'll just be early for Christmas 2021. Hahaha!

All of this to say.... Please keep praying!! We have so many friends who are struggling with their own trials of cancer. Please pray for them if you would!(Robert Hayes, Patty Fischer and Ashley Britt) I am so thankful that God hears us, He pulls us close when we are feeling so hopeless, and He fills us up when we are empty. I keep praying for strength to keep going. I honestly can't complain, and consider it an honor to be a caregiver for someone I call my friend. The Dartt family has been so good to me through the years, and it's an honor to give back this way. I pray for a healing on Stoney, but more importantly, that we will all see and glorify God throughout it all. That others will see Christ in and through us. Please be in prayer for us as we continue to fight this cancer, and survive relying solely on the promises of God!!

February 4, 2021…

Prayers needed today....Things were too goo to be true! Stoney is headed to ER for fluids and hydration. They discontinued our orders for fluids at home about 2 weeks ago, but I think they'll be changing that now again. Haha. Just praying there isn't any more issues other than the dehydration. Also making adjustments to TPN orders since numbers dropped in last lab results. Never a dull moment!!

February 7, 2021...

Well, we left super early this morning from Nashville after changing our flight to get to Atlanta sooner. We came directly to urgent care after arriving at the cancer center, and within minutes they had fluids going and blood work drawn. They have determined his electrolytes are too low and have admitted him back to inpatient. They are also doing a Ct scan right now to determine why he is having pain. Concerned about the liver... we shall see. I'm beyond exhausted, and so thankful we got here and they are going to take care of him. We will meet with the care team tomorrow and we will see what that means for all of his other appointments. They will most likely fall off the schedule if he's still admitted. Another adventure!! We have no idea how long we will be here, but I guarantee it won't be a short visit because it never is when he's admitted. Please pray for this situation. Everything was running fine and we were doing great, so we aren't sure what's happening. Please please please PRAY!!

February 8, 2021...

Many of you have asked for an update since yesterday so here it is...

After being admitted through urgent care here at CTCA, they are monitoring his labs every 4-6 hours. His sodium and bicarb dropped more today which has postponed the chemo. They will not give the chemo unless his numbers are more stable, so we wait.... pain management came in and ran an X-ray on his shoulder to see what could be done. They are considering a steroid shot based on those results. Most of the pain he is experiencing is from the inflammation of the tumor burden in his liver pressing against the diaphragm which causes the nerves to spike pain up to the shoulder area. Another reason his electrolytes are acting wacky (after being so stable for a couple weeks) is a side effect to the 5FU chemo treatment he is having. So this is a journey that will remain complicated and full of surprises, but it's no surprise to God!! I have a room at the holiday inn express across the street and this morning I slept in and it was GLORIOUS!! The first time I slept all night in weeks. I am spending the day here in the room with stoney as he rests (medicine making him very sleepy). Been talking to all of our favorite nurses who have come in to greet us with smiles, elbow bumps and some secret hugs (shhh, don't tell). We are being well taken care of. They love us here, they care about us, and truly want to see stoney get well and succeed on his health journey. They encourage me as the caregiver, and I am so incredibly blessed to have this staff on our team. They are a second family and I love every one of them!!

I am so so glad my friends, Robert and Joyce Hayes are here. Robert is getting his 6th treatment this week and will be scanned in 2 weeks to see how he's doing. We've had positive results from our friend Ashley Britt, who has been treated here and it's amazing to see what God is doing. We will keep hanging on, following the Lord through the valley, and will look forward to the mountain tops ahead. Thank you for your prayers!!

If you'd like to help us out, here's a link you can share a gift! We love you all!!

February 9, 2021....

Today has been a frustrating day here at the Center. I have been waiting on answers, and yet waiting seems to be the only thing to do. Stoneys bloodwork has been too low for them to start chemo, then insurance wouldn't do it as an inpatient procedure, then there is talk of changing the chemo plan and treatment for him. Stoney has been nauseated all day and feels so weak, tired and sick. Barely been able to eat or drink and feels miserable. The chiropractor here helped him quite a bit, but it's going to take time.... I want to fix everything and I want it done NOW! I am not a patient person and those of you who know me, you know that. There are things I would like to see get done sooner and I have no control, but I have given it to God. The storm we are in has been brewing for months, some days a hurricane, some a tornado, and other just a really bad rain storm. But I'm reminded that when the devil tries to whisper words of discouragement in my ear, that it's just lies and deceit. That I can rise to be stronger resting in my Saviors arms and seeking His truth. Today, my friends Robert Charles Hayes and Joyce Hayes encouraged me to go to the chapel here at the center and sing with them. Just the 3 of us and no one else. After recording my song last night and sharing it (in complete fear), they asked me to sing with them today like we did many years ago when our families toured together. I agreed, and Joyce picked the most perfect song!!! This sums it up for me... no matter the storm you are facing, just hang tight to His unchanging hand "Until the Storm Passes By" and there will be a light shining from above letting us know that God's got us in His grip!!

Tomorrow is a NEW DAY!!! Hoping for more answers, trusting for better days, and believing our God for miracles!! I hope this song ministers to you like it did to me. I recorded it on my last album and it still speaks to me today as it did back then. Love you all and thank you for praying!!

Let's continue to ride this storm out!!

February 10, 2021....

Well I just wrote an entire update and Facebook refreshed and deleted it before I could post so I'm going for round 2!

I came in early this morning so I could meet with the doctors and oncology team. Finally at 2:00, oncology came in to give us an update (we've been waiting since being admitted Sunday!). The oncologist is moving forward with rounds 4 through 6 of chemo starting tomorrow and will do scans after that to see what things look like before changing anything. He is confident this will help, so we will trust him for now. Stoney is feeling weak, tired, nauseated and has no appetite but this can be from a multiple of things including chemo side effects, coming off a strong pain narcotic or just from his metabolic panel being low. This afternoon, we saw the first positive results in his numbers going in the right direction, so now we wait! (Again...)

Last night I didn't sleep real well with worry and wonderings... I finally just asked God to pour over me His peace...The Peace that passes all understanding. After the news today, I feel better because we have a plan, we have direction and can move forward. Do we know what's next? No... but we do know that the Lord has a plan, and there's not one thing I can do to change it. There is testing in our trials, provision in His promises, and strength in our storms! We must stop trying to figure it out, and let Him bring the peace and calmness to our lives.

Stoney was encouraged to have our friends, Robert and Joyce Hayes stop by for a visit after Robert finished his 6th chemo today. He enjoyed seeing another friendly face (besides mine) and talking with someone other than me. Haha. The nurses have been exceptional...today I didn't want to leave the room in fear of missing the Dr, so my nurse went down and got me Starbucks coffee so I could stay here in the room and wait. I sit here with stoney now (as he sleeps) just counting my many blessings. We are in a place that loves us, that cares for us and has no shame in speaking the name of Jesus. A nurse this morning we love came in and preached, pleaded and prayed over stoney!! Gave him a pep-talk on how to believe and claim the promises we know and start looking for the miracle that only God can give. It starts with us... asking and believing!! No other place (hospital/care facility) I know has the gift of encouragement in Christ like this place. Even had pastoral care come in and pray for/over us. Amazing!!

February 11, 2021....

I arrived at the center this morning after all my instacart items were delivered. Now that I'm here for at least another week, I needed some groceries for the room, and stoney needed lots of items as well. Today, Stoney is feeling horrible...nerve pain in his shoulder that they can't seem to correct without the narcotic that he doesn't want to take.

The chemo was approved to begin today within the next 2 hours and will run through Saturday. We are praying this will be another step closer to slowing the symptoms down, however with chemo there is a whole new world of side effects many of you know all about. His numbers today are still not where they need to be but they feel confident in moving forward. They will inject more sodium bicarbonate in him and limit free water to get better results. It's literally like a yo-yo game but they all seem positive in finding a solution. So we wait...

They decided to move rooms today due to chemo, so packing things up and changing floors and rooms. I'm trying to be positive and have lots of energy but I must admit this is so draining and when he doesn't feel good, it can suck the life out of me. So please pray that God will give him and myself plenty of strength for this journey.

The weather here in Atlanta is raining, gray and miserable which can often make our spirits low as well. It's a great comfort to me to know that the sun is still there behind all the clouds and it will soon shine again, just as sometimes the trials of life block our view of the good days we will soon have again. I know that the gloom can overwhelm us, but trying to find the sunshine today as we fight this disease!!

I recorded this song just because of the title and message it brings... I needed it myself.

February 13, 2021....

Today has been another rough day. Stoney is just not bouncing back like he has been. More pain, more fatigue, more sleeping, etc. Today the nausea has been better and I got him up out of bed for a little walk for the first time since we got here (last Sunday). He brushed his teeth bedside and has been able to nibble here and there, but really doesn't have an appetite.

Because the hospital was so short staffed again, they had to move us to a different floor again (this happened Thursday as well) which was super inconvenient but I would ask you to pray for CTCA and it's amazing staff!! The nurses are doing everything they can, there is just not enough of them!! Our healthcare workers are heroes and need major prayer coverage!

Yesterday I left the hospital angry.... angry that stoney wasn't walking, wasn't eating, wasn't doing the things he should be. I went back to the hotel early and just cried out to God to change my heart because I didn't know what he was feeling. I have not been in this situation before. I want to help, I want to fix and I want things to be better, BUT GOD.... God almighty has a plan and it is not our own!! So, I ordered myself a cake from Publix and ate it until I had a tummy ache. It was so good but a really bad decision. Haha!!

Please pray for us!!! We need miracle, and once again for these medical mountains in front of us to be moved!! The expenses are adding up, and I really don't want to leave stoney here alone right now so I am staying and trusting our great God for ALL THINGS!!

May we find peace, comfort and strength in these stormy days! Love you all!!!

During my nights in the hotel room, I would go back and not just cry and pray, but listen to some music. One of my favorites, sung by Janet Pascal, "It Won't Rain Always". It was written by Bill and Gloria Gaither, so you know it is a good song, but the lyrics go like this…

"Someone said that in each life some rain is bound to fall
And each one sheds his share of tears, and trouble troubles us all
But the hurt can't hurt forever, and the tears are sure to dry
And it won't rain always, the clouds will soon be gone
The sun that they've been hiding has been there all along
And it won't rain always, God's promises are true
The sun's gonna shine in His own good time, and He will see you through"

I love the meaning of this song, which tells us life is going to have its trials and storms, but God is there. He has always been there. There is Hope in the midst of our sorrow. Even though we can't see past the clouds in our way, He is there waiting to shine through when the storm is over, but He is also still THERE guiding us through the storm and all its clouds and rain. I felt like walking through this valley/journey, I was having a hard time seeing God there. I never felt like He had left Stoney and I, but that He was just a little harder to see at the time. I had doubts that slipped in, but also, knew the devil was the one putting those thoughts there. I am so thankful for music. Even in the hospital room with Stoney we listened to music, but never things that were deep or made him think too much. I did that later, alone, and wept….

February 14, 2021…

First of all, Happy Valentines Day to all of you!

Secondly, today was a better day and I credit God first, but also all of you who have offered nonstop prayers!! I am forever grateful, as I know the entire Dartt family is as well.

Today, stoney was more alert, more active in walking and felt some better. He was in pain most of the day, but opted out of pain pills and didn't need any nausea meds. He has complained about pleurisy in his chest so I had an X-ray ordered, and the Dr ordered an EKG. Both came back clear!! Praise God! Pleuritic chest pain which could last a couple weeks but nothing more. He had a few naps, and even got a shower after his walk! (I won't tell you how long it's been, but take guesses and it's probably longer! Haha)

I found him more optimistic today as well which made me happy. His labs were a little more stable, but since they can change overnight, they will keep watching. No plans for discharge as of yet, but we will continue to pray and see what Gods plans are.

I am so thankful for all of you who have jumped on to pray, and encourage us both. I would be completely lost without it. God is giving me just what I need spiritually, and seeing all of you pray and encourage us is helping me mentally. All I can say, is please DO NOT STOP!!! I need you to keep pushing us to believe, to stay strong and be filled with peace and comfort. You will never know much your prayers, sacrificial giving and encouragement is getting me through this. Let's keep watching God do the miracles He promises He would. Claiming His word and standing on His promises!!

February 16, 2021...

After a long day, I just got back to the hotel room (almost 10PM). It's amazing how the cancer journey is a roller coaster of emotions and experiences. Good days, followed by bad, then happy again.

Today Stoneys numbers were not great. They weren't critical, but not safe enough to talk about any discharge. I had to go to target and pick up some "essentials" for the next several days and purchase a few T-shirt's to wear since my supply is done. The laundry room at the hotel is out of service and I don't have time to go to a laundromat right now. Dr's have ordered stoney to drink as much Gatorade zero as he can along with orals sea salts (try drinking that... it's gross!) He had a rough day with fluid "losses" so that will most likely set him back in morning labs but we shall see what tomorrow brings. I ordered dinner to be delivered to the hospital tonight (he was sick of hospital food) and we ate together and nothing tastes good at all. All of his tastes have changed. He still doesn't have much of an appetite but since his protein numbers are dropping, I'm tryin to push him to eat.

He was laughing and making jokes with the nurses earlier in the day, but by evening he was taking a dive. Praying that things will get better!! He hit a button on the bed and it took him for a ride so we had a good laugh about that!

Planning on staying to the weekend, if not beyond. I'm trying not to worry or think about it, because there is nothing I can do to change it. It's all in Gods hands and we must trust Him to provide and supply every need!! The healer hasn't lost His touch so we will keep believing!!!

Keep praying!

February 17, 2021...

I'm tired tonight so here is the shortened condensed version...

Stoneys labs today twice in a row - 6am and 6pm were stable and only within a few points from normal range so the plan is to try for a Saturday discharge and evening flight home. Praying that the weather in Nashville clears up so we can actually get home! Chemo round 4 has been scheduled for Thursday, Feb 25-27, March 10-12 and finishing round 6 on March 24-26. Scans will be done 2 weeks after and future direction will be made. Our oncologist came in today with some very promising news and HOPE for the future so we PRAISE GOD for that!!

In the meantime, it's just pushing forward and taking it a day at a time. Stoneys spirits are more optimistic and our nurses at CTCA are just absolutely outstanding. I can't say enough about CTCA!! We have been so blessed by the staff and the care...they are officially our family and we have made so many wonderful friends!!

Keep praying as we do have more expenses ahead, and will be back again next week! God knows and is providing all of our needs through all of you and we greatly appreciate it!!

I will post more tomorrow with pictures! Stoney texted me at 6:30 this morning with his exciting labs and I couldn't go back to sleep, so I'm ready to crash tonight!! Praying for more good news and fun times with our great nurses tomorrow!!

Sleep well y'all!!

February 18, 2021...

Hey everyone, it's early for an update but I have some news and asking you to pray for us...

This morning the doctor came in and Stoneys labs still look decent, but they are not sending us home Saturday like expected. They want to keep him until Monday, and try to back off some of the things they've been giving him to make sure he could even be stable at home once we leave. This was extremely disappointing to us both, but here are the blessings...

We are hoping that the pain management Dr will be able to give Stoney the nerve blocker injection on Tuesday as an outpatient and we will be able to have other tests done during the week that we would have missed.

Secondly, it does allow a safety net to make sure Stoney doesn't crash at home, and end up in an ER before the next chemo. It's a great safe way to watch numbers while here in Atlanta under the most incredible care!

Needs.... well, here are some ways you can help and pray!! First of all, to save money on me buying any extra essentials, one of the nurses offered to take my laundry home and do it for me. Y'all, I kind of cried. There is a story there, but the fact she wants to help us right now while battling her own storm in her life just makes me appreciate God and His timing and His love for us and for her and crossing our paths. Just a WOW moment to be honest.

Pray for the financial need of 9 more nights in the hotel, food, and groceries here for me and the drinks that we have to purchase for stoney that the doctors have ordered. It does add up, and seems scary but again I have no reason to worry or doubt that God will provide and supply!!

Continue to pray for our spirits and mental stability. We are both ok, but the challenges can get into our heads and we must fight the devil to remain positive and optimistic that we will get to the other side!

I get to see my friend, Chad and Ashley Brit today who is fighting her own cancer battle here and is doing great! We are headed to lunch in just a few minutes... I will also get to see my good friends, Robert and Joyce Hayes this weekend and may even record another song for y'all!

Sooooo....blessings in the storms! Praying for all my friends who are struggling with weather storms, personal storms and this unknown life that just seems to take us on a ride. My thoughts?? Enjoy the ride... no matter its highs, lows, and even upside downs... there will be something to learn and to come out stronger than before!!

For those of you who want to share in helping us fight...Here is the link for PayPal, I do have Venmo, Zelle, and you can always send the old fashioned way to our home if you feel led...

Blessings to you all, and here's to facing the storm with our heads up, and hands open as we take on the rain!

February 19, 2021....

Today has been a good day (for me!). Yesterday I got to have lunch with Ashley Britt (and her husband Chad) after she was disconnected from her chemo. She has had a 70% reduction in her tumors just after 6 treatments so it was so much fun to catch up and share testimonies and praises!

Then today, family of mine from Florida, were passing through and stopped to take me to lunch. They wanted to pray with stoney, but due to covid restrictions they weren't able to come in. I had so much fun laughing and sharing memories with them that after they left, I actually cried a little. It was just so nice to have family stop by!!

Stoney is doing well, BUT....they titrated down his bicarb fluids last night and just as the Dr expected, it dropped 4 points back into abnormal range. So, now they are working on ways to correct it, and figure out how to sustain this at home. This is the prime reason they did not discharge him and I'm so thankful!! Stoney was disappointed and feeling low about the news, but I tried my best to encourage him and to be thankful that we are here and they are working hard to figure this out!

Tomorrow I will go over and play some games with him, continue to get him walking, and watch some TV. We need prayers for upbeat spirits right now!! Prayers for motivation in fighting the good fight and pressing onward!!

One of the amazing nurses, who we love so much, took my laundry home last night and brought it back this morning smelling wonderful! I just feel so blessed I can't even explain it. I've fought back tears today many times (failed a few) when I think about the many ways God is providing for our needs. Not just financially... but spiritually and through other people...new friends! This journey is definitely not one I would have chosen, but finding ways to enjoy it, and seeing Gods handiwork is more gratifying than anything in the world. So... here's to more adventurous days following the Lord, and finding purpose each day in all the surprises He has!!

Thank you so much!! Please keep praying!!

February 20, 2021

Very tired tonight so will keep it short... Stoney had some disappointing labs today with his bicarb. They are working on getting it back up, but in the meantime he's feeling blue about it and wondering if he will ever get out of here. He's not eating much, and feeling the struggle with taste. Nothing is good to him anymore. Also, the loss of fluid is back up, which is the reason his numbers dropped. We keep fighting and pushing on. We are trying to come up with the funds we need for the extra week, but also trying not to worry about any of it. All of this is in Gods hands!!

Praying for a better day tomorrow with more blessings and positive results!!

February 21, 2020

Well, Stoneys labs were decent enough they discharged him back to the hotel! He ate all of his dinner tonight in bed and the TPN was delivered to the hotel in time for me to hook him up! He's hoping for a good sleep.

Tomorrow we will get bloodwork to make sure he is stable and then Wednesday he will have the nerve blocking procedure to help with his pain.

Thursday he will begin round 4 of chemo and Lord willing if all goes well, home on Sunday! Much will depend on how daily labs, but for now this is progress and we praise the Lord!! We will pick up a load of medications tomorrow (holding my breath) and see our friends, Robert and Joyce Hayes!!

God is good and we take it a day at a time! Please keep praying, and I ask special prayers for myself as now the responsibility is all on me to make sure he gets what he needs!! Just keep breathing...I tell myself!

Much love and thanks!!

February 23, 2021...

Stoney was feeling rough today and has been pushing through his weakness. His labs today were not great, but not critical. We will go back in the morning to see the results of tomorrow's labs and meet with the oncology team. He will then have a procedure at 3:30 to relieve some of the pain he is experiencing in the back, shoulder, and neck. His numbers showed some dehydration today because his symptoms are increasing again but we are praying to see more results after the next chemo treatment on Thursday. We are praying very hard they will not re-admit him tomorrow or Thursday!! Please please please keep praying for us. We need all of this to resolve before we fly home Sunday!!! Praying for good days ahead of these bad ones!! God knows, He cares and He sees!!!

Feeling emotionally drained tonight and praying for some medical mountains to be moved!!!

February 24, 2021...

His labs this morning were better and fairly stable, which we hope we can maintain through the TPN. Tomorrow he will begin chemo round 4 as long as things are normal and stable in the morning.

I'm feeling a little overwhelmed but trusting our Great God to cover us under His wings. I was able to sit outside in the sunshine today and just breathe a moment of Gods goodness, say some prayers, count some blessings and write a poem... He turns sorrows into sunshine if we let Him!

We were able to sing some songs in the chapel with our friends, Robert and Joyce Hayes, so that was a comfort and also fun! You may see some videos appear on Facebook in the next few days!

Right now, I ask you to pray for Stoney as he is in recovery and that he will be calm and at peace and that the pain will be gone!! He needs relief so badly!! Thank you so much!!

…UPDATE…

Tonight, I'm still sitting at the cancer center waiting for Stoney to be discharged from recovery. He was suppose to be out at 5:00 and that was almost 2 hours ago. He had a procedure to help with nerve blockage. The tumor burden in the liver was causing pressure on the nerve shooting pain through rib cage, shoulder and neck. As of a few minutes ago, the nurse called and said he was having trouble in recovery with blood pressure at 80/45. They were giving him fluids and other things to help bump that number up and will hopefully avoid admitting him tonight. They went through the spinal cord so it was more invasive that we had thought.

…EVENING UPDATE…

Well, it's been eventful tonight. At 7:55 the recovery nurse told me that plans had changed.. stoney passed out on the bedside commode after blood pressure dropped to 65/38. He passed out for a couple minutes, and they got him back and started fluids. Unfortunately, it wasn't enough to let him leave so he is in the ICU here at the center. When I left a little bit ago it was back up to 90/54 which is better but his labs are terrible! So... we wait, we pray, we trust and we learn...and most importantly, we lean on the Lord as He shows the next steps. Wont lie, I'm nervous to see what's going to happen next, but I am trusting God to deliver on His promises.

The night was filled with adventure and surprises. A very sweet nurse who had seen me up on the floor where Stoney was roomed saw me in panic and asked if she could help. I told her what happened and she offered me a ride back to the hotel so I could pick up a few things to bring him. I had to call Uber/Lyft to take me back and forth after that, and it was not as easy!. I had a couple of breakdowns and was so mad that I had to pay nearly $45 just to have a car take me 2 miles. The price you pay when you don't have a car. Hahaha.

Bottom line....I'm settled back into the hotel room, stoney is stable in the ICU and we have everything we need and hundreds (if not thousands) praying for us, so I shall not complain but praise His name!!

Off to sleep for me, with an unknown day ahead tomorrow! Chemo may be on hold if things don't turn around... I'm not sure what part of the rollercoaster ride this is yet...the straight down, upside down, the corkscrew, backwards.... who knows?!! But like any ride, the course will change and a new view will be in store!! I'm hanging on!!! TIGHTLY!

February 25, 2021...

Today I woke up early to hear Stoneys labs were critical. It was so disappointing. I got ready and got to the cancer center and stoney was miserable. He was in so much pain, nauseated and barely able to have a conversation. Being in the ICU, he has a different team of care over him and things were not handled as quickly and promptly as they have been before. It was like starting over on his care. Our nurses were terrific, kind, and most generous in their care. I am forever grateful to the nurses who are our heroes daily. As the struggle of power differs and continues between the doctors, Stoneys chemo which was approved to start today has yet to begin. I am not a happy person (caregiver) about this but there's not much I can do. I have done my part, pled the case and now we wait to see how God directs. I'm honestly the most exhausted I've been on this journey tonight. Neither of us expected yesterday to go the way it did. Looking back, I still can't believe how good and decent he was, and how the day ended in ICU. I stand 100% dependent on God my father to calm the nerves, to spread peace over me (and stone), to continue to pour out His grace, as I find strength in His promises. We will not be going home Sunday as planned, but that's ok cause there is something we need to learn by being here. There is always sunshine in our sorrows if we look for it.

I sat outside yesterday during Stoneys procedure with a piece of cheesecake and some coffee, and this poem came to me all in a rush. As I share it with you tonight, and ask you to pray continuously for us, I would ask you to ponder the amazing love of our father God in your own life, and who you know that needs to hear about the the precious gift of Jesus. Show them love, kindness, and joy...each day is an opportunity, don't miss it!

POEM:

My Savior and My friend...
A poem by BJ Speer

He's turning sorrows into sunshine
As I pray for Him to lead
He's proving promises a plenty
As I lean on Him and plead
He's giving blessings that overflow
As I trust Him with my needs
He's showing Grace most abundant
As He always intercedes
My Precious Savior walks with me through the darkest of my days
He leads me by the waters and hears me when I pray.
My Gentle Shepherd shows me where to hide when I am scared
He strengthens and equips me in ways to be prepared
My loving Father holds me when I'm lonely and in loss
He reminds me of His sacrifice that came at much too high a cost
My Faithful Lord provides every need and every care
He's proven time and time again He never leaves, He's always there!
If you don't know my Lord and Savior and there's emptiness in your heart
Let me introduce you to a friend, who will never part
He will love you and forgive you and enter if you ask
There is just one small detail, just one little task
You must accept Him and Trust, that His word is true
He'll erase your past, forgive, and make your life brand new.
A gift like this so simple that anyone can receive
The choice is up to you, will you trust Him and believe....
He's turning sorrows into sunshine
As I pray for Him to lead
He's proving promises a plenty
As I lean on Him and plead
He's giving blessings that overflow
As I trust Him with my needs
He's showing Grace most abundant
As He always intercedes

February 26, 20201...

I really wish I could come here tonight to share better news, but that's not the case. Stoney has had a rough day. He took pills at 6am on an empty stomach which has made him nauseated all day long. After blood work this afternoon, labs showed his kidneys were suffering. The functionality is not great, creatinine going up, his BUN number was high (72), and his output is nearly nonexistent. The reaction he had from the procedure Wednesday has put him back a ways. There have been some issues with one of the doctors here that has been resolved, and we now have a great staff working hard to turn things around, but we are going to need massive amounts of prayer, as well as Stoneys fight to push himself! There is only so much the hospitalists can do, so we pray and let God show His hand. This is a new low in his health care, so it's a bit shocking and overwhelming. He has been dehydrated many times and it has been fixed, but the kidneys not functioning the way they should is all new. It's hard to look at this situation and say "it's over or maybe things are coming to an end" when we have a God of miracles, but one must consider the what if's to the situations. Stoney always said that every day he lived passed his diagnosis day, were gravy days. I am praying and believing the Lord for more gravy days, but my heart is very heavy!!!

This is where faith steps in...this is where everything we have believed and trusted in comes to reality. Yes, we believe God can heal, but if He doesn't, how do we respond? Are we angry, or do we praise Him in the center of it all. I would like to believe in a miracle, but Gods miracle might be different than what I'm asking.

I am not in any way saying stoney is in his final days... he could live 30 more years if God chooses. Cancer is just a word not a death sentence. What I'm saying is may we (I myself) learn to accept Gods plan in how things continue. Trusting the one who knows, who sees and who cares.

I would just ask that people spend some time really praying for Gods Will to be done and that a healing would take place. That's what I would like to see, as much as the rest of you.

On this end...things don't look great, but God sees something we can't. To Him all things are perfect and beautiful, so let call upon Him to show us what He has! May we continue to be held in His hand!

February 27, 2021....

Last night was super restless for me as I just couldn't rest. I prayed each time I woke up, then would get a few minutes of sleep... I woke up this morning and checked Stoneys labs in the portal (I can see everything electronically which is great) and saw his numbers were worse, scary and some critical. My heart just ached and felt horrible. I quickly got ready and headed over to the center to find stoney sitting up, alert, eating and drinking! I just started crying... I was so happy!!! Leaving last night, I really was preparing myself for the worst. Anyway, he had eaten his breakfast and taken his pills and was feeling good. They rechecked labs and ran many other tests at 4:00 this afternoon, and all of his numbers are moving back into the normal range. It's not an overnight fix, but Lord willing within the next few days he will be back to where he was. We will then discuss plans with oncology for what's next. I believe that Gods people praying made the difference. I believe that a miracle took place, because that's what it was going to take. Our favorite Dr here came in tonight and was shocked at how good he looked compared to last night. I'm not stepping off the praying bandwagon though!! We need continuous prayer for more good days and decisions on what's next!!

I cancelled our flights tomorrow, and extended our hotel through next Friday. It stinks, but we are where we need to be and once again I believe God will provide what is needed to be here.

Stoney was ordering his food today with the staff, and when she said "what would you like for dinner?", he said "I think we will order take out tonight!" Hahaha. I loved it. I thought he must be feeling better! So, I have ordered Japanese food which is being delivered tonight to the center in just a few minutes. I think he deserves the reward!

We still have many hurdles to jump over but we are on the right path, and I am trusting God to take care of us!! The Goodness of God is amazing! Feeling blessed tonight!!

Thank you!! Please keep praying without ceasing!!

February 28, 2021...

Today was another good day for stoney. I spent another 12 hour day with him watching tv, playing some video games and ordered Mexican food for dinner! Had some good laughs, and naps

His numbers are moving in the right direction and we continue to wait and watch to see what's next. The biggest problem now is the loss of fluids (due to the cancer). Not to be gross, but to give you just an idea of how bad it is, he is losing 10-12 liters of liquid a day!! So they have to find ways to replace it through IV and orally. Still balancing the metabolic acidosis which is a huge issue right now. Keep praying that they will figure out the best option to deal with this at home. We still do not know about chemo or if they will go another route this week. Lots to be determined...so thankful his kidneys are getting better!!

Not sure when we will get home, but the important thing is getting him better and stronger!! I am so grateful for your prayers, and for the incredible nurses at CTCA who are taking such wonderful care of stoney and even blessing me each day with their love and care!!

We press on!!!

March 1, 2021...

"Oh taste and see...the Lord is good"

Today has been a good day overall with some prayer request I will give you! Stoneys labs were near perfect at 4:00 today!! Just a couple things that need to improve, but we are on the right path. His kidney functions are fully normal now and at this point they will pursue chemo tomorrow.

Now for the Prayer request... his tumor/cancer markers are pretty high and keep climbing even through the chemo treatments. This could be bad, but also without doing scans to know for sure, we must wait for the oncology team to look everything over before making any further decisions. Our oncologist does have a few things up his sleeve but we aren't sure when that's gonna be played so we wait patiently (which again, is not my strong suit) and trust the Lord. We have already seen Gods Goodness just through this weekend. I enjoyed my day just watching tv with him and talking about the good Ole days on the road and many memories we shared with so many people around the globe. God has been so good to our families...we have no idea what the week will hold, but I'll learn to Rest under His wings, knowing God holds the plan.

We do have many financial needs, so I'm just sharing one of the many links to leave a gift, but more importantly I would beg you to continue those prayers to our Heavenly Father for a healing only He can bring us!

I am so incredibly humbled by your love and compassion...your sacrificial giving and encouragement has just overwhelmed me and has kept me fighting for Stoney and given me the calm in the storm I've needed. Tie that all together with our Loving God who pours grace upon grace over us, I have no other words but "I'm blessed". Thank you!! Please continue....

March 2, 2021...

Tonight I come to you with a major prayer request. My heart is very heavy...chemo was put on hold while oncology discussed some plans. They decided to run 2 MRI scans and a CT. Their thought is there must be some progression due to the increase in symptoms. Stoney lost 16 liters of fluid in a 24 hour period so they are definitely concerned because I couldn't handle the replacements at home even if they let him go. So based on the results, they will make a plan to move forward. We may not know what the plan is until tomorrow or Thursday as we wait for oncology to discuss the options. Either way, it's not great but we know that the Great Physician is in charge and has THE ULTIMATE PLAN!! I am trying to take some deep breaths tonight and not be scared of what lies ahead. God has led each step through our lives up to this very moment, so I have no doubt that when the time comes to move forward, HE will cover us, protect us and show us.

I have had to extend the stay through March 11th for now. I will have been here for over a month at that time. I continue to meet the most loving and caring people each day. I have been able to share joy as well as tears with my new friends here at the center. I am able to talk about Jesus and discuss our trials and our blessings. I have met people that I would never have met if not walking through this valley. So there is a message to learn, there are still pieces of the puzzle I need to find and place, and there are still tears that need to be shed along with praises of thankfulness. Regardless of what is next...HE ALONE IS WORTHY, and HE will hold me and keep me close. Pray for

Stoney to have peace tonight, along with comfort and a good sleep. He is very tired.

Pray for me to have the strength to keep pushing, the joy to keep sharing, and the comfort of knowing I'm sheltered in The arms of God!

I also had some discouraging news today about another dear loved one diagnosed with cancer and my heart is just so heavy and aching. May the Lord return soon and take us all home!! Heaven is sweeter each and every day! Stoney was listening to my dad sing tonight in the room. My dads "Keep Believing" album. I have not listened to my dad in awhile, nor that album and what a message indeed...Let's Keep Believing!! God is BIGGER THAN ALL OUR PROBLEMS!!

March 3, 2021...

Hey everyone!! Tonight is a rough night. Not so much physically but mentally. Stoneys labs today were great!! We've come a long way and they just couldn't look better in my opinion.

However, the scans done yesterday have brought us some very disappointing news. The scans showed disease progression in the liver as well as large lymph nodes. It also showed some inflammation in the esophagus as well as a collapsed lung. Soooo, after taking it all in and processing it, we now have to wait a little longer. Tomorrow, oncology will be in to discuss further options and the plan of attack. We are obviously upset, but we also know there will be (hopefully) a really good plan in place tomorrow that we will forge ahead knowing God is leading. I left stoney just a little bit ago to come back to the hotel and get a good rest before going over in the morning and waiting all day to see oncology. No time set, so I just need to be there and ready when they open. Thankfully it's less than half a mile away so I'm close!! Please pray stoney will sleep. He's feeling broken, tired, worn, and weary. Heavy hearted with an unknown course ahead of him. I am feeling hopeful and optimistic knowing that God is with us...He has never left us, He has a plan (maybe not what we want) and is ever present in our time of need. My mom posted Ephesians 3:20 today in a post of prayer for another dear loved one and I'm claiming it tonight!!

As I sign off just asking to be still in your thoughts and prayers for us, I would just like to throw in the request for peace and rest and that we would all be able to cast our anxiety and care upon Him.

I leave you with this tonight... my stay here (for almost a month this time around) is not in vain. I have met incredible care providers, hard working nurses, cleaning personnel, pastoral care operators, and have made some life long friends. I have heard from people across the globe inspired by what we are going through and how it is encouraging them in some way. People, who I don't even know, have given sacrificially. God is using this story, our testimony, our life in some strange way. He is giving purpose through the blindness and despair. As I wrote last week in a poem, He is truly turning my sorrows into sunshine. That doesn't mean I don't grieve or don't care about Stoneys issues, it means He's giving me the ability to cope and accept that in which we cannot change. He is covering me and holding me daily and I feel it. I pray this upon stoney. I pray that he will feel wrapped tighter in HIS arms than ever before.

Thank you for your prayers and gifts. I will respond to each one of you at some point for the precious gifts and words of encouragement sent. Just give me some time...

Pray for tomorrow's plan and meeting with oncology and hopefully we will have some brighter news to share!! Goodnight and much love to you all!!

During this time in Atlanta, I did my best to reach out and get to know each person by name. I made it an effort to learn one name a day, and to pray for them. I would greet them by name when I arrived, or when I saw them in the hall. This was not limited to nurses, but to all the people that worked and cared for Stoney. They each carried a specific responsibility, and they each held a very special place in my heart. I met some very real, genuine people. People I will never forget, people I will live my life praying for. We take for granted our healthcare providers, our nurses, the culinary and cleaning crews. Without each of them fulfilling their very special job, a care center would fall apart. They bring so much joy and love into the rooms on a daily basis and for me, they brought hope…

March 4, 2021...

Oncology has been in to see us today.... I was here at the center at 8:30 so I wouldn't miss it, and the anticipation and anxiety was overwhelming!! Haha. I'm pretty sure I walked 2 miles in the room here just pacing. Finally, he came in and after reading the scans, he didn't seem to think it was as bad as we had thought. There is disease progression in the liver and the left side is heavily impacted by the tumors. The lymph nodes are there and they show progression as well but this is really about the liver right now. They can't get us out of here or really move on until we handle the liver first. So, the plan is try a chemo embolization, which stoney has had similar procedures before. One lasted 3 months, and the other 5 days! This is slightly different though as it will Involve chemo beads. We are hoping insurance will approve it to be done tomorrow, but if not, hopefully Monday or Tuesday at the latest!! We feel grateful that there is a plan, and we are not at the end of the line for treatment. Now we just need prayer that they will push this through to be done tomorrow!! He is walking the halls better and moving around...BP stable and he's eating a little better.

We will then stay over 2 days after the procedure to make sure there are no side effects and then go home!!! They will schedule a higher concentrated platinum infused chemo 3 weeks later and resume that treatment plan.

More time here...but good news!! And we have a great staff and wonderful people around us 24/7!! I'm thinking I may sleep better tonight! Haha!!

I praise Jesus right now!! Giving Him all the Glory for this new plan!! Praying it will work and be successful and get home (possibly as soon as next week!)

Keep praying y'all!! God has a plan...he is moving and working and we MUST KEEP TRUSTING AND BELIEVING!!

March 5, 2021...

This morning Stoney messaged me to tell me they paused all food and liquids after midnight in the hopes that they could have done surgery today. There was a small chance, but by 10am we found out that it couldn't happen today. However, chemo embolization (a form of liver directed therapy) is scheduled Monday at 3:00pm. The plan for the weekend is to maintain his labs and bloodwork and make sure his blood pressure is stable. He is trying to do his breathing exercises and walk to help build up his collapsed lung. The amount of fluid he's losing is unreal...almost 20 liters in a 24 hour period, so getting to this procedure is crucial!!!

We've had a good day joking with nurses and doctors, making new friends and being at peace. I was discouraged this morning when the procedure didn't take place, and we heard the surgeon we love will be out all next week and it's a new surgeon we've never had. We later found out he's a really great doctor and that the Lord may have worked it all out on our behalf, because HE does that you know?? Hahaha!

Today at 1:00 a precious family member and dear friend had bladder cancer surgery. They were able to remove the tumor and won't know until next week if any further treatment will be necessary. He was able to go home and is resting well!! God is so GOOD!!

We've ordered dinner here at the center tonight and I am getting ready to leave and head back to the hotel shortly. I am praising the Lord for His goodness, His Faithfulness and the overall amazingness of His plans. Not our own, nor our timing, and yet it all seems to work out just right.

Please keep praying we have a smooth weekend, with no hiccups and that things will just continue to improve. We are both longing to get home!!! (And are families are all waiting for us to get there!)

Praying He continues to supply our needs, as He's done and promised!!

March 6, 2021….

Stoney is hanging in there and holding his own, however, he's losing so much fluid each day. The amounts get higher each day so we are praying hard that this procedure Monday will help and really give relief for awhile!! We need your prayers….we REALLY REALLY need this to work!!!

He was able to walk today, but was having some tummy issues, so nausea meds were needed. I think he is nervous about Mondays procedure, and rightfully so. Tomorrow marks 1 month that we've been here. We had only been gone from here for 10 days from when we were here 3 weeks! He told me today, he just wanted to go home!! I sure hope that happens next week for us!!! God knows!!

In just 42 hours he should already be in recovery and resting, so I'm asking that for the next 42 hours specifically, that you would just really bring us both before the Lord in your prayers!! Whenever you happen to think about us, please say a prayer!! God is in the business of healing and can still perform miracles, and that's what we need!!!

We love you all and appreciate each one of you and all you've done for us!!

March 8, 2021....

PRAY PRAY PRAY PRAY!! UPDATE!!

Ok guys, here we go!! A very important day on our journey!!! Anticipation and anxiety growing! Not gonna lie

At 2:00 they will take stoney down to pre-op. At 3:00, they will begin the surgery which should last 60-90 minutes. He will then go to recovery for an hour before coming back up to his room here. Major prayer request to mention to our Father...1. That Blood Pressure will not crash (like previously) and he will remain stable through the procedure and recovery. 2. That they will be able to get as much coverage in the liver on these tumors (there are many tumors-10-12) and he will see immediate effects and relief. 3. That recovery will be better than expected and less painful. They will be going through the groin not the wrist like he thought. 4. Praying for his lungs to continue to clear and strengthen and we can get home soon.

This is normally a very easy procedure, but in Stoneys case, it's more risky. He's not their normal patient here so we are ready for anything. We've had many nurses and even doctors praying for him here so we are believing for a miracle!!! We have been warned about some different things that can happen, but we are just going to plan for the best possible recovery ever!! Claiming it in Jesus name!!! They will be making sure he gets labs every 3 hours for 48 hours to make sure his numbers don't go the other way. It is a very CRITICAL 48 hours for him!! Please pray for him and myself for peace and comfort and calm. The Lord Jesus goes before us, He's following behind us, He walks beside us, He looks down over us, and He's under lifting us up. Most importantly, He lives within me! Leaving today in the hands of the GREAT PHYSICIAN!!!

Many needs...He provides and supplies...love you and appreciate all of your prayers, support and encouragement!! Updates coming this evening!

Stone Dartt Update...AFTER SURGERY UPDATE....

MARCH 8, 2021...

Just sent this to family!

Dr Krebbs (the surgeon) just called me personally to tell me Stoney did fine through the surgery. He took some extra time and covered the left lobe of the liver with as many chemo beads as they could, giving him some extra coverage. The surgery was only supposed to be 60 minutes but he took an hour and 45 to make sure things looked good. Kim Dunn, (good friend and assistant to Dr Krebbs) just came in the room here with me screaming with joy that Stoney did really well and that the coverage looks great. Obviously the next 48 hours are critical in care and watching the numbers. His bloodwork could go too far the other way if the main symptom (watery stools) completely stop. He is getting a CT scan now to see what the coverage looks like and Dr Meiri (head oncologist at CTCA) will read it and tell us what's next in the plan in 3-4 weeks on Wednesday. All in all it was a huge successful from what they can tell. Now recovery will be the key objective!! Keeping his blood pressure stable and pain under control is a large issue they will watch closely. Thank Jesus for your care, for your love, for your continued protection. For peace and for comfort. You alone God are worthy of all our praise in good and bad. We trust you, we praise you!!

Thank you to all who have prayed!! Keep going!! Pray us home this weekend!!!!

March 9, 2021...

First of all, THANK YOU for all the amazing birthday wishes. I can't believe all the comments and kind words. I'm just so grateful for you all caring so much! Today I arrived at the center just in time to see my friends, Robert and Joyce Hayes get off the shuttle behind mine. Joyce told the drivers it was my bday and they all sang for me!! As I walked down the hall to see stoney, the nurses all said Happy Birthday to me making me feel like a celebrity. I visited with stoney for a couple hours before Robert and Joyce kidnapped me for an afternoon of fun! Newnan (where the cancer center is) is the home of Alan Jackson and carries lots of historical significance, so we toured the town center, had coffee and lunch and shared so many laughs. I toured with Robert and Joyce probably 18 years ago, and who would have ever imagined God allowing our paths to cross here at the cancer center all these years later and to have them celebrate my birthday with me?! I needed the break, I needed the laughs, I needed the sunshine. I feel so blessed today and am beyond words to express my gratitude!!

I treated the nurses, housekeeping crew and culinary team on the third floor (Stoneys floor) to cupcakes as a THANK YOU for all their care and kindness they've shown. To me, it was my way of celebrating with a team of amazing people who love us, care for us and who have become my friends!! Each one here holds a very special place in my heart!!

As for stoney...he is doing well. Blood pressure remains stable, he is sleeping a lot, and numbers have moved higher and movements have slowed. It's a good day with much to be thankful for in his care. Oncology will be in tomorrow to discuss the CT scan he had post surgery, and develop a discharge date and plan for the future. Keep praying for him to get stronger, to eat more and continue healing. They are still monitoring everything very closely and we have a ways to go but all moving in the right direction!!

Spending my birthday in Atlanta was very tough for me, because those who know me, know I love to celebrate! I was missing my mom, my friend Liz, and many others. I was missing the fact that Stoney couldn't even celebrate my special day. I enjoyed going into the town of Newnan with Robert and Joyce Hayes for lunch and coffee and treats. I enjoyed being able to bring in cupcakes for all the nurses on our floor. I enjoyed all these things, but it seemed like it wasn't enough to satisfy the longing my heart. I just want to get out of this place. I just wanted a change of scenery, but I knew God had a different plan.

I remember listening to Joyce sing a song in the chapel that they were posting for their YouTube followers. It talked about the Goodness of God. As I listened to Joyce (and her smooth as honey voice) sing this song, I was reminded how good God is in every aspect of our lives. From the moment that we wake up, until we lay our heads down at night, we live within His goodness. His mercy never fails, ALL my life He has been nothing but GOOD. How had I forgotten this? Why had I let myself doubt His goodness, His greatness and kindness? He has held me in hands, He has been so faithful, so why couldn't I sing of it? I tried to be a "good positive person" with people at the center. I tried to be brave, to be strong and of good courage, but I was weak, I was hurting, I was broken. Then to be reminded in a simple song, about His goodness, brought things back to reality for me. *Psalm 145 says "I will exalt you, my God and King, and bless your name forever and ever. Every day I will bless you and praise your name forever and ever. Great is the Lord, and greatly to be praised, and his greatness is unsearchable. One generation shall commend your works to another, and shall declare your mighty acts. On the glorious splendor of your majesty, and on your wondrous works, I will meditate...." -NIV.* Here God was blessing me daily, and I was too blind to see His mercies anew. Sometimes it is so great to be reminded isn't it? We get so caught up in the hustle and bustle of life, we tend to forget. I love this little chorus from a southern gospel song...

"Even in the valley God is good
Even in the valley he is faithful and true
He carries his children through
Like he said he would
Even in the valley God is good"

March 10, 2021...

Today was one of those days after a procedure that just hits you hard. Stoney has been very inactive today and has felt achy with an elevated temperature. This is all normal after the chemo embolization so it's not a shock but definitely not easy either. He did not walk, nor use his breathing machine, and appetite has been rough. Oncology came in today and gave us an update, but unfortunately no clear direction until scans are done again in 28 days. They want to wait and see what response the actual procedure had before directing us to the next step. At that point, he will choose a chemo pill (which is what we hope for) or come back for rounds of chemo that are more intense and last for several hours in one day. Soooo...we wait some more! Hahaha! I get the idea that God is teaching us to wait a lot? Lol.

On a positive note, if numbers continue to improve and remain stable, we could potentially go home Friday!!! There is a chance we could stay through the weekend, but so far it points to Friday as the discharge day. So we are praying hard for God to allow that to happen. We have some expenses we will need to square up on before departing but trusting God to provide....

Please continue to pray for a great day tomorrow and positive labs and news!!

Thank you so much!!

March 11, 2021...

I appreciate the prayer I requested earlier, and here's why?...

Today, Stoneys number one symptom (huge losses of diarrhea) began to increase and his metabolic panel became harder to stabilize. They are watching everything very closely, but to both of us it's very scary since this was the main reason we came here 5 weeks ago!! I called oncology and talked to our care manager, and she believes we must give this a whole week before we should be concerned. As the body adjusts to the treatment, and chemo continues to work, he will have good and bad days. The main objective is to have enough going in to equal what's lost. That's the hard part and a major mathematical equation. Word on the hall is they will release stoney tomorrow if they feel there is a way to maintain his electrolytes within his TPN (food IV bag we do at home). I am terrified to leave with things being up in the air HOWEVER, I am praying for Gods will to be done tonight and that the Dr will make the right decision in the morning. If we can go home, praise Jesus, and hopefully we can manage. If we need to stay longer, praise Jesus we are here and they can handle it. I've extended the hotel just in case!!

So many unknowns tonight and anxiety, but I am trying to rest in 1 Peter 5:7, and cast my cares upon the Lord for I know HE cares for me!!

I ordered dinner for us and when I went down to pick it up and came upstairs he was already asleep. So I ate my food and left his food there and snuck out back to the hotel. As I sit here watching the Disney channel (just need a break from the emotional dramatic shows) my mind is racing all over the place and I keep catching myself doubting what I know God can do. It's dumb isn't it??? We pray, we believe, we SEE His goodness and faithfulness and when we have a weak day/moment, we forget all of that for a time. Today, one of the most precious ladies at the center, miss Leisa Dannielle Harris, reminded me to LEAVE IT THERE WITH JESUS!! She said, "we've already prayed for it, you gotta stop the worry and leave it with Him....BJ, stop being nervous, STOP worrying!!!" You know what??? She's right!!! We talk about how big our God is and what He can do, but do we really let Him take control? We do badly want to figure it out and fix it on our own and we CAN'T!!!!

So tonight, I pray that ONLY GOD will take our burdens, take our heavy concerns and work all things out on our behalf so that we will KNOW that He in control and that His plan will be perfected. Hard to do, but I'm asking Him for it.

For the past 5 weeks, we've watched God work...why should it be any different tonight. I'm scared of the unknown, but that's what our lives are filled with. Each day is unknown…it's how we choose to leave it and learn it.

Pray for us both as I know so many of you have! We have so many needs, but again, trusting God for every part of this puzzle!! Until tomorrow…..

March 12, 2021…

Today was a ROUGH DAY!! I think we experienced all the emotions today. This morning, Stoneys labs were not good. They took a hit and so the decision was made to keep him until Monday. This was music to my ears, because I was scared of him going to the hotel and if something happened, what would I do over the weekend?! They are working very hard at getting his numbers stable so that we can manage things at home, but the large volume of output is getting high again, which causes them to wonder if it's safe. Obviously, this is disappointing to us because we wanted and thought the procedure had worked….however, we are also only 4 days into the recovery and the chemo can cause this issue, along with the long acting injection he had so we have no idea what's going on right now. The most difficult part is seeing things unfold and becoming nervous that nothing worked and we are back to where we started. Stoney is really feeling defeated and depressed more than I've ever seen and that scares me. We both need lots of prayers this weekend to push through and trust the Lord we can get home and things will get better for stoney. It's just very upsetting right now.

I walked about 2 miles today, ended up at a target to get laundry detergent and then found out when I got back to the hotel, the newly repaired washer was broken again!! Soooo…not sure what I' ll be doing this weekend for clothes but I'm certain I should have bought febreeze to just spray the dirty clothes. Haha. I have heard from so many people the last few days, and it means the world. If I don't respond, I'm sorry. Some days I feel like I just can't explain, talk, or even feel. This weekend is 5 weeks and with the expenses running up, and the unknown ahead, I start getting a racey heart but then I realize God is not surprised, so why should I be?? We will have what we need when we need it, and God will continue to show us each step. My heart is heavy, but I'm trying to lean on Him and leave it with Him. We aren't meant to understand His plan, that's not in our design. We are only suppose to TRUST….please PRAY for us and this journey… not an easy one as many of you already know!

March 13, 2021....

Today, I waited so long for transportation, that I gave up and rented a car for 2 days. For those of you who don't know, we flew in and only intended to be here for a few days so I haven't had a vehicle in 5 weeks!! Just depending on their transportation here. They've made some layoffs here, so not many drivers means waiting awhile on weekends. My impatience got the best of me today. So now, until Monday, I have wheels and at a very discounted rate for being a caregiver with CTCA. Stoney was in better spirits today, he walked, he napped, I was able to work on my phone and get some business done, etc.... His numbers were not stellar but not horrible. They are making progress here, but his fluid loss is picking back up, which is getting scary because there is only so many limitations and restrictions we can do at home. Praying that these numbers get better, and turn around fast!! There is a chance they may even keep him longer past Monday if needed, which we both agree is wise if it means leaving healthier!

The weather was incredible today and I only regret not going out and enjoying more, but we had fun today just watching tv. Lots of HGTV!! It's not good for me to watch. Haha!! Too many ideas! Lol

We are trusting the Lord to continue to work and move and to give us peace and comfort about what's next. Our minds can tend to go to some dark places, only because of what we've been through here already. The truth is, God could turn this around tomorrow morning if He chose too!! We are both learning to rest in His hands and walk into the unknown expecting a blessing and miracle. If He chooses something different, we will learn to accept it and follow Him through it all.

Thank you for your prayers, your gifts, your love and encouragement. Tomorrow marks 5 weeks of being here and we are homesick for home and family, but we know we are where we are needing to be!!

March 14, 2021...

Today was a very relaxed day of getting numbers up to normal. Things look decent and we are praying will be even better tomorrow. I was able to get myself a coffee, and pick stoney up a smoothie on the way in this morning. The way things stand for now, the only way we can come home is if Home Health

Care can guarantee the amount of fluids that I will have to administer to stoney daily... a 16 hour TPN bag, 3 liters of lactated ringers, and 1 liter of bicarb. If they will agree to those terms, we could go home and handle things from there until April 7th when we need to be back. The amounts of loss for stoney are hanging right at 12-13 liters a day so as long as we can replace it, we should be ok. He will not be able to work obviously, and will remain on somewhat bed rest, but better to be home if possible.

Things could change tomorrow as we all know, but we are trusting the Lord to give us the answers to be safe! Today, he was able to shower, he shaved his head and beard and went for a walk. We watched some sermons on the Hillsong network, and then HGTV. He was very tired when I left a little while ago, but each day is progress and he is fighting the best he can!!

We will press forward, and see what the morning holds!! I am so exhausted tonight and can't wait to turn these lights off and drift away...sleep well y'all!

March 15, 2021...

Today was the first day of sunshine and fresh air for stoney in 5 weeks!!! Our nurse, Patrick, took stoney to the rooftop lookout for some moments of fresh air and it was amazing!! Stoney did some good walking today and looks and feels great. His bloodwork looked good too! HOWEVER, since his symptoms (diarrhea) are picking back up for a higher level than wanted, they are keeping him a little longer for observation. They want to make sure that we can handle everything at home, because at this point, it would be very difficult to stay on top of it without careful restrictions and large volumes of fluids to give at home. AND... they are considering another chemo embolization to attack the other side of the liver that has a tumor burden as well. Stoney was extremely disappointed today with the news of NOT going home, but I feel the right decision is to wait until every detail is covered so we don't have to turn around and come back. They still are working things out, and until then we need to do our best and be patient. NOT EASY!!!

Sooo, extended hotel stay, and other expenses to deal with, but God is using His people to care for us and we certainly feel His love and care! As we were told, this is not a sprint but a marathon...and we will continue to push forward and beyond!!! Keep praying!!!

March 16, 2021....

It's just after 11pm and I just got back to the hotel. It's been a long day with lots of adventure.

I'll start from this morning... a dear couple who both work at the center met me at my hotel with 1/2 dozen donuts that were out of this world!! They have continuously checked on me and made sure I had everything I needed and I feel so incredibly blessed!! The rainy weather had me feeling blue but the SWEET morning treat had me feeling better!! Got to the center and parked a mile away (so it felt like AND in the rain) which had me wondering if by now I should just print a "I work here" badge and park with the staff. Haha!

I was able to have coffee with my friend Ashley, and her mom, which made for a wonderful visit! Ashley's treatment is going so well and she's doing great!! Please keep praying for her!!

Stoney was feeling very achy today and not the Best but we had chiropractic visit and it helped him. Later in the day, they moved us to another room and out of ICU!! The doctor came in and gave us a new plan today...they started a very high dose steroid on stoney today that will be given every 6 hours for 2-3 days before the step down begins. They want to see if this will help slow down the bowels for a few days. They may or may not send stoney to the hotel for the weekend and will then move forward on Monday or Tuesday with a second chemo embolization. Sooo, long story short...(maybe not so short) we are here for 9-10 more days! Ugh... I stayed all day, ordered dinner in and played Nintendo with stoney in the room. The nurse said we should hook it up to the tv and encouraged us to enjoy, so we did!! This has been home for 5 1/2 weeks so we are certainly finding ways to make it all work. Lol. I even ended the day with more sweet treats, when a nurse tech brought me a key lime flavored cupcake!! I must admit, it was a "sweet" day!!

We will trust the Lord to provide for us, to care for us and to guide us through the next many days. We would appreciate more prayers and that this steroid will not negatively effect stoney like it did before. (No sleep, anxiety, suspicions, etc...). He is not a fan but we are hoping this will help! Keep praying and fighting with us!

March 17, 2021...

Happy St Patrick's Day!! I hope all of you are enjoying your day and whatever festivities you may be partaking in.

Today, the weather here is rainy and we are soon to be under a tornado warning/watch. I enjoyed my day just watching stoney play video games. It was strangely relaxing...we had visitors from the nurses, doctors, and our housekeeping friends. We went for a walk in the hall and Stoney can't get very far without talking to everyone! Haha. Our doctor today said he was like a celebrity in the hall. We've been here so long that everyone knows us, and we've gotten to know all of them and our love for each of these people is stronger everyday. The care here is unbelievable and I would ask you to pray for the CTCA family as they care for so many people around the US who come here each day!

We will remain in the hospital for another day or 2 while they make the decision whether to keep him here for the weekend or send him to a hotel. The next chemo embolization will be scheduled for Monday or Tuesday, based on a surgery spot. We are praying this will make things even better for stoney and put us on a path home next weekend. Lord knows after 6 weeks, we will be ready to get home!! In the meantime, we will take each day at a time rejoicing for what HE is doing. That Stoney is feeling good, and able to eat and enjoy his days... the steroid they put him on is not creating as many problems as it did before so please keep praying!!

Continue to pray that our needs will be met, for strength and good health for myself and that I would get better sleep. I am feeling the strain physically and just need a boost!! Even coffee doesn't seem to do its job these days.

We love y'all and appreciate the daily prayers and encouragement!! Here's to more good luck (St Pattys humor, we all know it's called BLESSINGS) and good days!

March 18, 2021

Today we formed the new plan for stoney. They will actually keep him in the hospital for the weekend and do the procedure Monday and then wait to see how things go. They are talking a chemo pill he will take after they do scans in 3 weeks to attack the lymph nodes.

I feel good that there is a plan, but I feel like I'm barely holding on these last few days. I'm so tired, and just keeping having faith that things are gonna go great and we will be headed home soon. I know it's God that is getting me through these days, but I shouldn't complain. I see how hard these nurses work all day long, then go home to their families (most with small kids at home) and do all their parent jobs. I'm amazed! Sooo, I will keep quiet and continue to pray for strength and more good days!! I'm also looking forward to cooking myself and not eating fast food.

Short post today....counting our blessings!!

I found myself doubting some days if we were ever going to get out of this place. Were we going to get to go home? Were we going to need to move to Newnan? That thought crossed my mind many times, and at one point we had raised money in the thoughts we would need to, just to be closer for treatments. I fought the battle in my mind about what Gods Word says. I tried to go back, and stand on the promises I grew up listening to church and reading. I remember talking to my mom and she said, "BJ you know I love you. I am praying for you, and remember Jesus Cares." I had sung that old hymn every night in concert for 2 years. It clung to it when my dad was dying, I quietly reviewed the words when I was feeling depressed at other moments in my life, so now, once again I was faced with its lyrics that remain ever so true today…

"Does Jesus care when my heart is pained
Too deeply for mirth and song
As the burdens press and the cares distress
And the way grows weary and long
Oh, yes
He cares
I know He cares
His heart is touched with my grief
When the days are weary, the long nights dreary
I know my Savior cares
Does Jesus care when I've tried and failed
To resist some temptation strong
When for my deep grief I find no relief

Though my tears flow all the night long
Oh, yes
He cares
I know He cares
His heart is touched with my grief
When the days are weary, the long nights dreary
I know my Savior cares
I know my Savior cares"

My favorite verse is the last…"Does Jesus Care when my heart is pained to deeply for grief or pain, and my sad heart aches, til it nearly breaks, is it ought to Him, does He see?" Could He honestly see THROUGH my grief and pain? Was He listening to my prayers, my cries, and seeing my tears? I know HE was! His heart was touched, and He was teaching me a lesson in waiting, and watching. I kept quoting "He sees, He knows, HE CARES!!"

March 20, 2021….

6 weeks!! 6 weeks tomorrow we will have been here in Newnan!! In some ways, it's gone fast. In other ways, it feels like an eternity since we've been home! I sit here in the chair with stoney for 12-13 hours a day and somehow manage to complain about how tired I am when these nurses are on their feet working 12 hours a day nonstop not just for us, but many others. It's a wake up moment for me to just say "thank you" Lord for all you've given to us THROUGH this journey. The people, the financial provision, the care, all the things that I catch myself doubting or complaining, and why?? We have everything we need!! Yes, we want to go home this next week, BUT God has allowed us to be in the absolute most wonderful place I can imagine for this time. I've said this before, and I'll say it again... these people have become our FRIENDS!! It sure makes it easy being in a hospital room when you can laugh with nurses and doctors, talk about our faith, and families, our adventure, play video games, order food from the outside, etc... AND...ALL OF YOU have helped make that possible for and to us. Your gifts have sustained us, your prayers have comforted us, your encouragement has pushed us and your love has overwhelmed us. I can only ask that you continue a little longer as we have a few more days to get through before we know more...

Here's how you can pray!! That Stoneys bloodwork will remain steady. So far, 3 days in a row they have been stable and looking good with the steroid they gave him. Tonight, there is signs of extra "liquid movement" that could throw things off very quickly. Monday, he is suppose to have another chemo-embolization on the other side of the liver so we are praying it will give more relief but also target the tumors more effectively for a longer time. Lastly, for a quick and comfortable recovery. No hiccups or problems, no strange drops in bloodwork or blood pressure and to be able to go home Wednesday or Thursday. I've been listening to a great song called "Sometimes it takes a mountain", and I'm finding that this mountain we've been faced with has taught us more about believing, leaning and resting in and on Him! He loves us so very much and wants the best for us, but we often have to learn more about WHO HE IS before we can see WHAT HE HAS for us. We are both remaining optimistic for a good week with a great ending in sight!! Until then, PRAY PRAY AND PRAY SOME MORE!!!!!

Trusting Him for ALL our needs!

March 21, 2021...

Another day of just waiting and being patient! Fluids were rolling and labs looked good! The procedure will be tomorrow but we are unsure of the time because it will be processed as an emergency procedure from the inpatient side of the hospital. So, I'll be over early waiting to see what the details are!! He won't be able to eat or drink after midnight tonight to prepare for the day. We even had a little ice cream.

In the meantime, we had lots of wonderful visits by some of the amazing nurses, and docs! In fact, we had one nurse tell us today that she was gonna miss us because we were her favorite patients! And another nurse that brought us a home cooked meal that was BETTER than any restaurant y'all!! I'm talking the REAL DEAL with ALL the fix-ins!! BBQ ribs, pork, collard greens, Mac and cheese, corn bread and red velvet cupcakes. It was her day off, and she drove all the way in just to give us dinner!! We have cried more tears in the last couple days NOT because of pain or disappointment but because of the incredible blessings!! We have been reminded by so many each day of the GOODNESS OF GOD!! I stand amazed each day and wait to see what God is gonna do!

This morning I ran through the drive thru at Starbucks and bought some coffee for myself and a few nurses. The traffic was heavy and I allowed a couple cars to go in front of me and then a lady who seemed very much in a rush, tried to cut me off. She was so rude!! I smiled and waived even though she was gesturing something different. She even got out her camera to video me as if she was intimidating me, and as if I did something wrong?! I just smiled. Then she rolled down her window and yelled profanity at me, so I rolled down my window and said "Jesus loves you, but it ain't your turn"...when I got up to the window to pay, I told the lady how rude she was and then I asked how much her order was...she told me $5.55 so I said..."I wanna pay for it, and just show her what kindness should look like". As I drove off, I thought to myself, what if the world just showed more kindness. Bought a coffee for a stranger (even if they were the absolute most rudest person), cooked dinner for a new friend or neighbor, shared a kind word... we are here to love one another and to show Christ in a dark world. We are trying to do that here, as well as have become beneficiaries of the same. Kindness goes a long way!!

I also got to see my friends, Robert and Joyce Hayes when they arrived at the same hotel tonight to get hugs. It's been a good day...

Well, I'm off for a few hours of sleep before getting to the center to find out what the day holds! Please pray for Stoneys procedure tomorrow!! We are trusting the Lord to bring him through and that these tumors would just die!!

Keep praying!!!

March 22, 2021...

Stoney was put on no food and liquids last night at midnight to prepare for his surgery. This morning we found out his spot had been given away and the surgery would be tomorrow at 2:00. As bloodwork results came in, it honestly wasn't a bad thing. His numbers needed some work so today we have focused on getting things better for tomorrow. He will be no food or liquid tonight again at midnight which is miserable for him! We are hoping by tomorrow night there will be better news to report!

I was able to get out for a little while this afternoon with my friend, Joyce Hayes and then tonight she and her husband Robert and their pastor David and I all went to dinner. It was very nice to get out and laugh, tell stories and have some fellowship. Roberts treatment is going well and I'm so glad that I get to see them every couple weeks here!

I brought some leftovers back here to the hospital for stoney to enjoy, and I would ask you to pray for him. He is miserable in pain from his shoulders to his neck. The referred pain from his liver is really bothering him tonight so please pray!!

They will take him down at noon for pre-op, surgery at 2, and recovery at 4!! Praying for God to really guide the doctors to get all the tumors this time and that stoney would have complete relief!! We need a miracle!!

In the meantime, continue to pray for me as I continue to do the best I can be here with him, which is a blessing. I'm weary and ready to go home, but hopefully soon!!

March 23, 2021...

Stoney has been back in the room for a little while and made it through the procedure fine. They had to give him extra doses of morphine for pain, so now they want me to try and keep him awake for a few more hours so his breathing won't stop. Lovely. Haha! I'm out of tricks... it's gonna be a long 2-3 hours. Haha!

The surgeon had good news and bad news. The good news is when he got in there, the tumor they worked on a couple weeks ago still had a steady supply of blood flow from the tumor to the liver. So he worked hard on that again really trying to cut the blood supply off. He did some work on the other side of the liver but not as much as he wanted. He is hoping this works, and having faith it'll help, however there is a chance we come back in 2-3 weeks and attack the other side again. Slightly disappointing that it didn't go like we thought, but we are happy he took the time to work on the biggest tumor and that we CAN come back and try again. We should see if things look good within a couple days.... the bad news is they went through the groin instead of the wrist and so the pain is a lot worse...hence the extra doses of morphine!! Please pray the pain will subside and he will get some rest. He can't eat until he is alert, and awake long enough to communicate. Miserable, uncomfortable, and excruciating were his words... We are also hoping to see oncology tomorrow or Thursday up here to determine the next step in the process. I'm just praying they don't keep us here another 2 weeks until the next procedure. Praying hard that things will turn around quickly and we can go home!! God knows...

Keep the prayers coming!!!

March 24, 2021...

Today Stoneys pain has remained high most of the day, but treatable with morphine. He is eating more and drinking plenty. The best part of the day for him was going 28 hours without pooping! Haha! I know that sounds gross to some, or strange, or even funny. This is what we've been praying for!! His movements have slowed down and his heart rate is normal for the first time in 9 months. Things seem to be working very well this time around and his labs are stable and only on TPN, no other fluids!! Huge victory for now!! Praying things stay this way for many days, weeks and months!! They are discussing discharge Friday or Saturday so keep praying with us for more good news!!

I was able to get out with my friends for dinner and play some games today while stoney slept. I had a very nice escape today for a few hours and feel so blessed!

One the nurses from the night shift stopped by today (on her day off!) to deliver stoney a picture she bought him while out shopping. He had played her some Dartt music the other night, and she played him some of her Christian music, so it was so sweet to bring him a plaque of one of our title songs, "The Lord Bless Thee". We are certainly going to miss all of our friends here, but it will be nice to go home for awhile, Lord willing!!!

We thank the Lord for His many blessings and hope we are on a good clear path towards home!! We were discussing today that stoney has spent ALL but 10 days this year in the hospital. Over 100 nights since December 1st. We pray for God to continue to guide and direct in the upcoming days, and we will rest in His blessings in the meantime! Please pray for some surprise financial needs we have tomorrow and Gods will to be done!!

Keep praying and don't stop!!! We love and appreciate all of you and could not do this without you!!

March 25, 2021...

Today, Stoney enjoyed his first decaf coffee in 4 months!! He was very happy to have a few sips! He was feeling better, and has shifted off the morphine to a different pain killer. He has been sleeping a lot today, which is a side effect from the chemo embolism. We got word that discharge was in our future for tomorrow, but as afternoon labs came in, the possibility became less likely. With the drastic change (decrease) in stools, his numbers are all over the place. Some numbers high, some low and other that aren't quite sure where they are gonna land. So, they will draw again at 10pm, and 4am and see what things look like before making their decision but will most likely keep him another day (which typically means all weekend). I'm kind of bummed, but also know we need to get all this figured out before going home.

We also found out this afternoon that our Chief Oncologist here was leaving... we are both in complete shock as he is one of the most brilliant oncologist and specializes in neuroendocrine cancer for over 40 years. After talking with one of our favorite Nurse practitioners here today, she told us we would still have some access to his new office, and that it all might be a blessing in disguise. I began to quietly think, Lord... you knew Dr Meiri was leaving, you know Stoneys situation and you know our future. Maybe the plan is even greater down the road... "All things work together for good to those who LOVE the Lord". I'm not going to be scared, but I'm going to welcome the change that God has allowed because it might mean something even bigger and better for stoney. In the meantime, I'm going to remain in prayer for God to change Stoneys labs to be more normal tomorrow and that we will soon be on our way home. We are being tested to see if the devil can steal our joy, and I will NOT stand down!! I will STAND UP and praise the Lord for the amazing things He has done thus far and for what He's going to do!! To God be the Glory!!!

So, keep praying for miracles!! God's got this!

March was quite eventful to say the least. With more procedures and failed treatments, it seemed like we were headed into another new phase. While I tried to be optimistic again, I had to face the hard grip of reality that things may not get better at this point. I think Stoney knew that too.

We were excited to be finally going home after a long stay in Atlanta. Over 7 weeks stuck in the hospital, and missed celebrations with family and friends. Finally, we were going home! The night before we were to leave, there was a bad storm rolling in. We had seem reports of Tornado warnings, but never thought we would have an issue where we were. Stoney called me at the hotel and told me to turn on the news. I sat there and watching every media channel reporting that a very large tornado was headed straight for Newnan, and our specific area was in the middle of the track. Stoney was worried about me, and I was worried about him. They started moving patients out into the hall, and Stoney told me people were getting very concerned. Some patients had to be rolled out into their beds, while others like Stoney could walk to the hall and sit in a chair. The nurses had their hands full as they moved an entire floor of patients to safety. Stoney sent me pictures and told me to seek shelter. I was staying at the Holiday Inn, and there were no current signs of problems. I didn't want to go down to the lobby and thought I would be fine right where I was. The media showed the storm moving closer and as I looked out the window, the wind stopped, the rain stopped, and the power went out. It was dark outside, with no power on the inside. No more TV, and my phone was sounding off alarms. At the that time, the wind picked up, hail was hitting in the windows, and I heard people running through the halls and knocking on doors trying to clear the rooms. I quickly put on my flip-flops, and ran downstairs to find an entire hotel full of people waiting in the lobby. The generators were on, but they went out for a few minutes. People were watching on their phones, and even in the hotel, cancer patients fighting for their lives had been dragged out of bed to seek shelter. I remember being so scared in that moment, but not necessarily for myself, but for Stoney and the patients and nurses at the center. I had heard that the funnel had touched down just blocks away and I knew that the Cancer center fit that description. I could not reach Stoney for a little while and I became paranoid. Is this how it was going to end? Maybe it wasn't going to be the cancer at all.

Finally he picked up his phone and we began to discuss the past few minutes and the events that went on. When they took him back into his room, there was debris that had blown into his room from the window. Trees were down all around the center, and parts of the roof had been blown off. Rocks had been thrown up to crack windows, and cars were damaged outside in the parking lot. It was a rough night for many, as the morning news brought devastating pictures to the town of Newnan.

URGENT!!

Please pray for Stoney and the CTCA staff. There was an F4 tornado that came through Newnan tonight. I've been in the lobby of the holiday inn while power went out and was a scary few minutes.

However, stoney, and all the patients were evacuated to the hall and after power went out, generator came on but the building was shaking and they could feel the wind. When he called me to make sure I was ok, the sirens were going off, because a part of the building was hit. He is ok but everyone is very much shaken and upset right now. Please pray!

March 26, 2021...

Well...after the storm cleared and sun came out, it was a new day of many blessings!! Stoneys bloodwork came back picture perfect and was cleared to leave!! Home health is sending all the bags of TPN to the house, his brother Don came down from Nashville to pick us up and we are on our way home!! Lord willing we will be home by 8-9 tonight!!! What a miracle, what a blessing!!!

The nurses, housekeeping, pastoral care all came to see us before we left, prayed with us and gave us the best send off!! Tears of joy as we head home, and tears of love for the staff at CTCA who helped take care of us and to get us on our way home!! Pray for many of the nurses and their families who were personally hit by the devastating tornadoes in Newnan last night. The wreckage was terrible, and will take some time to recover!! We praise God for our safety through the night!

Please pray now for safety as we drive home!! We are so excited!!! God is so good and stoney is feeling great!!! Praise you Jesus!! Thank you so much for your constant prayers!!!! We will go back to Atlanta April 13-15 for scans and a follow up for chemo treatment. Praying for no problems and good days! Stoney will not be able to work for several weeks so please pray for his financial needs during this time as well.

March 29, 2021…

I haven't posted much this weekend, basically because I've been super busy and haven't stopped since I've been home!!

Stoney is doing better each day!! There have been tears of joy as he is getting stronger and feeling so well. Tonight he even ate a big dinner of salad greens and veggies...things he hasn't been able to eat in 6 months. Even had some coffee!! He is in complete shock and so thankful for all the prayers and support that you have shown!! Truly a miracle and blessings that we continue to be grateful for!

I'm enjoying time with my mom and friends, and trying to get the house in order after 7 weeks of mail, and mess.

Keep praying for smooth sailing and Stoneys strength!! God is so good!!! Continue to pray for our needs as we remain home and trust God to supply our needs during this time off.

After the many long nights in Atlanta, spending most of the year there, arriving home was refreshing. It was nice to be in our own beds, and environment. To see family and friends once again and to try and find some sort of normality after the insanity. Our time at home would only last a short while though, as more problems were mounting on the horizon. I was making new plans for Stoneys future that I had hoped would save his life. Including branching out of the confines of the cancer center, and reaching for the help from a well known surgeon in Denver, Colorado. I would find this to be my final push and cry for help. I researched many long nights, when Stoney was sleeping, for someone who would operate on these tumors. The list was limited, but I found one…Could he be the answer?

11

Leaving Time

Revelation 21:4 - "And God shall wipe away all tears from their eyes; and there shall be no more death, neither sorrow, nor crying, neither shall there be any more pain: for the former things are passed away"- NIV

Who would have thought that at this time on the journey, we would be approaching the final days of Stoneys life. In just 3 months he would be gone. At this point, I was still thinking we had years of living to go. We celebrated Easter with his family, and his Birthday on April 12th we actually celebrated in Atlanta with a big shot in his bum! Things didn't seem to be as bad as one would have thought.

April 7, 2021…

We were happy to get stoney out and about the other night to walk around town. We even made a stop in front of the Ryman auditorium. Beautiful Nashville nights!! Pray for stoney as he is having a little trouble with his tummy right now but he is pushing on and we are hoping for a good visit to Atlanta next week. He is overdo for his monthly injection so we are praying the ones he takes at home will be suffice for now.

We are trying to catch up on things at home and grab some naps here and there. I feel so exhausted and yet there is so much to do. God is so good and I feel so blessed for all He has done!! Please keep praying and don't stop!!

April 9, 2021…

Prayers for stoney today as he is becoming more symptomatic again!! We go to Atlanta Monday and there's a chance they will do another chemo embolization surgery if things keep getting worse. I'm just praying for a miracle!! He was doing so good, and still feel good but the symptoms have crept back quickly. Prayers needed!

April 11, 2021…

A little Sunday morning update!

I finally had time to get an ultrasound on my neck this week for a lump that I found about a year or more ago. Thankfully it's just a fatty hilum lymph node with nothing to be too concerned about but something to watch in the future. So very thankful!

Stoney on the other hand has been having more progressive symptoms each day. I've had to run extra LR fluids each day to keep up with his losses. We will go to Atlanta in the morning for bloodwork and his injection, then scans Tuesday and oncology Wednesday. They will not do another chemo embolization this soon as you can only have a limited amount and they don't want to use them up too quickly. We are praying the monthly injection does the trick and will sustain him for awhile. It's concerning to see things revert so quickly but that just means the tumors are slightly more aggressive and not being handled by the chemo like hoped. He will most likely start a chemo pill this week that will target the 2 lymph nodes that are cancerous along with the liver and pancreas. He is doing and feeling fine and happy to be home. Nervous about what's next and how quickly things may change but praising God for getting this far!! Praying for many more good days and possible new ways to handle this disease this week!

We love and appreciate you and your prayers and support! Please keep them coming! You keep us going!!

April 11, 2021…

Tonight we celebrated Stoneys birthday a night early. Since we leave very early in the morning for Atlanta, we spent this evening cooking on the grill and having some good laughs. Stoney looks good despite the increase in symptoms.

I ran 2 bags of lactated ringer today along with his TPN. A lot more fluid loss today, so very happy we will be in Atlanta tomorrow and praying for good advice on what to do next!!

I would like to wish my best friend, Stoney, a very HAPPY BIRTHDAY! It has not been an easy year, but we have both seen God work in our lives in a mighty way. He has fought this cancer battle as hard as possible, and it has been an honor to stand by him in support and caregiving. I pray for him every day and wish him good health and many more future "gravy" days!! I look forward to vacations and fun times, but more importantly a pain free, symptom free life!! Happy Birthday Stone Mountain Dartt!!! Here's to many more incredible days!!

Stone Dartt Update... Tuesday April 13, 2021....

We arrived yesterday at the cancer center and began with bloodwork, his monthly injection, and a couple of other appointments. We were certain things would be bad since we were up all night prior running extra fluids due to the severe losses. We were positive it was going to be bad results. The labs resulted at 4:30 and were all normal which was a shock and a birthday surprise for Stoney! We praise God!!!! We then ordered dinner to the room because we were exhausted and celebrated with non-dairy ice cream. (Stoney can't have any dairy right now). Then night fell, and around we went again! Stoney was up nearly all night losing about 4.5-5 liters of fluids. We are thinking from a food reaction but also could be the cancer growing in his liver.

This morning he is getting an MRI and Ct scan and will get more blood work to make sure his levels are ok and that we can manage and stabilize things from home. These are amounts that have only been handled by the medical team up to now, but I have the ability to run up to 3 liters of fluids from home a day. After that, it's back to the hospital! We don't want that to happen!! Please pray that Stoneys injection takes effect today!!! Sometimes it can take 4-7 days before it's in his body but we really need this to work sooner!!

We are so grateful for all of you who have truly walked this journey with us. Who have prayed for us daily, messaged us notes of encouragement and financially chipped in to keep us going!! We are praying that when the scans are read tomorrow morning, we will have more HOPE, more direction, more positive feedback, so we can forge ahead with whatever treatment God has for

Stoney, and for strength/whatever my part on this journey needs to be. Praising my Savior ALL THE DAY LONG!!!

Stone Dartt Update....Wednesday, April 14, 2021...

We have arrived back in Nashville this afternoon. A very chaotic morning with miscommunications on some things, so we did not get bloodwork like planned, but the visit with the oncologist was good and bad. Stoneys liver is considered to be doing well and better since the embolizations he had in March. Much improvement in the left liver lobe, but slight enlargement on the right side where he has not yet had the treatment focused. The cancer unfortunately has increased size in lymph nodes and a spot on the lung (which we think is new but he never really discussed that). They are starting him on a chemo pill next week that will be 14 days on/14 days off, plus an additional pill that will be taken the last 5 days of every cycle. The Dr said the progression was to be expected since stopping treatment in January to focus on the liver. He was also positive on us moving forward with contacting a surgeon I found at Rocky Mountain Cancer Center in Denver, Co (Dr Eric Liu) for a de-bulking surgery. They actually spend 6-8 hours going in the liver removing each tumor and possibly the lymph nodes depending on where they are. This is outside Atlanta's treatment center so we will be basically treated in 2 places if Denver takes our case. We won't have that appointment until the first week of May so we won't know if surgery is even a possibility yet. We will continue on the same routine now with TPN with no changes to the formula and give extra LR fluids at home for every 3 liters of loss up to 9 liters (of loss) a day. After that we will have to go back to the center and try for another chemo embolization procedure if nothing is corrected by the injection. It was mixed emotions of good and bad news, but the most important thing to remember is God is STILL IN CONTROL!! Nothing shocking or new to Him! We are trusting the Lord to open and close all the right (or wrong) doors and that Stoney will remain strong enough to take the chemo pills with little to no side effects. We leave it in the hands of the Almighty!! Please pray for calm nerves and a stillness as we listen to Gods leading through all of the decision making process. We appreciate the love and support and gifts you have given to keep us moving forward on this journey. It's truly the only way we would have made it thus far!!! God is so good and we keep following Him, are blessed to be covered under His wings at this time.

I was watching Stoney's health deteriorate even with all of the stuff they were throwing at him. Something was not right. I began researching online about other procedures that could be done and I found one called "liver de-bulking" and it was only performed by a couple surgeons in the world, one being Dr Eric Liu in Denver, Colorado. I wasn't afraid to make contact, not afraid to reach out, because what were they going to say? NO? The cancer center did not doing any procedure like that, and had no problem with us reaching out to ask. They didn't think he would do, it, but told us to call. They could see Stoney was struggling, and that he was not making good progress. All the nurses and even doctors would say, "you look good though…" Stoney always smiled, treated everyone with kindness, and he ALWAYS wore his fedora every visit. It was his signature move! Everyone recognized him and complimented him on all of his hats.

I asked Stoney if he minded me trying to contact the Dr in Denver, and he said whatever I had faith for, to do it. So, Rocky Mountain Cancer Center, I was coming for ya!

April 21, 2021…

A quick update on us.... Stoney is on day 3 of the chemo pill and is feeling tired all the time. He is also in horrible shoulder pain, which is deferred pain from the liver. He is hoping to get another cortisone shot when we go back May 4th. I am doing ok, but have my hands full with even more pills than before, as well as keeping the fluids going through the night. His bloodwork has been continuously safe and normal, which means we are doing the best at home.

We have received an early appointment with the surgeon in Denver, CO on Monday. This will take place on Zoom to determine if he will take Stoneys case and operate. Your prayers are very much appreciated!!! This is HUGE!! The surgery could remove the tumors in the liver and give stoney a few years without symptoms, between treatments. We are praying for the Lord to lead!! It's very invasive and scary, but trusting the Lord to open/close the doors. Please pray for our needs to be met on this journey!! God is so good and we are trusting Him in ALL things!!

April 26, 2021…

We just finished our meeting with the surgeon in Denver! Super nice guy and we are very happy with the news. We were hoping for a tumor de-bulking surgery, but he offered something less invasive to try that could happen within the next few weeks. A radio embolization... giving higher amounts of radiation directly into the tumors. This will hopefully decrease the size of the tumors, allowing symptom relief and the possibility for a de-bulking surgery down the road. He would also go in and remove the cancerous lymph nodes as well as any other tumors around. We feel very happy about our appointment and look forward to being treated by him. He is one of the top surgeons in the US and we are hoping things work out well. We will have the expense in flying to Denver and staying for 4-5 nights, but we will trust the Lord for our needs once again. Overall, good news today for the future!! In the meantime we go back to CTCA next week for injections and other appointments. Please keep praying for us to make the right decisions, for stoney to get stronger and feel better as the chemo pill has been hard on his body, and finances for the future of his medical journey!! God is in control!!

STONE DARTT UPDATE - Wednesday, April 28, 2021...

Today we have some news....

Things have changed and moved quickly. We will leave Sunday for Atlanta and begin at 6:45am on Monday morning at the cancer center for appointments, bloodwork and injection that will go through noon. We will then fly to Denver, CO Monday afternoon and meet with surgeon Tuesday morning for a "mapping procedure". On Wednesday, at 1:00 Stone Mountain Dartt will have a radio embolization at Sky Ridge Hospital in Lone Tree, Co. they will keep him for a couple days and Lord willing, we will fly home Saturday afternoon where he will recover for a couple weeks. He has been very tired from the chemo pill and has lost more fluids (which I am able to replace for now). We are so thankful that our team in Atlanta are working together with the new team in Denver to make this possible as it is something they don't offer there. We will NOT be moving care to Denver as some have asked. This is for a procedure that is not offered in Atlanta. Denver will also operate on stoney in the future to remove tumors once they have shrunk (after radiation) which is another procedure the Atlanta facility will not do. We are nervous and anxious about this new adventure, BUT also very excited that Stoney could experience more and better relief for an extended period of time (Lord willing).

Here are our needs that we are requesting prayer for!!....

1. The total cost of airfare, hotel, rental car, and other up front expenses in Denver is $1200. We have already booked it and used credit for now as things needed to be in place.

2. Prayers for Stoney to have a successful procedure with no complication, including tumor lysis which has happened before. That we can come home as planned and not have an extended stay in Denver

3. For this procedure to last far longer than the others have. This will be hard on Stoneys body, and he will continue with the chemo pill for at least 3-4 more 28 day cycles so strength for him, and not to be sick.

4. For safe travels!!

5. For me (BJ) personally. I am weary, tired, I have fought some depression lately, and need an abundance of supernatural strength and stamina to push on! (AND PATIENCE!!)

God knows and we are so blessed that things have moved quickly. We are thankful for a great, kind and helpful team in Denver and we look forward to being a LIGHT as we minister to them through our valley!

April 29, 2021…

PRAYERS APPRECIATED FOR STONEY....

Stoney had a horrible reaction to the second chemo pill that was added last night. Up all night throwing up. Please pray for him. They have pulled him off of it today. He is also headed to Vanderbilt hospital right now to have a chest X-ray due to a cough and tightness in his chest. Please pray!! So much going on...it just doesn't end!

…EVENING UPDATE …

After an X-ray, as well as CT scan, imaging showed no fluid in lungs or pneumonia. It did show some collapsing due to inactivity. He is suppose to do some breathing exercises. The scans also show extensive spreading of the cancer in the lymph nodes which is very scary since that is new from scans a couple weeks ago. We will discuss it with the Atlanta team tomorrow. His bloodwork was all normal, which is a miracle in itself. For now, we are praising the Lord for the victory today. Also, due to the horrible night on chemo pill, they have decided to hold him from taking it for now. We are hoping the pain subsides, and his symptoms will decrease and that we can just get to Atlanta and on to Denver for further treatment!! It's an adventure for sure, filled with uncertainty and fear; however, we are children of the ALMIGHTY GOD, and we know who holds our future. We will try to stand tall, trust in all we know, and believe that God is going to take care of the rest.

Please pray for our spirits to be lifted, and for all things moving forward!! We need a touch from Heaven above!

We had a few zoom calls with Dr Liu, as well as Dr Nutting. I must give my high praises to both doctors who gave us their complete attention, and walked us through every step. I can't even begin to tell you how kind these gentlemen were. They were busy surgeons, and took my calls, answered my questions, and cared for Stoney. They both wanted to see him get better and live life to its fullest. Dr Liu was quite shocked at Stoneys progression each time I sent him scans and reports. He couldn't understand how or why things were growing and moving so fast, as this was not normal in the Neuroendocrine world.

I also was amazed at during this time, how quickly God provided the funds when I asked for them. People were involved in our journey. They cared about us, and wanted to see us get well. I had people message me personally and ask me if this new adventure to Denver was truly worth it, and did I feel Stoney could make it. As hard as I wanted to slap back, I just said YES! I know people were worried about us both, but it just upset me that people were almost wanting us to give up after fighting so hard. My heart had one goal…to get Stoney better, whatever that took!

When the staff in Denver told us that the recover for this surgery would only last a couple of days, I knew in my heart that would not be the case for Stoney. As you have read time and time again, Stoney does not respond to the "normal". As everyone has said at the center, Stoney is unique! He was already tired, already weak, and now his body had been compromised and fighting. Our trip to Denver carried its own weight, and I had so many doubts about this decision when it was over. As you read the events over the next several weeks of May, you will see the change that was happening in Stoneys life.

May 2, 2021…

We are at the airport and beginning our very busy long week!! MANY PRAYERS appreciated this week!! Calm nerves, clear direction with surgeons, radiology, tor Stoneys body to handle everything they are doing, and that I can stay strong and healthy!!! We know God is in this! Trusting and Believing for a miracle (or 2!).

May 3, 2021...

Well, an eventful day it's been, and strangely it's only half through. Haha! We were up nearly all night for starters. Stoney had a horrible night with symptoms and pain, and I was up all night giving fluids to keep on top of the loss. This morning his labs were all normal, which was shocking to us, and we were able to meet our new interim oncologist. I got to visit with my friends, Robert and Joyce Hayes, who are being treated here this week which was great for encouragement. Then we got to the airport in Atlanta to head for Denver and we have been delayed 3 hours here due to thunderstorm in Atlanta AND snow in Denver. Sounds fun doesn't it? We are both so exhausted, and stoney feels terrible so please say a prayer that we can get in tonight and get some rest. That all his medication I have on ice in the suitcase stays cold, and that we can safely make it to the hotel to start our appointment in the morning! Always an adventure!! I' ll be doing all the driving when we get there, and that's kind of a new thing for me (especially in an unfamiliar area) so I'm a little nervous

Keep praying that God will clear the path ahead and we see results very soon!!

May 4, 2021....

"May the fourth be with us!" (Star Wars fans)...

We arrived in Denver last night at 10pm (after waiting 4.5 hours in delays in Atlanta) and had a fiasco getting the rental car. We eventually got to the hotel, hooked him up to TPN and fluids (thankfully safe-barely) and to bed by 1am!! I was up through the night changing his fluids trying to keep them going.

We arrived at the center this morning in Lone Tree and he had his angiogram/ mapping procedure at 1:30. He is now in recovery and doing well so far. The surgeon believes he has a clear path to attack the tumors in the morning, but due to a few changes, it will take a little extra time in surgery. The staff and people here have been incredibly kind and wonderful and we are praying for a good and uneventful day tomorrow. No surprises!!! Please pray Stoney has a good night and can get to surgery!! God knows!! PRAY PRAY PRAY!!

May 5th, 2021….

POST SURGERY...

The doctor just came out and spoke with me. First of all, thank you for all your prayers! Secondly, the team here in Lone Tree is incredible. Dr Nutting is a first class surgeon and I feel God picked him out just for Stoney today. I asked one of the nurses if all the doctors here were this nice and she said "No! He's one in a million". Thirdly, he told me that he felt really good about what was done today. That he shut down 4 blood vessels that were feeding the tumor on the left side and got one on the right side that was pushing up against his diaphragm. He is confident that Stoney should see some longer relief, but that it would take a few weeks for him to be feeling back to normal. They will do scans in a few months and make a plan on what direction to go…de-bulking surgery or another embolization, but for now, all is GOOD!

Now Stoney is in recovery and doing ok so far. They will keep him here overnight, and as long as there are no problems, he will come to hotel tomorrow. We will Lord willing fly home Saturday!!!

Please keep up the praying, and that all our needs will be supplied!! Thank you Jesus for today!!

May 6, 2021….

Stone Dartt Update...

Just a little something to make you cry! Haha!! Today physical therapy came in and wanted to make sure he could walk and move around. They found out he was a singer and asked us to sing. Well, I chickened out and stoney gave them a concert!

We are certainly living "God on the Mountain is STILL God in the valley" these days and so it's no shock it was emotional to sing the words.

Stoney is doing good today! Bloodwork was good and he feels good. Symptoms are calming down as well. They ran an echo this morning and are watching oxygen levels. If he passes the echo, the cardiologist should clear him to go to the hotel today! Keep praying and be blessed by Stoney sharing in song!

May 7th, 2021...

3:33 am - prayers appreciated. headed by ambulance to hospital ER! Stoney having medical issues

5:48am - UPDATE... they have done bloodwork, and X-rays and CT scans. Waiting for results but they are treating him for an infection. His picc-line is not pushing anything through so they are trying to see what's going on. Dr tells me that the chances of us going home tomorrow are slim at this point. Could be 3-5 days here based on results. Praying for a miracle and we can treat this with pills or something! We need a miracle!! Do not want to be stuck here longer! Please PRAY!! This was totally unexpected!

Well, they are admitting Stone back into the hospital here in Colorado. His symptoms and scans point to pneumonia or at least fluid on the lungs that they plan to drain later today. There are some other issues that are related to post surgery from the embolization he had, but most of those can be managed. I have cancelled our flights, extended hotel and car and now we WAIT.... like my mom said this morning, the devil heard Stoney testifying by singing to the nurses and didn't like it, so he's testing our faith. I must admit, I'm upset and disappointed about so many things, one being that I will miss being with my mom for Mother's Day but I know getting Stoney strong and safely home is a priority. I've been sitting in a wooden chair in the ER since 4:00 this morning and I'm running on fumes, but I'm not going to let the devil steal our joy. We are here for a purpose, and although I have no idea what that is, I will Praise the Name of Jesus! He will take care of us through it all! Praying for all of the needs to be covered and a safe return home...whenever that may be. Keep praying!! We need all we can get!

...AFTERNOON UPDATE...

We waited in the ER for 8 hours before a room opened up. Stoney is miserable in pain from the procedure that was done Wednesday. They did a Ct and found fluid on the lungs so they just finished draining about 625cc off. This should help his breathing a little. They also have him on an antibiotic through tomorrow morning to rid of any bacteria. He is sleeping now, which is something I wish I could do but they have me staying close by for a little while longer as things have fallen through the cracks and I'm helping with information. I have not had a moment to get anything to eat or drink since we got here at 4am so I'm about to run down real quick for something if I can. Please pray for Stoneys recovery to be quick. They are starting him on a water pill to drain a lot more fluid off the legs, ankles, feet and belly area. They are monitoring his electrolytes and hopefully we can leave by Sunday or Monday but the next few days will be critical in his bloodwork and pain levels. All prayers welcomed and needed! I must admit the view from the hospital window is breathtaking!! Snow covered mountains in the distance just shining Gods majestic creation through the glass! Amazing! Hoping for better night sleep tonight and even better days to come!

May 8,2021...

First of all, thank you for all the love and prayers. The outpouring of prayers is what we need, and what will keep us going, so don't stop!!

This morning Stoney is still in lots of pain and on more oxygen than yesterday. The Dr said his liver is very angry with the radiation so the recovery is going to be hard. We have lots of obstacles before us so we need prayer. He also said the harder the recovery, the more likely the tumors are dying so the struggle is a good thing, as bad as it feels to stoney! I will most likely be staying longer than I had even thought yesterday as they closely monitor him and get him stronger. There's more pain in his right lung area which had collapsed due to fluid (that was removed yesterday). With all the unknowns, I'm just trusting the Lord to once again see us through. It's scary being this far from home with no target release in sight, but I know we've been here before and God has not left us and never will. As much as I wish we were in Atlanta at a place we know and Love, with a staff that has become more like family, I'm thankful for the growing/stretching experience that God has put us in. There is something here for me to learn, or someone who needs to be encouraged through us. That's why God allows these things, otherwise life would be a cakewalk.

I'm praying I can be a light, and can show love and kindness through my fear, nerves and sometimes anger.

It gives snow here tomorrow, and I missed all our snow at home in Nashville due to being in Atlanta, SOOOO, I'm gonna enjoy it tomorrow here...in MAY!!!! Enjoying the covered mountains from the room today while Stoney sleeps and counting all the many blessings we've had to this point... and there's been so many!!! We will keep moving forward and believing for a miracles and many more good days to come. Thank you so much and please don't stop those prayers!

Sunday, May 9, 2021....

First of all, Happy Mothers Day to all you incredible moms! It is a special day to honor the very special women in our lives! I wish I was with mine today, but I'm so thankful she is home and doing well!

Stoney is still very puffy/swollen from fluid build up. His metabolic panel this morning was good and stable but his blood levels were not great. Mostly from the radiation he's had and his body processing it all. They are watching closely to see if he will need a blood transfusion, which we are praying against. Trying to replace numbers with supplements for now. The biggest issue at this point is the right lung has collapsed so after draining the fluid off, he desperately needs to build it up again. He's depending on so much oxygen right now that they really need to get that down in order for us to go home. They are hoping he will make progress over the next few days, building the lung up, and then send us home on a temporary oxygen pump (to travel with). His breathing has been greatly affected due to extra fluid weight, and high heart rate so strangely enough the reason we are staying longer is respiratory and not the liver issues! His body is experiencing lots of changes with the radiation so it'll be a process to get back to normal but the surgeon is still confident in the procedure that was done! So, the goal is to go home Wednesday or Thursday for now. It really all depends on Stoney and his willingness to work hard. They have taken him off the pain pump and gone to pill form now so that's good!! His appetite is coming back, and that's another blessing.

Today, Mark and Lynn Toney Holland stopped by the hospital and brought me lunch. We sang for them in Florida for many years, and it was so nice to see a familiar face here in Colorado! I am so grateful for the many people God has placed in my life through our many years of ministry. The years come and go, but the people God places in our lives are always right there when we need them. It was a Godwink today.

Please pray for strength and endurance for both Stoney and myself. I am weary, slightly depressed and just want to go home. Stoneys health and safety first obviously!! I feel wrapped in His arms and covered in prayer, so thank you to all of you and PLEASE don't stop!!

May 10, 2021....

Good morning from Denver! We are still here, and after the morning report I have extended our stay through Friday now. Stoneys metabolic panel looks decent but his hemoglobin dropped low enough to force them into giving him a blood transfusion. He is very nervous about it and not thrilled, but no alternative. His breathing is also still very labored and he's on oxygen. They said after his right lung collapsed, it would take time to restore its capacity but they thought it would be sooner than this. He is now working hard at using the spirometer and taking deep breaths. They will hopefully get him walking today at some point. His heart rate spikes with any movement. He is off pain meds though and liver enzymes are now normal so there are some blessings in it! Haha! I hate that we have had to extend this long and now even longer, but there is a purpose. His body has been through so much the past few months and even beyond, that it's just having to work harder. Please pray for a quicker recovery. That his lungs will expand and become normal soon!! I have had to cancel some plans to stay here longer, but I'm trusting the Lord to supply the needs and restore Stoneys health, and that life may resume to normal ASAP!! We need some relief.

Love you all and thanks for everything!! Please keep the prayer chains going, and feel free to share a gift below if you'd like to support this journey!

May 11, 2021...

God has such a sense of humor!! Last night when I left the hospital at 9:00, I felt like I was back in Maine, driving in a blizzard!! I came only to be here in Denver for 3 days. Checked the weather beforehand and new what I needed to pack. Never expecting to be here longer and in a snow storm! Haha. So, here is a pic of this southern boy in flip flops and snow! Woke up this morning with the ground covered and roads slightly icy. Hahaha!! In the middle of May!! Oh my goodness y'all, last night I was dying laughing alone in my tiny little rental car, thinking...Lord, you are stinking hilarious!!! So... that's my funny today.

The Dr just came in and gave the update on Stoney for today. Yesterday with the help of the water pill, they were able to drain 3.7 liters of fluid off him and will try again today. They got the oxygen down from 5 to 4 yesterday and today they are going to try to pull it down to 3. (Remember 2 is our magic number to go home). They will also get him walking today, or at least try and send him home with a walker to start. His labs were really good and liver functions are nearly normal now so we are just pushing along. They are hoping to get us home Friday but it all depends on Stoney and how hard he is willing to push! Please continue to pray for more progress!! We both feel Gods presence and strength, so don't give up on us!! Pray us home!!! Thank you and love y'all!!

May 12,2021...

Let's be honest, I'm so tired of this junk! I'm tired of sitting in the hospital day after day for long hours. And before anyone decides to go off on me, let me remind you I've been here in the hospital with Stoney for more than 129 nights since December 1st. People who have have walked this journey understand and get it. If you haven't, you will never understand the heartache, the fear, the loneliness and frustrations of it.

It has been a rollercoaster of a journey. To the point where you don't even know how or what to pray. It's always different for the patient and the caregiver. Both require grace and mercy, as well as love and kindness. I must admit I've been lacking lately of all of the above. My intensity and drive to push Stoney to get better and get home has been met with laziness and tiredness by him. My fear of the expense of being here matched with the unknown of his recovery and ability to push harder. My emotions have been getting the best of me I will admit! But this morning I was singing the old song, "Great is Thy Faithfulness", then when I arrived at the hospital the mountains were a clear view and in the midst of my anxiety I felt a Peace. I became so frustrated with Stoneys lack of trying that I walked down to the rental car, played an album by my dear friend, Tiffany Coburn, said a prayer then walked up to the room with my big boy pants on and said, "we are not giving up today". As I sit here next to stoney while he sleeps. The room quiet, the fear of the unknown, I am comforted with the fact that I am not alone. While the future is uncertain, and the days ahead are unknown, my ability to lean on everything that I was taught as a young child about Gods faithfulness is so comforting to me. Focusing on scripture and songs in a scary situation is helping me breathe, bring peace and stability... I almost left the hospital today with some built up anger, but instead I anticipate to see what the Goodness of God will bring to us here in this hospital room.

How has God been good to you lately and have you thanked Him for it? These trials are not easy, and I have a multitude of people watching me, how I respond and how I handle the daily news, hardships or praises. It's not easy being happy all the time or being so positive...it's a CHOICE! The presence of God is REAL, sometimes we miss it because we are so caught up in ourselves and our own feelings of despair and selfishness that we forget He's still there. I'm guilty. Today, I'm pushing my "reset" button, praying for a better day, with better results and a brighter tomorrow!

"...all I have needed, THY hand hath provided. Great is Thy faithfulness Lord unto me…"

May 13, 2021...

Good morning everyone! First of all, thank you so much for your prayers and for the kind comments yesterday. You brought tears to my eyes as I read through each comment and felt humbled by your love and support. It's a new day, and as we figure things out, I know I have the strength to push forward because all of you are praying and I can FEEL IT!! It is a gorgeous day today and the view of the Rocky Mountains are what I need to give me some energy and sunshine in my soul.

The goal is to discharge Stoney tomorrow (possibly morning) and for us to get to the airport and fly home with a temporary oxygen tank. Here are the obstacles that are before us right now....1. To change our flights, the cost has increased greatly due the fuel issues on the east coast (which is weird how it could effect the airline fuel in Denver) but it's about $300 more each than what we paid to change our flight to get home. 2. The oxygen backpack is not covered with Stoneys insurance and will cost us $512 to rent. That's for a whole week, but the medical team feels he won't need it once we get home *because of the altitude issues. I will have to ship it back when we get home. It's a temporary travel requirement and they don't feel comfortable releasing him to fly without it. 3. Lastly, the additional cost in rental car is $124. So, these are the urgent prayer request, financial needs and requirements to get us home. Once they run bloodwork and other tests this afternoon, they will give me the green light to book the flights and make all our travel plans. It's been a little overwhelming and I must admit, some anxiousness just because of all the details to attend to. The staff here has been amazing, and I can't tell you how grateful I am for their listening ear to what Stoneys needs are (with info being communicated from our Atlanta team). The hospitals (all 3 we have been to) in Nashville have been absolutely the worst in dealing with Stoneys case, which is why we don't like to be treated there and go to other states! As strange as this trip has been, and inconvenient and even expensive, they have done an absolutely amazing job with his care plan, so I just want to praise the nurses and docs here!!*

We will move forward and do what we need to do... continuing to trust the Almighty God! As our faith strengthens, and comfort grows, I want to truly express my sincere gratitude to every one of you who has reached out and messaged me, cared and supported Stone and myself on this journey. Life is never easy, but the road in between is where I've learned to rely solely on the firm foundation of Jesus Christ!!

Keep praying for us!!

May 14, 2021...

Thank you all for praying so hard!! Here we are... we have boarded the 3 hour flight home to Nashville! It's been an incredibly draining day and I'm ready to get home and into my own bed!! It started at 6:30am...I was able to get Stoney showered, dressed and cleaned up amidst horrible symptoms he was having today. We aren't sure if it's the nerves, the after effects of surgery, the cancer, etc... it's just been a rough day. I drove through traffic to the airport with sweaty hands, returned the car, hauled 4 suitcases by myself through the airport and got Stoney in a wheelchair and to the gate! I was soaked when we sat down! Haha. I had all the oxygen requirements ready and praise God that all went splendidly. He has had to rely on the oxygen a little heavier today just because of the stress. Anyway, we survived and I know it's because of the grace of God and ALL OF YOU praying!! I'm currently multitasking today making arrangements with a respiratory therapist next week for Stoney to see to make sure oxygen won't be a permanent fixture at home. The Dr will order scans in 3 weeks as well to make sure tumors are shrinking. We go back to Atlanta May 24th for his injection and that's as far as I've gotten for now. I'm exhausted, I'm weary mentally and physically and need your prayers to continue our journey at home! Neither of us are working right now, so we are learning how to survive through that drama as well. Haha. I'm telling you, NEVER a dull moment!!! Hahaha!! By Gods grace, I will not quit!! Love to all of you for getting us this far! I seriously cannot thank you enough!!!

May 15, 2021…

We made it home last night around 9:00 and stoney made it without oxygen all night long! This morning, he is struggling with breathing, coughing and high heart rate along with his fluid loss. I'm just trying to read him and figure out what to do.... I can handle most things at home, but it's always scary having 100% responsibility for someone! Your prayers will be much appreciated as we continue on this journey and wait to see how the radiation continues to help his body and fight the cancer!

A simple 3 days event lasted 2 weeks! It was unbelievable how God provided for all of our needs out there. It was so expensive, and since it was not covered like our stays at the Cancer center, the bills piled up so quickly. Yet, God spoke to people, and they gave. They shared their love for us with their gifts and we made it home once again. I stand amazed at the goodness of God. Now that we were home, Stoney had work to do! He was now on oxygen off and on, and he needed physical therapy to expand his lungs. They were collapsed and the only way he was going to get them expanded was to exercise and use a very intense breathing machine they gave him. Well, the machine sat on the end table next to the couch, and would carry it with him to any room and lay it down, but never use it. I would encourage him to walk, but he never felt like it or he made excuses on why he couldn't walk. I knew that things had changed, and I knew he was not himself. He was falling behind each day, and he was getting more tired. He was arguing with me, and I just didn't have the strength to push him. I called his two brothers to come and help me get him to walk. They did their best to help, but I just don't think Stoney wanted to do what he knew he was suppose to do…

May 17, 2021…

Today, I'm praying for GRACE!! Being a caregiver has been one of the absolute hardest things I've ever done in my entire life. I watched my mom care for my dad with such elegance, humbleness and grace and I always thought, "how is she doing that?" It's a thankless job sometimes and also mentally exhausting. Since being home, Stoney has been able to be off oxygen but has been so symptomatic in other areas its effecting his attitude. He's angry, he's frustrated, he's unhappy with nearly everything and who gets the brunt of it? Me!! Yay!! Lol. I have asked God why on earth nothing is working but it's not for me to ask...I just hurt for him to not have any relief. He is suppose to start the chemo pill next week and I know that's gonna make him feel even worse. He's up all night in the bathroom and not sleeping (thus I'm not sleeping) and I wonder where is God in all of this? Now, if I was an unbeliever, I would stop with that... but I know I have Jesus Christ walking with me...in fact I know He is carrying me these last several months because there is no way I could do this on my own. Growing weary on the journey is so normal and so easy...it's how we pick ourselves up and press forward that matters. I admit, I'm exhausted (I'm human!) but I also know the joy of the Lord is my strength, and I can run and not grow weary with the help of my Lord and Savior! I have to somehow close my ears off to the hateful words and tones that hit me in the face and learn to show love and receive grace. I would ask you personally for your prayers that I may feel strength like never before and find grace in the broken mess. That stoney would be encouraged and see results good enough to push on and find Jesus loving on him in this trial. It's a struggle!!!

I have been on this journey with him for 28 months now and for the first time I'm stepping away for a couple days with my mom. I have called in the "backup team" and taught them how to run TPN, fluids, pills, etc... His nephew will stay here a few nights with him for emergencies while I take my mom away for a much needed rest. I feel like I am cracking, breaking down and I desperately need a few days to just sleep and know that stoney has 100% care. I beg you all to pray that NOTHING goes wrong while I'm gone, that I get some rest, and that stoney manages here at home. This is something I have struggled with doing but I feel if I don't do it, my consequences will be even worse.

I'm so grateful for the outpouring of love and support and would ask you to continue!! Heaven is looking sweeter everyday!!

MAY 19, 2021...

As I am away and enjoying some time with my mom, the drama continues with Stoney at home. His calcium levels are very high, in fact critical. Home health care came out today to draw more labs to submit to find out why these numbers are high and to see if they can correct it without him going to an ER. Unfortunately the next 24 hours are critical in his care, because if certain signs are seen he will have to go to the ER in Nashville to get stable and then do a hospital transfer to Atlanta. Right now he is just very nauseated and added cancer symptoms. He is achy and miserable. No appetite and just barely do enough to get pills down. Being away and hearing this news is so hard on me...I'm torn as what to do, but trying to hold my ground and stay away as planned. I really need everyone to step up their prayers the next few days and pray they can find a way to lower his calcium without going to the hospital. That would be the biggest prayer!! They are making changes to his TPN which will start tonight as well....prayers for me to remain calm and clear minded. To be able to REST, and trust the caregivers at home to jump in and do what's best for stoney. I am enjoying this time with my mom!! We had a long talk last night, sharing memories and creating new ones that I am so grateful for!! It's just not easy letting it all go right now

Thanks for praying!! We need miracles!!

As I was in Florida, with my mom, I was handling calls from both of the surgeons. They were calling to check on Stoney, but also concerned about the reason he was not getting better. This was highly abnormal for them to be reaching out to the patient/caregiver, but they thought he should be further advanced in his recovery. I took a call one evening outside of the hotel and spoke with the Dr about how concerned I was, and his thoughts were that we maybe needed to wait another couple of weeks, or get him on a different chemo pill right away. This is where I was caught in the middle of a dilemma...Do I listen to the new surgeon who we had only met via zoom, or do I take the advice coming from Atlanta where we had been receiving care for 2 years. It was a tug of war of the soul. Ultimately, my goal for Stoney was to get better and I didn't care where that treatment was going to come from, as long as he had it.

I hate the scripture that says, "I waited patiently on the Lord and He inclined to me and heard my prayer..." One, I am hight impatient and two, I had been waiting so long and not seeing my prayers answered! However, "WAIT"... a small word with so much meaning. I thought a good word analogy should be "Wondering Alone In Trouble". But, we aren't alone. The whole time I was worrying, God was there walking WITH me. Remember the old poem, "Footprints in the Sand"?...I was having my sand moment. I couldn't see the footsteps next to me, because He was actually carrying me. He was closer than I knew.

I had a nice visit in Florida, but since I did nothing but wrestle with mind games, I was glad to get home and have my feet firmly on the ground where I could get things done, and move the mountains that needed moving...Meaning Stoney "Mountain" of course...

May 21, 2021...

As my break comes to an end, and I will be heading home, Stoney still continues to struggle at home. Today, his sister in law is taking him to a lung specialist at Vanderbilt. We aren't sure what they will find or say, but trusting the Lord in all things. I have been dealing with the doctors in Atlanta and Denver this week, trying to get them on the same page. Our biggest problem is that our oncologist at the cancer center has officially left. He was a neuroendocrine specialist and now they no longer have anyone that really specializes in that department. However, the Doctor in Denver is Neuroendocrine only specialist, but understands our desire to be closer to home. He has shared some amazing ideas and helpful benefits, but the Atlanta team doesn't want to lend their ear just yet. I would ask you to pray very hard about how we proceed. Spend more and go to Denver, or stay in Atlanta and hope they get on the same page. It's a struggle, but we are confident that we have a great God who will work all these details out on our behalf... we just have to stay patient. (Again, not my strong suit)

In the meantime, stoney is losing 9-12 liters of fluid a day and it's been rough to stay on top of, but started a new medication last night that over the next week may begin to help. He is very weak and not feeling good, nausea and no appetite.

Thank you for all your prayers and support! This is a very difficult journey and it carries a lot of stress! We just need to ride on the wings of our Savior!

May 23, 2021...

I'm asking you to pray for Stoney tonight and tomorrow. He is feeling terrible and worn out. He can't eat anything without feeling nauseated or sick. He was at the ER the other night and walked out because it was taking so long, but he has more fluid on his lungs that needs to be drained off. We leave for Atlanta in the morning at 7am for a busy day of appointments and his injection. Hopefully we will be back tomorrow evening if all goes well. We won't have enough time for them to drain the fluid, so we will need to make that plan later this week. It will be 3 weeks on Wednesday since he had his embolization in Denver. We were hoping to see better results by now but still trusting the Lord to see us through. His ways are higher and better, and although we do not understand nor can we see, we will follow and trust!!

Asking you to be on your knees in prayer that relief will come soon to Stoney's body!! We would love to see a miracle, but just days of some laughs, free of pain and some good meals would be an improvement and a blessing!!

We are facing a new series of financial complications, but WE KNOW He who is able to provide and see us through! God has been ever so present even in the darkest of days! Thank you so much for your love and support!! Keep praying!!

May 24, 2021...

Our day started at 5:30 this morning....got stoney breakfast and disconnected him from all his many wires and contraptions. Haha. Our friend, Liz, drove us to the airport on her way to work and we got to the gate just in time to walk on! Stoney has had to use a wheelchair all day today which is kind of hard for me to process, but I'll get there.

We arrived in Atlanta, made it to the center and then was told to go directly to urgent care there by our care manager. She (Kristen) is AMAZING!! We would be lost on our journey without her! They drew his labs there, and we met with nutrition and nephrology there, and then they ordered an ultrasound to try and drain the fluid off Stoneys lungs here as to not go back to Vanderbilt this week. However, upon looking at things, they did not feel he had enough fluid to safely remove it. Instead, they urged him to use the spirometer and walk!! Haha. Umm...I think I've been pushing for that for 2 weeks now. Haha. He has been feeling so bad lately and has had no energy but sure perked up when we saw one of our very special nurses, Elaine!! She made our afternoon!!

We got his injection, and barely made the shuttle back to the airport! We are aboard our flight home and liz should pick us up again on her way home from work and Lord willing be tucked in at home tonight. It has been a long day, but we are blessed. I have been a little short with stoney a few times because I want him to do better... I have to stop, take a breath, say a prayer, and then smile and just go with it. His bloodwork today was mixed good and bad. They will start him on a medication to lower his calcium this week and monitor his other electrolytes daily, even adding his Octreotide to his TPN during the night. All good things considered I guess. They all said his lethargy is from the radio-embolization and could last another couple weeks. It's normal for most patients with that much radiation to feel this way.

We will go home and push forward, and fight this horrible nasty disease on all thrusters! We do have many needs as Stoney will be unable to work for a few more months, so more prayers appreciated!!

We feel so blessed to have so many of you pray for us, follow us and cheer us on!! It is that tenacity that will keep us going and fighting!!

Here's to another day!

May 28, 2021....

I've had several people message me and check on Stone and I the last couple days and figured I needed to make an update. Honestly, it's been very depressing around here because some days I feel nothing is going to get better or change...it feels kind of lonely since Stoney doesn't really talk much and seems highly withdrawn. Mainly he is in pain, exhausted from the radiation and never hungry. Just making him eat enough to take pills is hard enough!! My days consist of changing LR bags, refilling his drinks, getting pills together and talking with the medical staff everyday. They feel like Stoney went into the Y-90 procedure already weak and tired (after already having 2 chemo embolizations) and so the recovery is taking longer for him. He has no energy to exercise and some days I feel like he's giving up, although he has assured me he wants to push and get better! His brothers have been over this week to encourage him to walk and use the spirometer which has been successful once a day.

I would ask you to pray that things turn around quickly for him. That he would feel encouraged and happy. We need JOY here!! I have I Love Lucy, The Lucy Show and Here's Lucy playing through the day just for laughs and a happier atmosphere...and every now and then I get a laugh out of him. I like those moments…

Pray for my sanity...my spirits to stay high and that God would fill me with peace and understanding. I have decided to go back to work full time June 1st! I will have my travel agency back open and will be booking cruises, vacations and group tours again. I think we all need vacations!

Financially, we are struggling since stoney has been unable to work and people have asked about disability. If we file disability, he will lose his special financial aid in Atlanta. It's a catch 22!! We are just trusting the Lord to sustain us, and keep us covered! We have what we need today... and God will provide the needs tomorrow. We continue to press on, live in hope and trust the Lord in and through ALL things!! Keep praying for us!! We truly need a divine touch!

June 3, 2021....3:30am

I could say, "1 step forward, 2 back"..."here we go again..." or "Thy Will Be Done"....

After Stoney's good day Monday, things began to turn. He began to talk less, sleep more and the pain has become intolerable. His brother, Don, has been with us a few nights helping me out so I can take care of things and have a small reprieve but last night after Stone Mountain Dartt walked, it became clear that something wasn't right. We talked for quite awhile about all the details and made a plan for Don to take Stoney to Atlanta's urgent care at CTCA. I have a medical appointment today (Thursday) and upon hearing from them later today, I will drive down to Atlanta and switch with Don. I have spoken with the surgeon in Denver who is waiting on scans that should be scheduled Monday or Tuesday (or maybe even tomorrow now) to decide if surgery is an immediate option. He has wanted to wait until there was more shrinkage, but he is willing to move forward with a more complicated operation if it's the last case scenario (which we may be up against now).

I got up, and got stoney packed (clothes, pills and some electronics just in case they keep him)and saw them both off and now as I lay here in bed trying to think about a few more hours of sleep, I ask for Gods perfect will to be done...whatever that may be. I told my mom yesterday it's the hardest prayer in the world to pray. Just knowing we must be ok with whatever Gods plan is. To trust Him, to seek Him, to Lay it down and leave it with Him. My heart hurts for stoney and to have watched him suffer the last many months through this horrible disease has been painful, and life changing for me. To see the graciousness and goodness of God through all of it, and yet struggle with the unknowns and uncertainties that the trials bring. I would ask you to pray that Stoney will feel peace and comfort waiting in the urgent care...that the scans and bloodwork would show us just what we need to see, and that we would have a clear plan ahead of what's next for the surgeon in Denver. That stoney would have relief from the pain and nausea...that joy would flood his soul once again.

The next few hours and days hold many surprises, as it does for so many of us lately. I lay here thinking that God told us "I'm with you always, and I'll leave you never". I feel His presence of peace, and I'm trusting in Him for direction on what's next. (And also that we won't be stuck in Atlanta for very long).

Thank you for your prayers and support...this journey has proven to be eventful and at times scary, but yet eye opening to Gods faithfulness and constant care!

Until we know more...

....UPDATE...

Stoney spent the day in urgent care awaiting news to what's next on this journey. They did a Ct scan with contrast and found the liver is enlarged from all the radiation and may even have new tumors unfortunately. There is fluid on both lungs and he will be having a procedure tomorrow at 1:00 to remove it then Lord willing will be on his way home. The nausea and gagging from eating is part of the liver cancer getting worse so prayers needed!!

In the meantime, I sent the scans and imaging to the surgeon in Denver and we are waiting on a call tomorrow to find out what's next. There is a chance we may be going to Denver next week for a major operation to remove half the liver and all the cancer infected lymph nodes. We will hopefully know more tomorrow! This is scary and yet exciting. Also, the last option left on the book! I will update you with that info later and what all is involved. We are going to need major prayer coverage and miracles to get there and get through it all!! But we have seen God provide and guide in the past so this is no exception! Please keep up the prayer chain. We need to be covered and surrounded!!

Many asked what the de-bulking surgery would entail if the surgery had moved forward. They would open Stoney up, remove all the tumors in the liver, the lymph nodes, and even the tail of his pancreas, giving him a reconnection, and naming it something with way too many letters and something I couldn't pronounce even if I tried. It was intricate, it was complicated, and it was dangerous. It would have also saved his life if he had been able to receive it about 6 months prior. Unfortunately, the Cancer Center never gave us that option, nor recommended it. They only pushed surgeries and procedures that they could control at the center. It is a disappointing thought to think we could have done something to save his life, but in the end, isn't God's time table perfect? Truly, we wouldn't have changed Gods plan with our own anyway…Its another Romans 8:28 - All things work together for good to those that love the Lord (NIV)… You have to keep bringing back the scriptures at every point, because God in His sovereignty and perfect wisdom had a plan that I could not wrap my mind around. I had to trust the unknown. I had to put faith into action. "Forsaking All, I Trust Him". Easy? NO.

June 5th, 2021…

Stoney got back home last night (or should I say this morning at 1:00am)… he had 800cc of fluid drained off his lungs. He was in pain and not feeling well. His labs showed extreme dehydration so I spent most of the night running fluids. He is not eating much and can barely get his pills down. His kidneys showed some decline in labs as well but hoping the hydration would help. The Surgeon in Denver cannot operate right now, so we are waiting on insurance to approve the Pet Scan so they can get better images. In the meantime he will start a new pill this week and have his Octreotide increased in his TPN. It has been a very difficult few weeks (months!) but we are taking it a day at a time, trusting Jesus each day, and resting on His promises. It's very sad watching this journey first hand but I know that God is receiving the Glory through the praise and thanksgiving AND that's what I pray we can continue to do! I pray that Stoneys pain is kept at bay, that he will remain comfortable and if new options and procedure arise, that he will be able to tackle it!

For now, pray for wisdom in the upcoming days and strength for each day!

June 7, 2021….

I have been wondering myself this weekend if Stoneys labs would look better or worse after I gave him many liters of LR (lactated ringer) over the weekend. Today, we received the results, and they weren't good! The bloodwork today showed Stoneys kidneys were fighting and although not in failure, it is in what they call acute failure. CTCA called me and based on his numbers, I will leave at 4am and drive him back to Atlanta where they will directly admit him m. At this time it could be 1-2 weeks but we really don't have any idea how long. At first I just cried cause we didn't get a good rest last night, and I'm so tired!! Then I just thanked the Lord that we are going to a place that has continuously been a safe haven for us. A place with loving kind nurses and friends who I know will take only the best of care for him!! I am not a fan of driving, but will make the venture in the morning trusting the Lord to take care of us! New expenses that God is already working out for us even though we don't know, scary days ahead that God is already preparing peace and comfort for, unknown procedures that God has already seen and is preparing the way for. As I can sit here and be bold and strong in my sharing of this post, my heart is truly tender, and even a little afraid of the days ahead. But HE has a plan, HE knows the way, HE holds my hand and HE cares for me and all my fears!! This trip is hard for me…each trip we take gets a little harder as this disease runs through his body, but I'm so glad that as children of God we know the one who rides on the wings of the wind, who walk before us, beside, and behind and carries us when we are weary. May we find comfort and strength in tomorrow and peace and joy tonight as we wait on the Lord…

Please pray for every detail, concern and need!! We walk in and by faith!!

On a side note, his Pet scan and MRI are both scheduled for Friday and once the surgeon sees that report, he will know better how to make a decision on moving forward with surgery. That's an answer to prayer today.

Thank you for your prayers and support!! Please continue and uphold us!! I'm weary….

June 8, 2021…

Today was a long day!!!! After 2 hours of sleep, a 5 hour drive, almost 7 hours in the urgent care at the cancer center, Stoney was finally admitted! His labs were slightly better than yesterday and there was a conflict of issues with one of the physicians at the center (that we don't really like) but we had a great team of 4 fight for us and worked hard to get Stoney admitted!! He has been in lots of pain today (more than usual) and so he's doped up on pain meds. He went all day with no food or pills, so got further behind…come to think of it… so did I!! Haha. I just realized a little bit ago that I hadn't eaten all day and barely had anything other than 1 bottle of water and a cup of coffee. Today was a JOB! And tonight, we are both exhausted. I got to the hotel with barely any energy left and the girl said, "we have no reservation for you tonight". I came super close to losing Jesus and nearly had a 3 year old meltdown in the lobby. Haha. Thankfully after 30 minutes, they managed to move a "sold out" hotel to a…."oh mister Speer, it looks as if we have something". Haha. God deserves credit for that one! Haha!

So now Im in my room with some food and barely keeping my eyes open. We are PRAYING for God to provide our financial needs here as we don't know how long we will actually be here, but also Stoneys physical health! He is so tired, so worn and so ready to have some good days. Please pray for him. When we got to his room, we had our friends, Patrick and Liz assigned to us and it made our day!! We got hugs and it brought a smile to both our faces. We love the staff here! (Most of the them…haha!) we will take it a day at a time, and trust the Lord to have His perfect will and way over us!

…I'm off to sleepy town!….

This would be our last trip to CTCA. This trip I made on June 8th was the very last time I traveled to Atlanta, for I would be there for 5 weeks, and come home alone. Driving down that morning was a feeling I have never felt. I knew when we walked out of the house it would be the last time Stoney would ever be there. I told Liz the night before at dinner that I didn't think Stoney would be coming home, and I remember her looking at me in disbelief. I had this gut feeling as if God was preparing me fo the drive, and for what was coming. Stoney knew too. I believe that with my whole heart. He never told me that, but I knew. He looked around the house, feeling miserable and sick, and the way he scanned the room, it was different. Something in his eyes just told me that he knew he would never see his home again.

The drive was long. We left while it was dark, and we had to stop so many times for him to go to the bathroom. He could barely make it into the restrooms, and had a couple accidents on the way. I listened to the Gaither Vocal Band for the entire drive, and Stoney slept. I knew he wasn't feeling well, because for one he never let anyone else drive, and two, he would sit there and tell you how to drive.

When we arrived in Atlanta and he walked into the urgent care unit, I felt like a burden was lifted off of me. I had made it. I had accomplished the task that was upon me, I had succeeded. Now it was up to them to fix him, and get him back to normal.

Our friends who checked us in when we arrived could tell Stoney did not look like himself. He was not as happy, not as engaging, nor did he have his smile plastered to his face. He was in a wheelchair, he was breathing heavily, and he looked liked he had not slept in weeks. Things were about to become real, and UGLY!

June 10, 2021….

Well, tonight I come with a heavy burden. The last couple days have been pretty hard to watch. Stoneys health is declining drastically and we are faced with extremely limited options at this point. The surgeon can no longer operate on the liver so a transplant is out. We have not made a definite decision yet as the entire family is weighing in and we seek the Lord direction on what to do. Hospice is at the top of the list for now, but not the chosen path just yet. We meet with a GI specialist tomorrow about a blockage in his abdomen and await to see his labs after sepsis was found and being treated for tonight. As I sat in the chair all day and looked at him, he is not himself. He is struggling. He is suffering. He is miserable. My prayer is that God will have mercy. That

He will show grace, love and compassion and no matter how hard this becomes I pray stoney will remain comfortable and at peace.

Tonight, I lay here at the hotel with a lot on my mind. It's hard for me to talk to anyone without being emotional but at the same time…what a future for stoney. I'm actually jealous! I guess I wish I was the one closer to go. Heaven is getting sweeter everyday and I long to go there more and more. Stoney will get to see my dad and they' ll probably have some good talks like they used to, along with some good laughs. It's easy to want to keep someone here because of our own desires, but when we look at the whole picture, this life here stinks!! No, really… look at what is going on in our world!! Tell me, who honestly wants to be here instead of Heaven? Perfected bodies that no longer experience pain, mental freedom with no tears or sadness, no death, no wanting of anything because we are shaped and perfected in the image of the Almighty. I'm just plain jealous! Haha. I will miss the bestest friend I have ever had, and I' ll suffer from loneliness and anxiety for a while, but when I think of the life he will have, I can't wish him to be back or want him to stay because I wouldn't be a good friend myself. "In this life we will have trials and tribulations…." God laid it out for us early on, so why should we be surprised by it? But fear not!! For I am with you always HE says!!

I leave you tonight with this thought… as we pray for Gods will to be done, if ever God was to perform the largest miracle in present day history, now would be the time. To blow peoples mind that cancer could be gone not because of a doctor but because of the GREAT HEALER! He hasn't lost His touch and can still perform a miracle. BUT…. If He doesn't, pray that the God of all comfort, the God of all Mercy, never will forsake us nor leave us. That HE would surround stoney with peace and pour over him a feeling of safety and comfort. That He would give us, his family, his loved ones a calm and stillness knowing that we are sheltered under the wings of our Great God!!

I close my eyes tonight knowing tomorrow is already prepared for us, and there is nothing we can do to change it.

As we all prepare to make big decisions tomorrow, please cover us in your prayers!!! We need them!!

June 11, 2021…

Today was another long day sitting, soaking in the moments that we have. Stoney seemed slightly more alert this morning, then slept more and was a little confused this afternoon. His kidney function is between 25-30% right now. He doesn't talk much to me, no real conversation so that's hard. His breathing is becoming heavier and labored and the thought of getting home is becoming more difficult. I have asked his brother, Don, to come down and lay eyes on the situation and help me make the decision on whether we can get home or not. Keeping him comfortable is the most important thing. He is developing a deep cough, probably early pneumonia from laying in bed for weeks, and is on an antibiotic. So much going on, so much suffering, but Gods hand is on him and we are following Him the best we can.

We will keep you updated, but for now it's like we are stuck in a horror movie. Please pray for safety of family traveling, peace in these days, wisdom in knowing what decisions to make, and comfort in these moments of fear. Your outpouring of love, support and kindness today has been overwhelming and I'm grateful!! Thank you all!! Please don't stop!

June 13, 2021….

I apologize for no update yesterday. It's been a lot! Stoneys brother, Don came down to help me be the family spokesperson in the decision making. Then my mom and best friend, Liz, came down to surprise me and be moral support. Friday the center opened their policy to allow more guest so it was perfect timing! The staff at CTCA have given a couple options to us at this point. Being where we want stoney home with family and friends, they are doing their best to tank him up on fluids and electrolytes, along with a heavy steroid so we can safely get him home. Being where he uses the bathroom every 2 hours and loses 10-12 liters a day, it's important that he can make the 5 hour trip with no stops. We are still working through details. Stoney and his family have chosen not do hospice right away, but to do palliative care at home as long as possible until hospice is surely needed. It buys a little more time with what we can do at home…The last few days have been very difficult on everyone and Stoney has seemed scared and unsure of the steps. Once we leave here, we will no longer be back to CTCA. A very difficult and hard choice! The last few days, nurses have been in with hugs and lots of love and we have been blessed and ministered to by so many!! It's gonna be hard to leave! We have cried and laughed and poured out our hearts...we have fought with decisions, and juggled the options. There were ultimately only 2 decisions, and they have felt this is the best. I will update you more tomorrow, but for now... I love you all and appreciate your prayers and support!! More to come tomorrow!! I've got to clear my head!!!!

June 15, 2021...

We have experienced such anxiety, hopelessness and even depression the last few days of not knowing what to do...then, trying to make a decision...then, hearing a new plan and pushing for a way home, and now another glimmer of hope or opportunity has come today. We had been given literally no hope Friday, and things looked totally different...BUT GOD! Today I had a call from an amazing friend, angel, nurse here at CTCA who wanted to talk to me. I met with her downstairs and she shared with me that she just had a heavy heart for Stone and couldn't stop thinking about "what if...". She researched some therapies and options at Vanderbilt hospital and upon my approval, reached out to a neuroendocrine specialist there and booked an appointment, which then I had bumped up to next Tuesday. With that in mind, we do NOT know if this will work, or if they will take the case once they see all his paperwork, but it's a bright spot today and it has given Stoney a "hope for tomorrow". I will say this...the journey has ONE end result, but if there is something that we can do that we missed, we would not forgive ourselves for not trying. That being said, Stoney has A LOT of work to do, and the entire thing honestly depends on his ability to fight. We have listened to several doctors, taken the advise of many nurses, and now practicing all those things into a survival mode. Stoney is receiving the information, and today has already pushed himself to do the things they have asked. He is back on oxygen and will probably have to take that home, AND he is getting a Plurex drain in his lung tomorrow so that I can pull off fluid at home. I have spent my entire afternoon fighting for his care and provision. I have talked with numerous people here about what's next, looking ahead and finding ways to make stoney comfortable from now until the time God takes him home, whenever that may be....

I won't lie and say things have been going smoothly. It has been a nightmare I really don't want to relive but I believe in HOPE. I have had some conflicts with people, I've disagreed with people, I've even had to ask Jesus to take the wheel and give me lots of Grace. BUT I BELIEVE IN JESUS making a way when there is no way. I believe in following the open doors that are ahead, and when they close, I know He is showing us a different plan.

This journey depends on the prayers of Gods people, the strength for Stoney to push that only he can receive from the Living God, peace for his friends and family, and an everlasting love that we can fully trust in.

We will hopefully go home now Thursday or Friday and have home health care continue to supply TPN and LR until we have the consultation with the Dr in Nashville. We will make a decision on final care at that time. Until then, we will fight!! We will press on! I'm asking God to give me, and all involved wisdom in making these decisions and looking ahead. We are going into some uncharted territory with these options and decision making so we need prayer!!

We will have a few immediate expenses I trust will be provided for… such as a portable bedside commode to travel with and new supplies at home.

I will leave you all to process this new information and pray for us with these choices we are making. Our hearts are so extremely heavy, but we are marching forward!!

God bless y'all!

June 17, 2021

We are still in Atlanta….LOTS OF PRAYERS are needed! Yesterday Stoney had a PlureX pump put in to relieve the fluid that keeps accumulating in his lungs. They drained 1.5 liters, which is twice as much as 12 days ago. After that procedure, Stoneys oxygen dropped and he is on 95-100% full high flow oxygen so the chances of us going home this weekend are a No-GO! In fact, we are at a point where we need some miracles OR complete peace. The next 24-48 hours are so incredibly crucial to where we go with Stoneys care once again. It has literally been a roller coaster!!! The emotions of the ups and downs are like gasping for air at times. Stoneys brother, mom and myself have shared lots of tears, and cried out to God to show us HIS perfect will and way!! I stayed all night with stoney last night and tonight, Don, is with him. It takes 3-4 people at times to move him and get him to the bedside commode. There has also been lots of "not making it to the bedside commode". The nurses and staff have been incredible through this as we've reached a new intimate relationship with them so to speak. Each of them share their love for stoney and our families and cover us in prayers and care.

We wait for the Lord to show the way….and it has felt like the wilderness at times. The goal? To press forward in keeping stoney comfortable, to tell him we love him and that God loves him and to encourage him to rest on the promises that we sang and read about for years.

I will have more information tomorrow I hope, but for now we have extended our stay through Monday! May the presence of God be ever so near and present!!

Thank you for following us on this journey and for sharing your love with and for us!! Strength for TODAY, and bright HOPE for TOMORROW!

While we arrive at this very critical moment in our cancer journey, I have struggled with how much to share about what went on behind the scenes. There was a battle that no one in social media world knew about that was going on because I chose not to share it. I have a war within my soul as what to share at this crossroad in my own personal story of the journey.

Will what I say make a difference, or hurt feelings, or harm friendships? I don't know… but, if I cant be honest with myself and share my heart, then I don't think I can fully grieve the way I intend to. Sharing our story, re-living our pain, is allowing me to release hurts, grief and sorrow. So, I will share, and hope for the best for whoever reads this.

While Stoney was receiving his plurex pump, I stayed in the room with Stoneys brother, Don. Don and I have been close for years, and there has never been an argument, or upsetting discussion that made either of us angry. We spent vacations together, watched movies, laughed and cried together. I had no hard feelings toward any of Stoneys family members for not being able to help me at any time. I knew it was easiest for me to be Stoneys caregiver because I could work from home. They loved me, and I loved them. We were one big family, and they gave me a platform to share my life with thousands of people in our years of ministry.

I have heard that grief brings out strange emotions in people, but I never thought it would happen within this family. While the room was empty, I shared my heart with Don. The doctors had thrown around hospice care, and asked me how I felt about it. The team of physicians caring for Stoney was about 80% in agreement for hospice, and about 20% for getting him back to Nashville in a care facility to see what happens. In my heart, I never wanted to agree to hospice, but if the hospitalist thought it was best, and that Stoney would be more comfortable in that environment, then of course I wanted that option for him. I did not want Stoney to suffer, or to be in this pain regardless of how he may have looked. I have come to the point in my life that when a human being is hooked up to fluids, IV's, they have drains to keep certain fluids out, and drains to put fluids in, then its not worth living anymore. How could anyone want to live like that, and how selfish are we to want them to live like that? Stoney was so swollen he couldn't walk, he could no longer clean himself up, so we were wiping him about 12-15 times a day, and cleaning large messes off the floor. He was having more accidents, and the control was gone. They were changing the beds several times a day, and mopping up the floors. There was no way I could manage this care at home, even if I had wanted to. We were doing things that I never dreamed I would be doing, and I would do it for the rest of my life if I had to. I loved Stoney, and I would have taken his place on this journey if I could have. That being said, I would never want him to live like a machine if he himself did not want to. I would stand by his side to the end of time. I think everyone knew that as they had watched our struggles from day one.

In that moment alone in the room, Don was expressing his emotions, and I tried to listen and understand where he was coming from, but I knew he was angry and I was taking it personally. Feelings were being put on display. I was biting my tongue, praying that I would not say something that I would regret. I was, at that moment, asking God to give me grace, and to show mercy. To be compassionate and kind. To be still and silent. The things that were being said felt like daggers in my heart, and those words began playing with my mind. I knew he was scared. I knew he was angry. I knew, because he told me. He was a brother losing his sibling, his heart was breaking and so was mine. He and Stoney were close, and they loved each other very much. I believe there was an emotion that had been harbored for many months, but I was just the one that happened to be in the room at the time. I began trembling, shaking, and then I bursted out into tears, and wrapped my arms around him. I did not know what to do, what to say. We both were losing one of the most important people in our lives, and we didn't know what to do, or how to respond, or even how to move forward. Ideas were being thrown around by so many people, and we didn't have time to process them respectively.

I am sharing this with you for the sheer purpose of love and forgiveness. As much as it hurt me, and yes I was angry for days, if not weeks for the accusations that were shot at me like flying arrows. My initial feeling was how could anyone say things to me after everything I had done, after giving up much of my life to care for someone I loved and appreciated. How could you question my care, my actions, and feelings after pouring out my heart and soul for over two and a half years? People say things in a moment of fear and anxiety, but I was human and had feelings that were valid, as did he. We were both losing someone, and our emotions were getting the best of us.

I fought off feelings of bitterness for weeks about how angry I was. God began to dig at me, while the devil fueled me. I knew that Stoney would never want discord within his family and myself. He loved everyone, and was the peacemaker in the family. He would want us to work it out, forgive and move on. And to be honest, I knew what I had been doing for Stoney was right, and the decisions I had made, were what needed to be done. He had made me power of attorney for a reason, and he left me in charge to handle all the big decisions, and I did not take that lightly. The nurses supported me and agreed with me. They continued to tell me they felt like I was being responsible with Stoneys care.

I put on a face and acted like things were fine, even though I felt like a wounded soldier. I would carry the heaviness and heartache quietly. I would struggle through the sorrow in the process of grieving. The fact is, God was going to take Stoney in His own time and there was nothing that Don, nor myself could do about it. Looking back, and seeing how it all played out, it was purely the divine power of God to see it all come together the way it did.

I can lay my head down at night knowing I have no regrets. I know that Don still loves me, and whatever bitterness he had against me has been laid to rest. Dealing with this stress had me so upset for the remaining weeks ahead in Stoneys care. I carried feelings of guilt and shame each day thinking I was wrong for all my decisions. I felt like maybe the family hated me, or felt like I was not doing all I could do anymore. Like I had given up on their son. I know today without a shadow of a doubt that they love me, appreciate me, and care for me. His mom and dad saw me hurt. His siblings saw my undying love, and I hope they believe in their hearts that I love each one of them. I never told Stoney the details of what went on in fear he may become upset and make his final days worse. I wanted him to believe that everything was alright and we were all going to be fine. Why give him something more to worry about?

June 20, 2021…

First of all… Happy Fathers Day to all the special dads, including mine up in heaven!! Secondly, I skipped posting a couple days cause I didn't know what to say. We have been on a real rollercoaster journey this past week especially as Stoneys care has been all over the place. Here is what I can share…

He is still awake and communicating with the help of pills, fluids, TPN, potassium, magnesium, and high flow oxygen. Without any of these things, it would be a very different story. On Thursday, the doctors and staff here thought it would be a good idea for Stoneys family to come down and see him. I believe this was a great idea. Through the weekend, his mom and dad, other brother and sister came down, his sister-in-law, his niece flew in from CA, his 2 best friends (one from Fl and one from Ca) came in, my mom and Liz were all here. It was nice for everyone to see him. To share memories, laugh and cry. Last night I had a great talk with Stoney for about 4 hours and we talked about everything and cried and shared lots of stories. He was coming to grip with what was going on. I told him I would support him 100% on whatever he chose. Doctors came in today and talked with family and Stoney has chosen to fight a little longer, to push a little harder, and so we will go on that journey with him. This means he will still be HERE in Atlanta. He cannot go home because of the oxygen issues, and I would need 24/7 care for him as well. So..I ask you to pray for direction, for peace, for grace and especially for STRENGTH!! I will not lie to you…I am beyond exhausted and I'm feeling it like I never have before but this is not the time for me to quit, so I'm gonna lace up my shoes and run a little further with him until he can't do it any longer.

We have a few expenses I would share that we need help with. The main one is the cost of hotel this coming week as I (and his brother Don) will need to stay here in town. We are switching shifts at the hospital so someone is with stoney 24/7. Also we had the expense of hotel for family this weekend… there is also food expense being here. We are just taking it a day at a time, trusting the Lord to provide our needs, equip us with the abilities we need each day to cope and process, and guide and lead the doctors in their decision making daily.

Please continue to pray as we walk through a very difficult valley. I cannot share many other details, and I don't need to, but I would ask that you pray God cover us with protection, peace and strength more than ever before. I'm finding it harder to breathe but I know who supplies the air I need!

June 23, 2021….

It is 2:00 in the morning and I am on the overnight shift here at the center with Stoney. We've been taking turns so that Stoney is not alone, because he has felt scared and hasn't want to be left alone. The room is dark, the TV is on, Stoney is sleeping and I am trying to get some travel work done, as during the day I am met with physician consultations, updates, Stoneys needs, etc.... As I try to write an update tonight, I find myself at a loss for words because its been a strange few days. One night a few days ago, I had a talk with Stoney about death and if he understood what was going on, and where things were headed because the staff wanted me to try and see where he was at emotionally with it all. He didn't seem to realize that we were out of options at that point. In the days that followed, his family came to visit, shared special memories, good laughs and encouraged him to fight for life, and we have seen a spark in Stoney that we haven't seen in awhile. He is pushing himself to walk to the bathroom for the first time in 2 weeks, he is taking his pills when they come, trying to make himself eat better, etc... He is still on high flow oxygen, but they have been able to reduce it each day a little. He is still on TPN and labs shift from day to day, and he still has a cancer that can no longer be treated, but he is still trying to LIVE! ...and who can blame him for that?

Part of me wonders if its a last minute rally, and another part of me wonders is it a miracle that God is giving us? I ride this wave of anger, and anxiety, then hope and excitement. If I allow myself to think things will go back to normal like it was before (which NO one feels will happen here at the center) I feel like I will have my heart broken if that plan fails. But what if I am not trusting God to do what so many people are praying for? Is my faith not big enough? Do I allow myself the chance to be hurt again, or believe that God can do what He said He can do. I have this wall up where I am trying not to get hurt, but yet am I not allowing God to show me how BIG He is? Stoneys brother, Don, is with me (along with my mom and friend Debra) and we hear 2-3 different doctors say different things. No one seems to be on the same page, or if they are, they don't all agree on the same thing or on the pathway moving forward. The nurses here have followed me for the past 2 1/2 years and have seen the ups and downs of this adventure and are seeing the toll it is taking on this weary body of mine. They have given me hugs, lifted me up with encouraging words, and given me the push I need each day. I have just been so anxious lately because I have wanted to know whats NEXT???? The verse of the day for me started with "Wait on the Lord..." A simple but difficult word.... I have told you before, I am impatient!!! WAIT is NOT in my vocabulary. But.... I am trying to realize that if God has a plan (which HE does) I cannot change it no matter how badly I want to. Do I want this journey to be over... selfishly yes, I do. (it would be a lie if said otherwise) Do I want to Stoney to leave us all? NO, I want him to be healed and enjoy many more days! Do I want God to have His perfect Will and Way?? Absolutely! However....that means I have to WAIT! We have these moments to enjoy with Stoney while he is here, and we must find a way to live in these moments with joy, because the day will come when he won't be here and I have no idea when thats going to be. I am a planner... I want the next 2 days, 2 weeks, 2 months all planned out, but thats not what God says.... He says "wait"....I will probably fail at some point,(many times even) but I am trying to honestly learn to wait and be silent and listen to what the Lord says, and follow what I am suppose to do... even if that means us being here longer than I want to.

There is a strong chance Stoney could pass here....there is also a strong chance Stoney could get to a rehab center in Nashville and work on getting stronger, and a chance he could even go home. BUT....we must WAIT and see what God decides to do. We have been thrown so many curve balls this past week, and I am SOOOO EXHAUSTED! I find the strength that I need each day and it somehow gets me through, because I know so many people are praying and I find such comfort in that.

We have extended our hotel for another week while we continue to make a schedule for Stoneys care. Day shift and Night shift... Until he is no longer afraid to be alone and not a fall risk.

We will take a day at a time, trust the Lord, and WAIT.....

"Wait on the Lord: be of good courage, and HE shall strengthen thine heart: wait I say, on the Lord." - Psalm 27:14 -NIV

One of my favorite music gospel music artist, is the Martins. I have listened to them for probably 25 years, and its strange how every time I see them on TV or see an album, they never change. They still looked the same as they did when I first started listening. They sing a song that I fell in love with one night while I was watching them on TV. As I listened to the words, the tears began streaming down my face. The song was called The Promise, and the lyrics to the chorus took my breath away….

Chorus 1: *Cause you know I made a promise that I intend to keep*
My grace will be sufficient in every time of need
My love will be the anchor that you can hold onto
This is the promise, this is the promise I made to you
Chorus 2: Cause you know I made a promise that I've prepared a place
And some day sooner than you think you'll see me face to face
And you'll sing with the angels and a countless multitude
This is the promise, this is the promise I've made to you

This song just hit a chord with me, because I was living the Promise. God was taking care of us. He was giving me peace, and growing my strength, I just couldn't see it as clearly as He could. His GRACE was sufficient in all my times of need. His love was my anchor that I was clinging to. Every word He promised was TRUE! I knew Stoney was going to be taking his heavenly journey soon, and I know that heaven is a REAL place. I knew that very soon, he would be enjoying all the benefits of heaven, and standing face to face with the Savior. WOW! What a moment, singing, rejoicing, proclaiming the Worthiness of the God we had sung about for year, and now he would be there. I was starting to get jealous!… and I had the promise that God was going to continue to take care of me.

June 25, 2021…

Last night I stayed with Stoney all night and we watched the Game Show network, Friends and some animal planet. He talks when he wants, and I listen. He wants so badly to be home, to be healed and to live life again. We don't know what God has for us right now but what we do know, is that He loves us!! The care at CTCA has been extraordinary and I am so grateful for our time here the past 2 and a half years. Now we have a new adventure that lays ahead… CTCA no longer has any treatment that can be done, and because of that they can no longer keep us here. So, today Stoney had a plurex put in his belly where they are draining fluids now from his lung and his stomach. They are filling up very quickly, and this allows him to be comfortable and not have to get anything new once arriving in Nashville. He had 8 liters drained last week, and 6 liters drained today off his belly, 350 CC every few days off the lung. He came through the procedure fine and now they are just monitoring him.

The next step now…a transfer is in place to move him by ambulance from here to a Long Term Acute Care Home in Nashville so he can be closer to home and have more time with family. This fee is $1200, and we will have to pay up front on Monday for the ambulance.

They will move him Monday around noon or Tuesday morning based on bed availability in Nashville. We will just keep following the plan and see what God has next for Stoney. He is on many rounds of pain meds, but still has a FIGHT left in him that is bigger and stronger than anything I've ever seen. I admire him… Please pray as I continue to work closely with CTCA and the care home in Nashville to make this a seamless transition for stoney. We will be saying a final goodbye to all our friends here in Atlanta, and to be honest, I'm not ready for that! They have been my family, and I love them all so very much!! Each one of them has blessed my heart in some special way and I just am so grateful for the time we've been here!

Thank you for your prayers, and please continue to pray that the transfer needs are met this weekend so we can get home. Looking forward to being closer to home, and having a lot less expenses from there. Thankful that insurance is covering more than we thought, and so blessed that God is opening and closing doors along the way to show us exactly what to do!!

Keep praying and have a great weekend!!

June 28, 2021…

I have waited a few days to post, because everything has been stable in a sense.

I have signed paperwork for the hospital transfer. I have worked with CTCA to arrange the ambulance to move him either tomorrow sorry Wednesday now. They are waiting on a bed to open up in Nashville. Stoney has been in more pain, is taking more pain meds and sleeping around the clock. We thankfully raised the money to get him moved, thanks to all of you!!! I am beyond grateful!! Until then, we again, WAIT on the Lord for His perfect Will and Way!! God knows my heart, He knows my wishes and desires, and I'm trusting Him to continue to guide us… keep praying that the Lord will wrap us up and give us the strength we need to press on!! So much love to you all!!

Why Should I feel discouraged? Why Do the shadows come?
Why does my heart feel lonely, and long for heaven my home.
When Jesus is my portion. A constant friend is He….
His eye is on the sparrow, and I know He watches me….

June 30, 2021…

Just thought I would share a brief update! We are still in Atlanta. We are waiting for the facility in Nashville to have an available bed. If we don't get one by Friday, apparently there will be an insurance glitch and they'll have to resubmit for approval. So in the meantime, mom and Debra and I are here with stoney taking care of him and being his company. He is also being showered with love from the nurses, our friends Robert and Joyce Hayes. I was also able to see my dear friend Ashley and her friend Kristen! It's been an emotional and busy week. I will say this… we've been on an emotional rollercoaster this week with decision making, and indecisiveness. Yesterday, I had my first major melt down and went back to the hotel to take a "mental health day". Today, I was blessed with goodies from Ashley & Kristen (donuts and cupcakes) before they left to go home. Then, our friends Robert & Joyce took mom and I to dinner and we shared good laughs and lots of memories. God knew just what I needed today. My friend Debra has been here pitching in and helping me around the clock, along with my mom who has given me a huge amount of mental support!! This journey is spinning right now, and we don't know what's next. Stoney is on a PCA pump (for pain) and is having fluid drained everyday. Some days he is really good mentally, and other days he's clouded and confused. All I know is that I have to put one foot in front of the other and take it a day at a time. Praying for God to do what He's always done… love us, guide us, protect us and provide for us. We live in HOPE!! Please pray for us…for me… I am weary and continue to lean on Jesus and my friends for support! :) Love you all!!

The situation with Stoneys medical treatments had come to an end. There was nothing more to be done, and now we were waiting and watching. The choice of survival was in Stoneys hands, as well as the hand of the Almighty. Stoney would refuse his medicine, and push food away.

During this time I would have been lost without the support of my mom, our friend Debra, and of course Liz who came when she could. Debra had just moved from California to Oklahoma and was between jobs, so she flew to Atlanta to help me care for Stoney. Debra works in the medical field so she was no stranger to all of the nasty details and what it takes to care of a patient. She would put her gloves on, and help me clean Stoney up. She would help me clean up his messes and stay all night so he would not be alone. I had truly been blessed with some incredible friends in my lifetime, but now they were shining stars. It was humbling for Stoney to have people take him to the bathroom and to clean him up; however, there was no choice. They were understaffed at CTCA at the time, and he needed 24 hour care. He was more care than what they had time for. They knew that, we knew that, and Stoney knew that. We took shifts in staying with him all night. When Don was there, we rotated the evenings and the days, and when Debra arrived, she jumped right in. Given that most of the doctors needed to talk to me, I would try to go back to the hotel for a just a few hours of a nap, and come back to get the report. I tried to be in 2 places at once for as much as I could.

Amy, one of the discharge nurses, was calling me everyday to keep me posted on beds in Nashville. Facilities that would take him. His levels and care was changing so often that insurance changed their minds on what they would offer. Secretly, Amy and I prayed that if God would allow, Stoney would stay at the center in Atlanta and pass peacefully. I wanted him to be there, the nurses who loved him wanted him to be there, and ultimately it was Stoneys choice, and he wanted to be there. God heard our cry. He knew our hearts.

Thursday, July 1, 2021….

Looks like we are here for the weekend in Atlanta. No beds available in Nashville until Monday. We will be moved based on ambulance schedule, so could be Tuesday since Monday is an observed holiday. Taking it a day at a time. Tonight I'm feeling frustrated, and in an emotional cloud. So many things I want to say, but what's the point. Like my mom always says, some things are better left unsaid. After being on this journey for 2 1/2 years and seeing all the things I've seen, experiencing first hand the ups and downs, the emotions…. I have no regrets. It has stretched me, taught me, and showed me so many things about who I am. I've never been too scared to run away from it, but I have become so emotionally attached that I can't hide from it. I've been hurt by some on the journey, but I've stood my ground, and I've stood behind Stoney 100% pushing him to fight as long as he wanted. I have nothing to prove, nothing to argue, and I've been honest the whole time about where we are on this journey, and I will continue. The reality of the situation is grim, but the outcome of the journey is beautiful and glorious, and the race will be finished well. You all have been supportive and lifted us up more than I could have ever imagined. You have even gone far beyond in your kind words to comparing me to some Bible heroes, however, I am just a vessel being used, nothing more. It has been an honor caring for the most amazing friend I've ever had! He told me today that every time I go to Disney from now on, I have to save him a seat…that I can and will do! I'm no longer afraid of the days ahead on this journey because I'm so secure in knowing Gods plan and picture is so much bigger and better. While we are here, we live and love each day. We give God the glory in all things like we have, and trust Him in the needs for tomorrow. We thank and praise Him for the blessings and the memories we share. While my mind is heavy on the details that lay ahead, I am comforted to know that today we have all we need and I'm surrounded by people I love.

I am blessed to have a support team here on social media who has followed us, prayed for us and given to us on our emotional rollercoaster journey!! I'd be lost without your love! Have a Happy 4th of July weekend, and pray for us as we continue pressing on!! Until Monday….

Have a happy 4th? How could we ourselves go into this weekend with joy and peace, knowing that the end was soon coming for someone we loved so dearly. That weekend my heart was angry, bitter, cold, yet joyful, kind and longing for relief. How could one hold all of these emotions at the same time? How could my heart feel so many things? I wanted Stoney to be healed, but obviously that wasn't coming. I wanted him to be set free, but I didn't want to say goodbye. That weekend the nurses were so kind and so good to me. They loved on me and our family. They surrounded us with so much gratitude. Thanking us…WHAT? WHY? We should be thanking them! Their around the clock care for one of the greatest human beings in the world was astonishing to me. BUT thats why…The were grateful, and thankful for the kindness that Stoney showed to them. Thankful for his temperament, his love and hospitable spirit. He loved on them everyday. He managed to smile through pain on some days just to show them he cared. The nurses saw that, they were touched by him. I can still see their faces as they worked that weekend knowing very well he was in his final days.

July 2, 2021….

I wasn't going to post until Monday, but we've had some news and a change of plan I wanted to share with you all so you can be in prayer. (Even more than usual). Since yesterday was the last day of the insurance approval for the facility in Nashville, they had to re-certify the decision today. After receiving all the information from the past week, Stoneys health showed too much of a decline and insurance denied him the long term care. Because he is now on a PCA pain pump, as well as declining labs, and draining more fluid, there is no long term care facility that will work with us. He is considered only as a Hospice patient at this time. So, we will be staying here in Atlanta until Tuesday, and then they will search for a hospice facility close to home. He will come off all his TPN and extra fluids, and be close to family in his final days. Due to the cancer spreading, there is no other options at this point. Please be in prayer for Stoney as he is processing this news, and for his family and myself as we move forward with this information. In the meantime, we are going to spend lots of time listening to music, watching tv and sharing memories.

Our hearts are heavy but praising the Lord that His arms are open wide and waiting!

As time was running out, I don't think I had fully processed all that was going on, and that July 4th would be the last coherent day for Stoney. Don, and his daughter Rachel had a wonderful visit with Stoney. His nephew Taylor, and his wife had a visit the previous day. Stoney was talkative, and yet quiet if thats possible. It was on July 4th in the afternoon that Stoney chose to withhold the fluids, the pills, and any medical treatment. He was choosing to go on his own hospice. Partly, we had decided that together that it was time. And partly because if there was any chance for him to pass in Atlanta at the care center, now was the time. They would not move him if he was unstable, and he would not last long once he made the decision to hold. His nephrologist said, 3-5 days. His body was only functioning because of everything they were giving him. Without any piece of it, he would not hold.

That night, we were watching the PBS 4th of July special in the background. Each once of us got a few moments to talk with Stoney in the room. Debra would sit next to him and he would share memories with her. Liz would sit next to him, and he would share special memories with her. Then mom. My mom struggled so deeply. She would go in the room with him, and do everything she could not to weep. She would stand behind him and pet his head, his shoulders with tears streaming down her face. She loved Stoney as another son, and losing him was breaking her heart. Since Sharon was not able to be with Stoney through this process, mom was fulfilling a role. She was also re-living the final days of losing my dad. Mom knew about death. She had lost her mom, her dad, her husband, and now an "adopted son". I remember Stoney leaning over to my mom and saying, "Paula, don't stop living. Don't stop traveling. Go and do it for me." I can still see my mom crying.

It was my turn. I tried to be tough, because I never wanted to be weak in front of Stoney. I was many times, but it was never my intentions and I always wanted him to know I was his warrior. He held my hand, he looked at me with eyes that looked like a puppy dog wanting something he couldn't have. I asked him if he was scared, and he said "no". I asked him if he was ready, and he said, "I don't think anyone is ever ready." I knew he wanted to stay and play, because he told me so. He told all the nurses that. He wanted to LIVE. He told me to make sure and go to the places we had planned. He told me to take care of his mom and dad. Then, he told me to REST. He said, "Beej, I know when I am gone, you are going to want to make plans, go on trips, and stay as active as you can. I want you to rest. Do you hear me?" Tears ran down my cheeks. I haven't rested in years. I don't even know how. Even to this day, I don't know what resting is, because there is always something to be done! One day, I will do what he wants me to, but for now, I can't.

He was getting tired, and now had been 6 hours without fluids, without medicine and I could tell he was ready to sleep. The phone rang, and he answered it. It was one of the younger nephews in the family calling to say goodbye. Stoney had the phone on speaker, and I could tell they didn't want to do much talking, but only hear their Uncle Stoneys voice once last time. Stoney talked, and engaged to an empty line and then told him he was tired and needed to hang up. One last "I love you".

Stoney told me he needed to go to the bathroom, so I ran over and cleared the way. Debra helped me get him on the toilet, and left the room while I stayed and talked with him. He looked at me with tears in his eyes and said, "I hurt so bad, I cant do this anymore". I started crying, and just acknowledged him. I wanted this pain and suffering to end. I now was being selfish in wanting him to have his heavenly healed body. Oh God, touch Him, or take Him I cried!

That night I laid in the hospital bed next to him, as he stayed in the recliner that he had slept in for 2 weeks. I put on Alice in Wonderland, his favorite Disney movie. I have only told a few people this story, but I will share it now publicly. I was asleep, and awoke to feel a breeze on my arm coming from the other side where Stoney was. It was like a feather going back and forth across my arm. I turned to make sure Stoney was ok, and he was asleep, but still breathing. I though, BJ stop dreaming! I turned back and tried to go to asleep again, and the same feeling happened on my arm. There was no vent blowing air, there was no window open. I turned and looked again and Stoney opened his eyes and looked at me, and then closed them. It was the strangest feeling and I don't know what it was, but I can make an assumption. I know that angels are around us. I know they are real, and I know they come to usher those passing up into heaven. I don't know if I was feeling the brush of angel wings watching over Stoney waiting for God to say, "Bring him home", or if I was imagining something. I don't know if Stoney felt it, or just happened to open his eyes at the same time I looked at him. I felt what I felt, and I know it was real and I will believe what I want to….

July 5, 2021….

I hope many of you had a good 4th of July holiday and even enjoying more time today. This weekend was really difficult, as Stoney made the choice to start comfort care earlier. He is in so much pain all over, and is so tired of fighting. With his puppy dog eyes looking at me the other night he said, "this is going to get worse isn't it?" What does one say to that? I told him, Yes unfortunately, but we will do everything to keep him comfortable to his last breath. They stopped all the fluids, all the pills, all the life lines… and just have pain meds dripping now. His brother, Don and nephew & niece Taylor and Rachel were able to spend some quality time with him. We have cried more in the last 2-3 days than we have in a very long time!! Through it all, God has been good! Last night, I stayed with Stoney all night and I had Disney movies playing in the background. Neither of us slept much but that's ok… he didn't want to be left alone. Today, he sleeps more and has increased pain meds running. His time on this earth is coming to an end, but HEAVEN is coming and there will be no more time to worry about. He told us he was just getting a head start :)

The next few days are going to be brutal, but praise Jesus we have His hope, strength, peace and comfort to carry us through. It is not looking like Stoney will be able to transfer to Nashville at all at this time, so we will remain here for now. Quite frankly, we are all ok with that!! This is where his journey started, so how perfectly fitting, it will be where it ends! The entire place here LOVE stoney (and myself) so much and I know we will be surrounded by more love than we can imagine. Please pray for Gods mercy on Stoney. That there will be no suffering or pain in this process. Quick and peaceful! As I work ahead on plans to have him moved back to our hometown, and what comes next, I ask you to lift us all up in prayers….Tracy, Sharon, Forrest, Don, Florence (and their family) and myself as we work through this difficult time. We will keep folks updated as much as we can. May we feel an abundance of peace that we never have before, and may Stoney be wrapped in the loving arms of His Heavenly Father for eternity!

On July 5th, Debra had stayed the night with Stoney and said he didn't communicate much, other than some mumbling. He had been in bed now for over 18 hours without moving, and his bowels had come to stop. On his last trip to the bathroom, he had left a dark tar movement, which gave the nurses warning we were in the final hours. When I arrived the morning of the 6th, Debra had warned me that his breathing had changed. I arrived early, and when I walked in the room I was mortified to hear his breathing to say the least. I was almost like I wanted to cover my ears and scream. He had the famous, "death rattle" that everyone talks about. If you have ever walked the valley of death with someone, then you know what I am talking about. It can be loud, and then it gets even louder. All I could do was shed tears, as I knew what was coming, but knew where he was going. I texted mom and Liz knowing they were on their way over so that Debra could take a nap. When they arrived my mom looked at me with fear. She knew… I was playing "Music of The Dartts" on Stoneys phone and it was going through all of their albums in order from earliest recordings to later. It still amazes me listening through the songs, how many of them about heaven featured Stoney as lead vocalist. He was singing about his new home for years, not knowing he would reach it before any of us.

His assigned nurse for the day was also named Liz and one of our many favorites. She was now just a part of our family. She kept coming in and checking on us and was giving Stoney more morphine to keep him comfortable and to help with his breathing. As the nurses came by to check on me and to see Stoney, they all had tears in their eyes. They loved him, and they hated to see him go. They had told us we were their favorite patients, and we had changed their lives. Stoney had brought them joy, and the feelings were mutual as they filled our hearts with love.

I was on facebook looking at some posts, when my mom said, "BJ, its time." I got up from the chair and went to his side. I held his hand, and my mom took his other hand. Our friend, Liz stood by his side and we prayed. We spoke to him, we loved him and we told him he would be missed and loved. His breathing had slowed down, and with each gasp we wondered if it was his last. The grip he had on my hand was so tight. He knew it was me. I believe that. I stood up, I kissed his forehead, and I said, "Give daddy a hug for me, I love you". He took once last breathe, and he was gone. We watched for him to take another big gulp of air, but he was gone. Nurse Liz, put her hand on my shoulder, and whispered, "he's gone. He's off the monitor". I just broke down. All the emotions I had held just came rushing out like a gush. I was shaking as I was holding the lifeless hand of my best friend in the entire world. I had stood by him, I had cared for him, I had loved him and now he was gone. My mom said, "BJ, look at his eyes…" Stoney had tears from his eyes coming down his cheeks on both sides. I felt like I couldn't breathe. I felt like I was paralyzed. I looked at my hand, still wrapped in his with a grip. As I shook, I pushed his hand off of mine and buried my head in his blanket, but felt the most comforting spirit I have ever felt. I knew in that moment, people were praying because we asked them to. I knew that Stoney was there, somehow looking over me, and giving me Peace to get up and do the next thing.

I stood up and hugged our beautiful, loving, caring nurse, Liz. I felt like in just the one hug, she was hugging me with a thousand arms. She was so special to Stoney and I, right from the day we met her in December 2020. She had now witnessed Stoney being ushered into the arms of the Almighty, and had developed an attachment to our family.

Then, I had to do what no one wants to do… I called each member of the family to tell them their son and brother had passed away. I heard each of them weep on the phone, and I did my best to keep it together. I told them I loved them and we would be getting things together and starting the trip home. A new chapter was being written in each of our lives. Stoney was gone too soon, but he will never be forgotten, for his legacy lives on!

July 6, 20201….

"Absent from the body is to be PRESENT with the Lord". Stoney passed this morning at 10:35 listening to his family singing "Count on the Shepherd" on his phone. Lots of tears but rejoicing as well. No more suffering. No more cancer! He is whole again!!

I told him to give my dad a big hug and took his hand, and with one last breath, he was gone. Pray for us as we make arrangements and move forward.

God is GREAT and GREATLY to be praised, even in sorrow!

12

Lifting Up Time

Ecclesiastes 3:1-8 - "There is a time for everything, and a season for every activity under the heavens: a time to be born and a time to die, a time to plant and a time to uproot, a time to kill and a time to heal, a time to tear down and a time to build, a time to weep and a time to laugh, a time to mourn and a time to dance, a time to scatter stones and a time to gather them, a time to embrace and a time to refrain from embracing, a time to search and a time to give up, a time to keep and a time to throw away, a time to tear and a time to mend, a time to be silent and a time to speak, a time to love and a time to hate, a time for war and a time for peace."-NIV

The moments following Stoneys passing were almost a blur. After making the calls to the family, I sent the girls back to the hotel to back up the suitcases and start loading the cars. Since we didn't know from day to day when Stoney was going to be making his heavenly journey, we were basically living out of suitcases waiting for the time to come.

I remember feeling hollow. I remember not wanting to do the next, but I knew it was necessary. Once the girls left, nurse Liz came back in the room and asked me if I needed anything. I told her I was fine, and we were just waiting on the local funeral home to come and prepare the body for transportation to Nashville. I stayed in the room with a body of the most amazing person I had the privilege of knowing. I tried not to stare, but it was impossible. I had never been in a room with a dead body before. I could see the color had faded, this skin had fallen around his eyes and cheeks. Lifeless. All I wanted to imagine, was Stoney sitting up in the bed with his fedora on smiling back on me, and instead I was looking an empty shell removed from this world. He had his red shirt on that I put on him over the holiday weekend. Nurse Liz had propped his head up and pulled the pillow in so he looked presentable. I was alone in the room, with a racing mind. I could not make myself get use my phone, because all I wanted to do was stare. I sat on the little loveseat by the window and wanted to cry, but I couldn't. I stared a little longer from a distance and wanted to know what it must have been like. Those were thoughts running through my busy mind. What did he see? Who did he see first? Was my dad there to greet him, or his grandmother he loved so much? Did he fall into the arms of Jehovah, Abba, our Father? In that flicker, that last breath, what did he experience or feel? I wanted to know!

One of the sweet ladies who was on the cleaning team, but had taken time off, asked if she could come in. Of course I said, yes, but I really wanted to be alone with him a little longer. She didn't stay very long, giving me my space, but wanted to assure me that she knew where he was. The past few days, people had come into the room to see him, but now there was a presence of sadness and the traffic had stopped. Liz kept coming in to check on me, and if I had my way I would have told her to come in and sit with me just so I wasn't alone. She had been with Stoney for so long, and I felt like she was a part of my family and I knew she wanted to weep with me. She had other patients on the hall to take care of that day, and I have no idea how she did it. I could never have had the strength to work a floor after watching someone you had grown to love die before your eyes.

The coroner came, and rolled in the bed with the famous body bag. He unzipped, and I just couldn't stay in the room any longer. I had seen it in the movies, and on crime shows, but to be standing in a room, where they unzip the bag and prepare to put someone in it is an out of body experience. I knew what was going to happen next, and I could not handle to watch. I asked if I could say goodbye one last time, knowing he was gone and couldn't hear or see me. Knowing it was an empty shell. I kissed his head and as I walked away, Liz met me at the door for one final hug. As I embraced her in that moment, I knew I would see her again. I knew just because we were leaving didn't mean our friendship was completed. This was a bond that would remain precious to us and our family for years to come. She asked me if I knew when the funeral services would be (which

I did, since I had already been thinking about what happens next the previous day), and said she wanted to come. I had never known a nurse or care team to come to a funeral of one of their patients, especially over 5 hours away. I didn't think much of it at the time, but told her I would send her all the details. Finally she said, "do you think at some point I could ever have one of his fedora's as a memory?" To me, I was honored she would ask, and I know if Stoney was still breathing he would have given the one he had. I assured her, I would make sure she had one!

I went down to my car, and as I walked down the hallway from the elevator, my heart just sank. All these people we had met over the past 2 years, that made a difference in our lives, I may never see again. Sure, we say "come visit us in Nashville", but do people ever do that? Not many. I made my way to the front, and my dear friends who had welcomed me each and every day (Mark and Saundra) gave me hugs and said their final goodbyes. I crawled into the front seat of my car and gripped the steering wheel and just wept. I think I could have filled a lake. I looked at my phone, and it was blowing up. Messages from people all around the globe sharing their love and kindness to me, sharing their gratitude for all I had done. I must have had 50 or more text messages, plus 30 or more Facebook messages, emails were pouring in…I became so overwhelmed I couldn't even look at them or read them at the time. My goal was to load up, and get home. It had been 5 plus weeks since I had seen my house, slept in my bed or fixed a decent cup of coffee. I just wanted to walk into the house and collapse.

After I composed myself, I drove just half a mile to the hotel, and met the girls, who were all packed and ready to go. Mom was going to drive home with Liz, and Debra was going to drive me home so I could handle correspondence. I wanted to respond to all of the messages, as well as begin preparations for the service since I knew several people who wanted to come, lived far away.

Being a passenger that day in the car thinking about what all had happened, the empty days that laid ahead was overwhelming. I turned on some of my favorite music from the Gaither Vocal band. The songs that played one after another were songs of heaven, loss, grief, pain and joy. They covered all of my emotions with their music. I would let the tears stream down my face, and tell Debra, "He is there! He is face to face with the One who created him, who we sung about." I just couldn't stop thinking about it or believing it. How had all of this happened so quickly in one sense, and yet so incredibly long in another. Processing the events of the last 2 months was something I was struggling wrapping my mind around. I tried to close my eyes and just pray. Pray for God to reach down inside of me, and flip a switch to press on. To remember "He whom I have believed, and am persuaded that He is able" to do abundantly and exceedingly great things. I prayed that God would bring back every verse, every song, every quote and every sermon that I had ever heard, to minister to my broken heart at this time. I begged God to touch me, and to use me going forward.

I knew work on the service needed to get started, so one of the first calls I made was to Wendell Calder, a family member, a pastor, a friend. I called him and told him Stoney had passed, but he had heard the news from my mom and his granddaughter. He shared how proud he was of me and wanted to know if there was anything he could do. I said, "yes, as a matter a fact there is". Stoney loved Wendell, and always enjoyed our weeks or weekends at camp when we would sing and he would speak. I grew up listening to Wendell, and have called him "Uncle" as long as I can remember. I could not think of anyone else to speak at Stoneys home going service. Stoney and I had talked privately a few nights before he passed about what he might like at his service. He chose songs, and thought it would be nice if Wendell could preach, but knew he was a busy man with a busy schedule. Wendell assured me he would move (even cancel) plans so that he could be there for me, and honor Stoney.

I called the funeral home, and talked to the director about dates. I knew people were coming from out of state, and I knew it would be expensive for many coming from far away. As I looked at the calendar, I just laughed. I knew there was only one date that would work for us, and it would be July 17. For those of you who may remember in the opening paragraph of the book, Stoney was a Disney fan, and there was no better way I could honor him by having the home going service on Disneyland's birthday. Disneyland opened July 17, 1955 and Stoney cherished the theme park, holding an annual pass for as long as I can remember. We both attended Disneyland's 50th birthday celebration in 2005, and so the date was just perfect. I asked Abigail if that date would work and she said it would. They don't like to do services any further out than that, but it shouldn't be a problem. Now I had 11 days to prepare a service that would honor my best friend.

Stoney had left me in charge of all his final affairs, so I made plans to meet the staff at the funeral home upon arriving home. I asked Stoneys mom, Sharon, to go with me so she could make any decisions that I might have missed. I also didn't want her to have any regrets about not having any say in the planning process.

Stepping back into the funeral home was surreal. Just 5 years prior to this moment, I was doing the same things for my dad who had passed with Lewy Body Dementia. This time though I was making different plans, and it was ripping my heart out. Stoney told me he wanted to be buried in his Haunted Mansion shirt, and a fedora. He said he wanted to be "fun uncle Stoney", not "stage Stoney". As much as I cringed at that request, I fulfilled it. Abigail, another Disney lover, thought it was the best idea. She thought it was just great that he was being buried on Disneyland's birthday, and the theming would be around one of her favorite attractions as well. The preparations seemed to go smoothly. I didn't care at the time how much it cost, I just wanted it to be perfect.

I called our friend, Ronnie Booth, to sing and he accepted. Actually, I called his wife, Kim, and she said he would do it. Same thing. haha! I called our friends in California, The Henry Family, and they said they would work on flying in for the service to sing. Later, we found out that the whole family couldn't come, but Amanda would come and sing the song Stoney had request, "I Call it Home."

My friend Debra stayed with me at the house so I would not be alone. The first time entering the house alone was not bad, because I wasn't truly alone. I had Debra. Later, I would find the first night in the house alone, was torture. But for now, she was there with me keeping the mood light and mind on peaceful things. She helped get dinner ready, clean up, and help with all the arrangements that were coming ahead. She was offered a new job through all of this, so she had to fly back to Oklahoma for a few days to start work, leaving me alone. My mom Liz lived next door, and I knew if I needed anything I could call. I needed to start my new life alone at some point so, now was the time. Debra was only gone for a few days before returning for the weekend of the service. In the meantime I kept myself busy by making 12 cheesecakes. Stoney's favorite dessert was cheesecake, and he loved mine. So I made, Key lime, lemon-blueberry, coffee, coconut almond joy, pineapple and original with fruit topping. It kept me busy, as each one takes about 4 hours start to finish and I could only do one at a time. I tried using my moms over to move things along, and we found our her over was off by about 50 degrees. When I went to pop open the springform pan, the cheesecake fell apart and leaked all over the counter top. I was so mad, but I just threw it away and started over.

The weeks following Stoneys death, I couldn't sleep. I was going to bed at 2 in the morning, and waking up at 7 or earlier. It was not normal for me, but I couldn't help it. I felt like God was allowing me to accomplish more things in the day. I knew I was not listening to what Stoney had told me to do (REST) but I could not help it. There was too much to do.

I had phone calls, and emails from people from all over letting me know they were driving or flying in for the service. Some were great friends of mine, and others family members of the Dartts. I decided to plan a huge dinner the night before the service for just those who were traveling in from long distances to allow them ample time to visit with Tracy and Sharon. I knew that Saturday would be so busy, and visiting would be limited.

When I make up something in mind to do, I do it. I had decided that I was going to cook for all 35 people, and set the funeral home's banquet room as the venue. I had friends who could help me decorate, but I was going to do the cooking. I am not trying to brag, but Stoney always told me I was his favorite cook, and I know now he was lying, but I thought I would humor him by preparing this meal. I planned the menu, and began preparations earlier in the week before folks started arriving. Along with making 12 cheesecakes, I had now added BBQ pork, chicken, loaded mashed potatoes, jalapeño mac & cheese and side salads. I enjoyed the work. It kept my mind off from going to darker places. It gave me satisfaction, and made me happy that I was doing something for Stoney. I think when you are a caregiver for so long, and then the journey stops, you crave purpose. I felt like I had lost my purpose now that Stoney was gone, and I needed something to give me joy and fulfillment.

As early as Thursday July 15th, people began traveling in. I had blocked hotel space at a couple of our hotels in town, and arranging some airport runs for several friends and family members. I was approving proofs from the funeral home, sending pictures, arranging the schedule for the big day, and more. I kept telling everyone I wanted it to be perfect, and people warned me to rest and that it will all work out the way it was suppose to. That phrase drives me insane! No, it's not all going to work out the way its suppose to unless I make it happen that way. I am a die-hard planner. I work hard, and focus on details to make sure it all goes well. If there is a crack in the road, I have cement and roller to cover it up. I couldn't imagine anything less for this day.

The morning of July 17th had arrived. I did not want to face the day. I made coffee, and was getting ready to leave when I asked Debra if we actually had to go. She said, "I'm afraid so…" We did not have a viewing the night before like most families do. Stoney didn't want it that way, and I hated viewings, so we agreed. I arrived with Debra, and Amanda Henry to the funeral home early as requested by the director. I was given the opportunity to go in and see him before others had arrived, and I honestly didn't know if I was ready for this moment. I had been with him alone in the room at the center for an hour after he had passed and this shouldn't have been much different. But, it was. There is something different about seeing a loved one in a casket. I dealt with this before, when we had my dads service there. Walking into a room, and seeing the casket before you at a distance, the appearance of their head on the pillow from afar. It feels like the longest walk you will ever make just to approach them.

With Debra on one side, and Amanda on the other, we walked up and paid our respects. I started to tremble, and heard Amanda say over and over again, "it's not him, it's not him". I am so glad they were both with me, because I am not sure I could have done that alone. As I looked at him laying there with his fedora on, haunted mansion shirt, and plastic looking face, I realized, "This really isn't him." I knew that, I did, but in that moment your brain and heart play a game. This broken shell, still swollen, still full of disease was actually perfected and healed. I just couldn't seen the new body. I wanted to stay forever, and gaze at him and reminisce all our memories, but I also wanted to remove myself from the room and its sorrowful atmosphere. The family was arriving, and the viewing was private for family and friends. I stood in the corner of the room in a fog. I know people were talking to me, and I most likely answered them, but I was somewhere else. I was thinking about the last time I had a conversation with him, the last time I heard him laugh, or say, "BEEEEEEEEJ...." I tried not to be critical of the terrible way he looked. No one looks good after they pass, which is why I don't like viewings or open caskets. I told mom if she's still alive when I die, and has to do plan my service, to find some good looking guy, stick him in the casket and tell him to wink at people every now and then just for fun.

I listened to the sounds of people's voices getting louder as more were in the room. I saw people cry, I saw some laugh as they shared memories or greeted each other with a hug. I saw despair on some faces, and joy on others. I had many things on my mind, and yet nothing mattered. I was awaiting the service, and yet wishing it would never come time. I've only experienced those moments a few instances in my life when everything is so present, yet so distant at the same time. It's as if you can see everything happening, but you aren't really there. I don't know if that makes sense, or if anyone else has experienced it. Maybe I'm the only weird one. I had asked our Pastor to open the service and share some thoughts. He pulled me over to discuss what he was going to say, and I remember crying. I don't know why at the time, but probably all of the emotions hitting me and knowing we were about to sit through a very emotional funeral.

I had found out just days before the service that 4 of the nurses from the Cancer center were coming up to attend. I broke into tears just knowing that they were coming, and wanted to share their love with Stoney and myself. One surprise that I was not prepared for, was Stoneys naturopath physician drove up and attended. There was just so much love in one place, that even now I am getting emotional thinking about it. The flowers, the hugs, the cards, the kind words. All so special, and yet humbling.

It was now time... The funeral director lined us up. I would walk in with Sharon on my arm. Stoneys dad was in a wheelchair and an usher would push him down in front of us, and behind the casket. Sharon had a bad hip, so she held my arm in one hand and her cane in the other. The remaining family members were all behind us, and I was not ready to walk the aisle had done just 5 years ago behind my dads casket with MY mom on my arm. The music we had chosen as the processional was my dad singing, "Finally Home." This was also the same song played as mom and I walked in for his service. Memories were flashing back, scenes in my mind were playing out like a movie. As we entered a room full of people, I stared at my feet. I did not want to look at anyone's faces, as I knew I would fall apart at a moments notice. We sat in the front row and the service began.

From Pastor Michaels opening of 1 Timothy 1:16, "may today we find a refreshing breeze" (NIV) as we remember the life of Stone Mountain Dartt, to the music of Ronnie Booth and Amanda Henry. From the standing ovation to the nurses who had given their time, love and care, to the message brought by Dr Wendell Calder. From the memorial video to the Salvation call, it all flowed seamlessly and I felt like God was honoring every aspect. Wendell closed the service with prayer, and we had 3 people raise their hands for Salvation, which brought tears to my eyes. We would later find out that the Live broadcast would reach people in all 50 states and 24 Countries. By the end of the night it had been viewed by over 2,000 people and counting. God was doing something through Stoneys life, He was working in the midst of our loss.

When the service ended, we followed the hearse to the cemetery plot just up a little ways from the chapel. We would then listen to the graveside prayer by Pastor Michael, before watching the entire casket put into the ground, and covered with dirt. We had special pictures engraved onto the lid of the vault of the Haunted Mansion attraction in the background, with some favorite family photos around the edges. As they started lowering him down, I had never witnessed this part of a graveside before. It was very real to watch him being put into the ground, and to watch them shovel dirt on top. I handed out roses to the women in the family where they then placed it on the top of of the site, and we said our final goodbyes.

Back in the reception room, people were eating, and sharing stories. We had so many wonderful comments about the service and said goodbye to our many friends as they would begin their journeys home.

I wish I had a clone of myself that weekend. I felt like I was losing my mind with all of the people that wanted to speak with me. First of all I am blessed, thankful, and grateful for every person that was there. Secondly, I was honored that they would want to come from so far away, to be with us. I was just fading mentally, and wasn't sure how long I would be able to smile and keep it together. I was exhausted, and yet would have done anything for that day to have lasted 48 hours alone. Meaning, I didn't want it to end. I enjoyed the fellowship, the laughs, the stories, surrounded by people we had not seen for so long. This one hour service and reception that

I had worked so hard, and planned for over a week was over, and I again, wanted more time. I had so many people help me prepare and clean up. My cousin and her husband came to see me later that afternoon to spend some time with me, but I was done. I couldn't talk to anyone, I could't hold my eyes open, I couldn't think. Debra told me to go to bed and she would take care of everything for me, so I did. I slept the rest of the afternoon and evening and when I woke up that night at 10:00, Debra was there to get me something to eat, and then make sure I went right back to bed.

I was covered with people who loved me, and wanted the best for me. They were worried about me, and cared so much. The feelings that poured over me the following days were alarming to me. I would have thought that I would be an emotional wreck. That I wouldn't be able to get up out of bed, or eat. In fact, I pretty much prepared myself for just that while we were in Atlanta and I was watching Stoney slip away. I knew I wouldn't be able to function on my own, and would suffer a nervous breakdown. Stoney was such a huge part of our everyday life, and handled so many details that I never thought about. He fixed everything that needed fixing. All of our electronic issues, phone and computer problems, we would give to him. However, the comfort was overwhelming. I felt a great sense of peace, strength and comfort. If you read all of the posts through this book, I mentioned over and over for people to pray for those 3 things. Now, I was experiencing them in my life first hand. Yes, I miss Stoney. Yes, I shed many tears and still do. Days don't go by that I don't think about our wonderful friendship, his laugh, and warm hugs. (just life Olaf) Living with the Lord by my side helps me get through each day a little easier than the day before.

I was (am) being sheltered in a spot like no other. I am feeling so much love from friends and family. I am feeling the presence of the Lord as I navigate my new life without my best friend. I am finding that the Peace of God is within me, and each day He is showing me new mercies and the freedom to live and laugh again. The loneliness is still there, and I believe will always be there to an extent. When someone we love passes, they take a piece of our heart with them. That hole never heals entirely, but it's covered by Gods goodness and grace. I am so undeserving of the amount of grace God has given to me over the past few years (and beyond). He has shown Himself more faithful than any other time in my life. He has supplied every need I have had, and filled me with so much love. He has brought the most dearest friends into my life, sheltered me from harm, and shown mercy in times of despair. I could not imagine walking this life without him holding my hand and guiding me through.

People have said to me how proud they are of me, or go on and on about how wonderful I was to take care of Stoney. Honestly, those comments make cringe, and sometimes cry. I can imagine NOT taking care of someone you respect and love. I cant imagine going through this life knowing God had a plan for you, but ignoring it for your own selfishness. We all have loved ones that deserve our time. Friends that deserve our care. Family who deserve our respect. I believe it is a choice we make to do whats right. When Stoney was diagnosed on January 12, 2019, I made a choice to stand by his side and serve as a warrior. I chose not to leave his side when the waters were starting to sink the ship, and I chose to listen to God when He spoke, not questioning the uncertainty that was before us. He had a plan, I chose to follow. Don't miss an opportunity to be used as a vessel by Him. To fight in His army. It is worth it, and you get to see God show up in ways you may have missed if you choose not too.

Where do I go from here? Well, the day after the funeral, I again couldn't sleep. I felt this heaviness on my heart, and no it wasn't covid. Stoney and I had discussed a plan for the future when he was in the ICU back in March to create a support base and even financial aid for nurses, and caregivers. We witnessed so many talented nurses burdened by the financial insecurities or family obligations. Single moms working all day in the hospital and barely getting by and struggling with child care. Other nurses who were working 3 jobs to support themselves and their families, plus going to night school or on the weekends to further their education, but struggling with student loans and debt. We met patients at the center who would be lost if it wasn't for an advocator that helped them show them where they should go for treatment. We met caregivers who struggled with depression, and loneliness because they didn't have a support team to help them move forward. Stoney had a heart for people, and an obvious love for nurses. He admired the way they took care of him, and he loved getting to know them each individually. He engaged them. He spoke to them and cared. He even taught me how to love them, and open myself up to them even when I didn't agree with them. We learned their favorite recipes, where they liked to shop, and travel to. We wanted to find a way to give back and make a difference in their lives. You could say that by giving them coffee, bringing in donuts and cupcakes was a start, but we wanted to do more. We discussed many ideas but when he started getting better and was able to come home, we quickly lost sight of this endeavor.

Fast forward to my restless nights, and heavy heart. I don't know how to explain the point when God puts something on your heart, and you reach out for what He says to do, follow, and then see doors open beyond your wildest dreams. I know that God says to ask, and it shall be given. He also says, "Seek, and ye shall find. Knock, and the door shall be open." I know I could take that verse out of context, but it's so true. I was seeking, there was knocking, and there was asking.

I made a few calls, sent a few emails, and within a week Moving Mountains Ministries was born. With a goal to provide financial help to struggling nurses, emotional care to those hurting, and medical support to those searching for answers. I had in my mind a logo with 3 mountains, one for each goal. On the middle mountain, I wanted a fedora hanging off of it to honor Stoney and that signifies the middle mountain is also his middle name. I mentioned in my many posts for people to pray for the mountains to be moved. That is what I am still praying today, and what I hope we can do together to support nurses, caregivers and those searching for answers. I don't have all the answers, but Jesus does. I know that by doing what we are called to do, He will use us and reach those that seem impossible to reach. I'm just answering the call. Moving Mountains Ministries may last a few months, or long after I'm gone. I'm hoping the latter of those. In the meantime, I am going to advocate for those in need, and do my part in caring for others. Stoney left a mark in this world, and I want to see it go to reach many more generations. I want people to know joy, to have hope, and to see Jesus in a dark world of fear and hopelessness.

All the proceeds from this book will go to support the ministry, and help fund a nurse in need, or someone who is in the process of losing a loved one.

As I focus these days on sharing the spotlight on nurses and caregivers, I love sharing their testimonies through our social media pages, and website. I want to close with a few testimonies from Stoneys nurses, who left an impact on my life (and his). It is because of them, Stoney and I had a vision, a purpose to give back and find a way to support those who give their lives each day. Stoney was, is, and forever will be my hero, but the nurses that stood with us and cared for us daily will always be OUR heroes…

"Ever since I can remember, I have had a passion for things with a heart beat… as a little girl I always found my self taking care of something, saving chipmunks and rabbits from my cats, even snakes and lizards when I had to! In 2006 my Mom was diagnosed with stage 3 Breast cancer and I quickly became her helper. I would attend appointments, help her after surgery, and I even got to shave her head during her chemo treatments! We made the most of it. It was then I quickly realized I wanted to be a cancer nurse when I grew up. With my moms diagnoses and some genetic testing, we came to find out my mother was a carrier of the genetic mutation BRCA2, also know as "the breast cancer gene". Fast forward some years, my sister was tested, and found to be a carrier of the BRCA2 gene as well. Those who carry this gene are put at a greatly higher risk of developing breast cancer at a young age than those without it, so that being said my sister then made the choice to have a prophylactic double mastectomy. Once again I found myself as a caregiver, drains, doctors appointments and more. Fast forward again, two years later I found myself in the same position as my sister… BRCA2 positive….. time for surgery…. Here I am the one that is usually the caregiver, and now has become the one being taken care of. At this point I was 110% positive that God put me on this earth to be a nurse. So that's what I did, fast forward once again I am a Registered nurse at the Cancer Treatment Centers of America, in Newnan, GA. This is my dream job! I finally made it. Within my first month at CTCA I met Stoney and BJ, it was love at first laugh! I knew from the beginning we would be peas in a pod! Time went on and we grew closer. BJ would bring us snacks, pizza after my shift, we would have "comedy hour" every evening and make jokes, laughing until we sometimes cried at anything and everything you could imagine. From the day I met Stoney, until the day of his passing, he was smiling. I would walk in every shift with handfuls of pills for him to swallow and he would greet me…. "Hello beautiful." He was always smiling. As I watched him grow more sick in

the last couple of months... I would sometimes Think to myself.... "Will he ever lose his joy??" The pain, the drains, the tubes and wires... his legs so swollen he could hardly move them, but He never lost his joy, never stopped smiling, never stopped rejoicing. The last few weeks when Stoney really began to decline things got tough for all of the nurses on the floor, and even the family. But that was when it hit me... I realized this was my assignment. My task from God. He took someone's else's suffering, and forever changed me, forever blessed me. Cancer and I have a love/hate relationship.... You see, I hate cancer.... But a part of me can not help but be thankful for it.. cancer has made me who I am. It's been in my life as long as I can remember. I have learned more from it than most could imagine. If not for cancer I wouldn't be where I am today, and I wouldn't have met Stoney. Although, I would have done anything in this world to take away his suffering, I can't imagine going through life and never knowing him. It's hard to put into words what my time taking care of Stoney really taught me, and the emotion that overwhelmed me when he passed. That morning I wanted to leave, I wanted to go home and bury my face in my pillows and cry. In one room we prepared his body for the funeral home, and in the next rooms down were several more patients to be take care of. Some happy with great news, some sad, some angry. It is tough learning to juggle so many emotions, when all I wanted to do was shut down. That's when I though to myself.... "What would Stoney want me to do?".... One thing he taught me was how to be resilient.... How to bend but not break... how to keep your joy and continue to serve others even when you are suffering yourself. So that is what I did.

As much as we grieved on earth we also rejoiced. Rejoiced in the life long friendships that had been made, the blessings that were brought to us through the pain, and most of all rejoiced in the fact that our Stoney was in heaven. I think of Stoney everyday, and I miss him dearly. but I know I will see my friend again, and he will greet me with a big smile and a "hello beautiful." Until then, I will be here on earth, taking care of my many patients ... some similar to Stoney... but never anyone quite like him. My heart is forever changed because of Stone Mountain Dartt. I will continue to do my work in his honor, staying resilient and rejoicing in everyday, and I'm proud to serve on the Nurses Advisory Panel for Moving Mountains Ministries that was created in his honor!"

-Liz-Hunter

Why am I a nurse? Growing up I had some unfortunate things happen to me. I remember nurses and EMTs always being so nice and eager to listen. I wanted to be that nurse who listened, wanted to help, hold your hand on your worst day, and celebrate big on your wins. I love how versatile nursing and how you can devoted yourself to others as a career.

What have I struggled with as a nurse? Nursing in current times is difficult for multiple reasons. Mainly with how poorly the hospital systems treat nurses, we have to fight to be given safe ratios so our patients can have the best care.

The trial I've faced with trial child care? Many nurses are mothers, we face the issue of leaving our babies 12-14 hours day. We happily do it because we want to give you or your family the love and care you need. But, I've never seen a hospital offer any help with child care, whether it's a stipend, childcare center built into the hospital or shifts that accommodate day care times.

What did Stoney mean to me? I'll never forget the day I met Stoney. I was down the hall in the ICU and I noticed a call light going off on IMCU, I walked down into the room to see what I could do because his nurse was busy. I walk in and instantly was in love with BJ & Stoney's demeanor. We talked for a FULL HOUR. Lol we talked about life, food, shared so many laughs, I wasn't his nurse but I feel like god called me into that room. Stoney to this day reminds me to 'rejoice'. Rejoice in the mundane, to just love and enjoy life for exactly what it is. Everyday I walked into the hospital, whether Stoney was feel bad or good, he put a smile on my face. I can't explain it, but he had a beautiful energy that just made you love him.

-Kaitlyn

For me I have wanted to become a nurse since I was a little girl. I never knew of any other path. All I knew was that I loved helping people and seeing the smiles on their faces. I have been a nurse for a little over 15 years and it was not until may past 2 years working in Oncology that I begin discovering my purpose as a nurse. When I began working in oncology I had just left a very abusive marriage and I had to go figure out how to raise 3 little boys on my own...I was in an extremely dark place in my life but unbeknownst to me God had a different plan for my life. What I mean by this is that God had placed me right where I needed to be. My cancer patients gave me a reason to fight and not feel sorry for myself. I quickly realized that no matter what kind of day I was having theirs was much harder and it humbled me. I remember the first day I met Stoney. I was his nurse in

the port room that morning and of course his name intrigued me but what also intrigued me was his will to live and his joyful spirit. I have never once since Stoney without a big smile on his face. Strength like that is absolutely contagious. He gave me strength just by being in his presence. His laughter filled the hallways and he went out of his way to make others smile during his own struggles. BJ you are incredible you never left his side and you fought right along beside him and you are the absolutely the best vernier I have ever met and your are also incredibly strong!

My point here is that we all have our own battles we are facing and you never know what someone else is going through but overall I do not save my patients, they save me everyday.

-Amber

"To be a nurse is something I cherish everyday. When I walk through the hospital doors, in my eyes, my patients are my family. My mentality is always "how would I want my family to be treated", that is what gets me through. When I met Stoney, I knew he was someone special. Not once during his entire journey did I see him with a negative mentality. Stoney always fought, & he fought hard. I always got so excited to take care of him, because he and BJ always made my day. To be in Stoney's situation and have such an impact on people says a lot about him. He never complained, his faith was so strong, he was always such a light and I will always remember that and take that with me every single day. It was such an honor to say that I was involved in caring for Stoney and I thank God for allowing me to cross paths with him."

-Alexis

MOVING
MOUNTAINS
MINISTRIES

ABOUT THE AUTHOR

BJ Speer is a Singer/Songwriter, Author, Owner of Where U Wanna Go Travel, Co-Owner of Alice Carter Designs, and Founder of Moving Mountains Ministries. BJ Spent over 20 years on the road, sharing his faith and love for Jesus Christ in Churches and on the Mission fields around the world.

Printed in the United States
by Baker & Taylor Publisher Services